IBERO-AMERICANA: 38

EARLY COLONIAL TRADE AND NAVIGATION BETWEEN MEXICO AND PERU

WOODROW BORAH

UNIVERSITY OF CALIFORNIA PRESS
BERKELEY AND LOS ANGELES
1954

IBERO-AMERICANA: 38

EARLY COLONIAL TRADE AND NAVIGATION BETWEEN MEXICO AND PERU

WOODROW BORAH

EARLY COLONIAL TRADE AND NAVIGATION BETWEEN MEXICO AND PERU

BY

WOODROW BORAH

UNIVERSITY OF CALIFORNIA PRESS
BERKELEY AND LOS ANGELES
1954

IBERO-AMERICANA: 38

Editors: C. O. Sauer, G. P. Hammond, J. H. Rowe, L. B. Simpson

170 pages, 1 map

Submitted by editors October 21, 1953

Issued May 21, 1954

Price, $2.50

University of California Press

Berkeley and Los Angeles

◇

Cambridge University Press

London, England

PRINTED IN THE UNITED STATES OF AMERICA

PREFACE

THIS STUDY is an examination of the sixteenth-century export and entrepôt trade of Mexico with Peru and of the navigation which bore it. Chapters i–vi examine the origins of the navigation in the Pacific; the development of the Mexico-Peru traffic; various aspects of the trade, navigation, passenger movement; and the inevitable government regulation and taxation without which few studies of commerce would be complete. Owing to the fortunate survival of the Cortés family commercial records, I have been able to give, in chapter iv, a picture of the operation of commercial and common carrier enterprises. Other private commercial records for both sixteenth-century Mexico and Peru are no longer extant. Chapter vii deals with the far-reaching changes which the China trade brought to the Mexico-Peru traffic and the consequent prohibition of any trade between the two viceroyalties.

The reader will notice that I have used archival materials primarily in Mexico and Spain. I have tried to find material in Peru, although from a distance, but a series of inquiries by the office of the United States Cultural Attaché in Lima and a personal search by Pedro Muro Arias, a gifted Peruvian student interested in the same topic, located only seventeenth- and eighteenth-century records.

In preparing this study, I have had much and generous assistance for which I gladly acknowledge my indebtedness. The directors and staffs of the Archivo General de la Nación, Mexico, and the Bancroft Library afforded their usual courteous and unfailing assistance. Luis G. Ceballos, Paleographer of the Archivo, gave invaluable assistance in reading sixteenth-century script. The Henry E. Huntington Library kindly permitted consultation of the Gonzalo Pizarro–La Gasca correspondence. John H. Rowe gave advice on Peruvian materials; Carl O. Sauer, much-needed help on meteorology; and Lesley Byrd Simpson, a very great deal of advice and his usual generous but searching criticism. I thank Ing. Ramón Escobar Tabera of Oaxaca for help in determining the sixteenth-century road from Oaxaca to Huatulco, and Pedro Muro Arias for a cordial and generous relationship. Muro Arias' history of the later trade will complete the study of the colonial traffic. My work was aided substantially by a grant from the Committee on Research of the University of California, Berkeley. A year in Mexico in 1951–1952, as a John Simon Guggenheim Memorial Foundation Fellow for other research, made it possible for me to find additional materials for this study and to verify tentative conclusions.

CONTENTS

I. THE BEGINNINGS OF SHIPBUILDING AND NAVIGATION ON THE PACIFIC COAST OF AMERICA

LAND AND SEA communication and trade among the various Spanish colonies in the New World began almost as soon as they were established. In the Caribbean, ships not only distributed goods brought from Spain by the galleons but also carried local products from colony to colony. In the sixteenth century Havana bought Mexican flour, and Veracruz received wax and honey by sea from Yucatán. In the Pacific, the principal traffic comprised cargo and passengers between Panama and Peru, for the galleons anchored on the Atlantic side of the Isthmus at Nombre de Dios. A considerable traffic also developed in local goods and passengers, not only among the various "realms of Peru," but also between the west coast of South America and the west coast of New Spain. Limeños drank chocolate from Central America and paid for it in silver from Potosí. Reaching beyond Guatemala, colonial ships linked the two great Spanish viceregal centers of the New World, Mexico City and Lima. The Mexico-Peru run was perhaps the longest and most difficult of the coastwise traffics in the Pacific waters of America; yet it was begun when Henry VIII at the mid-point of his career was detaching England from Rome and was well established when the English monarch died in 1547.

Communication between the two viceregal capitals was necessarily by sea. Moving baggage and freight overland by pack train or the usually illegal use of Indian bearers was so slow and expensive that water transportation was preferred wherever it could be used. Furthermore, the opening of a land route from Mexico City to Lima was made impossible by two formidable geographical barriers. In southern Costa Rica and northern Panama, unusually rugged mountains and dense forests made land travel prohibitively difficult. The Spanish were not even in a position to open a land route through this area until after the conquest and settlement of Costa Rica in the 1560's. Farther south, in southern Panama and the Chocó, mountains and one of the densest rain forests on earth made movement by land virtually impossible, so that, after the first painful attempts at exploration, communication from Panama southward was entirely by sea. Even today the difficulties of building a road through the tropical rain forest of the Chicó have left a three-hundred mile gap in the intercontinental road system.

Because it was an ocean navigation, the Mexico-Peru traffic came into being after the Conquest. The European conquerors and settlers reaching the Pacific shore found no native vessels making the long and difficult voyage between Mexico and Peru, nor, except along the coast of Peru, any extensive voyages at all. Why there was no direct communication between the two greatest cultural areas of the New World remains a mystery, since the Incas had developed great balsa rafts which could have made the voyage by taking advantage of the favorable currents. Nevertheless, there is no suggestion in the extensive Spanish records that there was such communication.[1] Native experience in ocean navigation hardly extended beyond the coast, and the conquerors had to chart the shallows, deeps, winds, and currents of the South Sea for themselves.

Linking Mexico and Peru thus meant an extensive new development involving shipbuilding, exploration, conquest, settlement, and trade, in the long arc of colonies established on the Pacific coast of America in the first decades of the sixteenth century. In this development all the Pacific coast must be considered. Two colonies at the center of the arc—Panama and Nicaragua—were more important than Mexico and Peru, for they provided by far most of the vessels, pilots, and crews.

Shipbuilding began on the Isthmus of Panama. To explore the new-found South Sea, Balboa began to construct ships in the summer of 1517. His shipbuilding was a tragic and heroic feat. Timber was cut on the Atlantic side of the Isthmus, perhaps because the trees on the Pacific slope were too small and stunted. Cordage, nails, anchors, pitch, tar, sails, and all other gear and supplies were assembled at Acla on the Atlantic. Everything was carried on the backs of Indian *tamemes* over the continental divide to the Río de las Balsas on the Gulf of San Miguel. According to the official version, 500 Indians died during the work; according to Las Casas, the true number was 2,000. With heavy loss of men and materials, and much difficulty, four brigantines were assembled in 1518–1519. The last of them may have been completed only after Balboa was beheaded at the order of Pedrarias Dávila, who promptly seized the ships, finished equipping them, and sent out an expedition to explore northward along the coast.[2]

A second set of brigantines was built in 1520–1521 by Gil González Dávila on the Río de las Balsas. Hearing of Balboa's death while himself still in Spain, he secured a royal order that Balboa's ships be turned over to him for exploration. The order was presented to Pedrarias Dávila in Feb-

[1] For notes to chapter i, see pages 131–133.

ruary, 1520, received with much ceremony by the wily old governor, who "obeyed" it, but with even more ceremony refused to comply with it.[3] Thereupon González Dávila broke up the ships he had brought from Spain, cut fresh timber as needed, and had gear, timber, and provisions carried over the continental divide to the Río de las Balsas for assembly. The four brigantines for which he had materials foundered before reaching the ocean. Somehow he persuaded Pedrarias to assign men and give assistance for building four more vessels. These were small and poorly constructed, but on January 21, 1522, the expedition embarked. It explored the coast of what is today Costa Rica and Nicaragua, although the ships required major repair because of damage by shipworms.[4]

Shipbuilding as practiced by Balboa and González Dávila was expensive and difficult. Caulking materials, nails, anchors, cables, cordage, sails, and other gear all had to be brought from Spain and transported across the Isthmus. The vessels proved easily vulnerable to shipworms—probably the teredo, which abounded in tropical waters. As early as 1514 the Spanish invented a method for sheathing the underwater parts of ships with lead, but the additional expense of buying lead and moving it overland was so great that the method does not appear to have been used in the first decades of navigation in the Pacific.[5] Even without lead sheathing, Balboa's four brigantines were claimed to have cost 50,000 ducats, a formidable sum.[6] Although suitable timber was soon found on the Pacific slope, shipbuilding still required a large amount of personal capital.

Because of the expense and difficulties, and also because Pedrarias Dávila, governor of Panama until 1528, was determined to participate in and control new ventures,[7] only a few ships were built on the Isthmus during the early and middle 1520's. Pascual de Andagoya, a member of the Panama City council and husband of a protégée of Pedrarias' wife, explored southward in two ships, which he may have built in partnership with Pedrarias. The partners who continued the southward exploration which led to the conquest of Peru—Francisco Pizarro, Diego de Almagro, and Hernando de Luque—built two ships and bought a third, one of Balboa's brigantines which had miraculously escaped destruction by rot or shipwreck. Luque, a wealthy priest, provided the money, but the ubiquitous Pedrarias Dávila was either a fourth partner or a sponsor in this earliest phase of the venture.[8] Other colonists with private capital and either official position or enough influence to win Pedrarias' consent, may have built ships in these years, but, if so, the vessels were speedily wrecked or disintegrated.

The most effective stimulus to shipbuilding came in the later 1520's and early 1530's through export of Indian slaves from Nicaragua to Panama. When Panama was founded in 1519, the surrounding territory had too few Indians to support the 400 Spanish *vecinos*. The most important men received allotments of no more than ninety Indians; the rest of the settlers had to be content with between forty and fifty apiece. Even these small numbers were soon severely reduced as the Indians died off from disease, abuse, and unaccustomed labor in mines and placers so that the vecinos of Panama were forced to look elsewhere for laborers in substantial numbers.[9] They found fresh sources of supply to the north through the new settlements at León and Granada, which were in a fertile area with a dense, sedentary aboriginal population but with no mines of sufficient richness to support settlers or fully occupy local labor. With an abundant supply of Indians and a ready market in Panama, the settlers of Nicaragua turned to slaving as their cash industry. They bought Indians held as slaves by other Indians, compelled the enslaving of more Indians as a form of tribute, and simply seized and branded whatever natives were available when a shipment was being made up. In the middle of 1526 at least one shipload of Nicaraguan Indians arrived in Panama. It may have been the first. After 1528, when Pedrarias Dávila moved from Panama to Nicaragua and devoted his considerable talents to organizing the slave traffic, export of Indians grew very rapidly. León and Granada became the centers for an industry that required not merely local levies but expeditions into surrounding regions as far as the Honduran coast. The procurement and shipment of slaves was carried on mainly by private individuals, although Pedrarias and other government officials were deeply involved in the slaving expeditions either as partners or through sale of permits to use the royal branding iron.[10]

The traffic in slaves fostered a rapid development of shipways and shipbuilding. In March, 1529 according to a report by Lic. Francisco de Castañeda to the royal government in Spain, five ships already were engaged in trade between Panama and Nicaragua, making the round trip usually in from fifteen to twenty days and exceptionally in thirty days in all but the worst weather. One of the vessels belonged to the Crown and the governor of Tierra Firme jointly, one to the royal treasurer Alonso de Cáceres and his partners, one to Pedrarias Dávila, and two to Pizarro and Almagro. Apparently the two partners in the Peruvian venture used their vessels between expeditions to Peru to earn funds and avoid the expense of maintaining them idle in port. According to Castañeda, Hernando de Soto and Hernando Ponce de León had built a sixth ship in Nicaragua, which was ready to be launched.[11] Later in the same year 1529 De Soto and Ponce de León sent this vessel and still another, probably built in Nicaragua by them, with cargoes of slaves to Panama. The voyage became noteworthy because Ponce de León, who went to Panama to supervise the sale, was approached by Pizarro, who wished to use the ships in his new Peruvian expedition. Ponce agreeing, both he and De Soto joined the expedition with a number of armed Nicaraguan Indians and perhaps a hundred Spaniards from León and Granada.[12]

Nicaragua had especially good resources for building ships. It had suitable timber and mast trees in the forests near the coast, pitch for caulking, *pita* and *cabuya* fibers, which could be made into cables and cordage, an abundance of Indian foodstuffs, and a port to supply the vessels. Until Pedrarias died in 1531, the development of shipbuilding was hindered by his determination to reserve slaving and exploration for himself and his friends. As soon as he died, his successor, Lic. Castañeda, allowed the colonists to build ships and engage in slaving virtually without restraint.[13] By late 1533 or early 1534 between fifteen and twenty caravels were reported as being engaged exclusively in the slave trade with Panama.[14] Some of them may have been built on the Isthmus but the majority were probably constructed in Nicaragua because of its superior resources. If all of these vessels were indeed caravels, they ranged in size from four to fifty tons and were decked over for ocean travel.[15]

The vessels engaged in the slave trade were more than half of the ships on the Pacific coast of the Americas at this time. In a letter of October 10, 1533, to the emperor, Lic. Espinosa reported from Panama that, including Alvarado's ships, there were more than thirty vessels in the Pacific.[16] Since all but three of Alvarado's ships had been built in Panama and Nicaragua,[17] construction on the Isthmus and along the coast of Nicaragua accounted for the overwhelming majority of the existing vessels. The export of Indian slaves from Nicaragua thus gave powerful impetus in developing shipbuilding facilities during the crucial years when coastwise shipping was beginning. It also did much to train mariners and pilots who assisted in the exploration of the coast and manned many of the ships built in other areas.

In contrast with the centers in Panama and Nicaragua, shipbuilding developed rather slowly elsewhere along the Pacific coast. The first shipbuilding on the west coast of Mexico began in 1522, shortly after the surrender of Mexico-Tenochtitlán. Cortés sent a party to explore the Pacific shore for a shipyard site. The party chose the mouth of the Zacatula River. Juan Rodríguez de Villafuerte was sent with forty Spanish artisans to build two ocean-going caravels and two brigantines for exploration of the coast. The Spanish artisans trained and supervised a large number of Indian allies who had gained some experience in building the brigantines on the lakes of the Valley of Mexico during the siege of the Aztec capital. Spikes, cordage, sails, anchors, caulking materials, and all other supplies except timber were hauled from Veracruz. Fire destroyed the first ships before they were completed, but new ones were begun, although because of virtual suspension of work during Cortés' expedition to Honduras, they were not completed until 1526. Two of them sank in coastal exploration and the other two were sent with Alvaro de Saavedra Cerón to search out the route to the Spice Islands.[18] For a permanent shipyard Cortés chose Tehuantepec, which could be reached by an easier land route than most west coast harbors and, in addition, could receive supplies from Veracruz via a ship and canoe route over the Isthmus of Tehuantepec that left only twenty leagues of expensive land carriage.[19] By 1528, when he left for Spain, Cortés had five vessels under construction. On his return, however, he found them rotten, the workmen dispersed, and the gear seized by the First Audiencia. He at once salvaged two vessels for rebuilding and began construction of two more at Acapulco.[20] In 1532 he had two ready which were soon lost at sea.[21] At the time of Lic. Espinosa's count of ships in the Pacific (October, 1533) Cortés had more on the ways but probably none fit for sea. Five years later, in 1538, he had nine vessels, although these were immobilized for lack of pilots.[22] Until the later 1530's Cortés appears to have been the only person building ships in New Spain.

In the early 1530's another center of shipbuilding was started on the northern coast of Central America at Iztapa in Guatemala, where Alvarado built his first three galleons for exploration to the west, and at Acajutla in El Salvador, where Alvarado established another shipyard.[23] Like the earliest construction in Mexico, Alvarado's ships were destined for exploration and conquest and not for trade. Rather, Alvarado, by buying ships built farther south and by enlisting seamen and pilots drew upon the reservoir of talent and shipping developed in the centers at Panama and Nicaragua.

Peru, after the Spanish invasion and settlement, did not become a shipbuilding center for some years. Its own coast lacked timber. In the middle

1540's it had repair facilities at the island of Puna near the southern limit of the coastal forest, but still built no ships. It was probably cheaper to build at Panama and Nicaragua than to freight gear, ironwork, and other fittings. Toward the end of the sixteenth century Guayaquil in the Audiencia of Quito, which could draw upon extensive forests, became notable for shipbuilding.[24]

In the early and middle 1530's the major Pacific coast centers for shipbuilding and shipping were clearly the Isthmus of Panama and Nicaragua. Between them these two areas supplied the overwhelming majority of the vessels, trained seamen, and pilots in the Pacific. Panama, which lay upon the most direct route between Peru and Spain, was the most important port in the Pacific just as its fleets were the most important in the supply of Peru. It became the major center for the pilots who in those years were charting the South Sea.[25] Nicaragua, with its superior resources and substantial production of cordage, sails, pitch, and timber, probably built more ships than Panama.[26] Nicaraguan vessels, men, and supplies took a major part in the supply of Peru, second only to that of Panama.[27] By the end of the 1530's a fleet of merchant ships sailed each year to Peru from the Nicaraguan port of Realejo (La Posesión) with provisions and goods. Another fleet sailed annually to Panama to help provision that city and supply the fleet which sailed between the Isthmus and Peru. Between fleet sailings from either center single vessels maintained communication and trade between them and Peru and with Guatemala and the Audiencia of Mexico.[28] It was on the margin of this far greater movement of shipping and trade of Panama and Nicaragua that navigation developed between New Spain and Peru.

II. THE ESTABLISHMENT OF COMMUNICATION AND TRADE, 1531–1550

We have no evidence showing direct maritime communication between Mexico and Peru before the fall of 1536. Movement of passengers, arms, horses, and supplies from Mexico to Peru, however, began some years before, perhaps as early as 1531 but certainly by 1533. In 1531 Pizarro landed at Túmbez and began his march inland. On November 15, 1532, he seized Atahualpa at Cajamarca and completed the first stage of the Spanish occupation of Peru. A rush to the rich new country with its vast stores of specie and hordes of docile Indians began from all parts of the Spanish dominions.

In the Audiencia of Mexico, circumstances were unusually favorable for migration to Peru. By 1530 it was clear that there were far more conquerors than encomiendas, and there emerged a rather numerous group of unprovided-for conquerors. At the same time, gold placer mining with gangs of Indian slaves, which had provided income for many of the Spaniards, was beginning to play out in all but the richest sites. In all likelihood, yields were never high enough to provide handsome returns for more than the largest operators and the lucky few who happened upon unusually rich deposits. Moreover, placer mining, either carried on directly with Indian slaves or indirectly through exaction of tributes in gold from Indian villages, provided the specie to pay for imports of arms and goods from Spain. As Luis de Castilla commented later, Spaniards saw little profit in remaining in New Spain for "there was no use in sending cotton cloth, or cacao, or maize to Castile, nor would ships come from Spain to pick up such products."[1] Disheartened, many of the conquerors and so-called settlers, those who came after the fall of Tenochtitlán, returned to Spain and the Antilles, or went on to Peru.

As early as May 13, 1532, the cabildo of Mexico City complained that Spaniards were leaving in such numbers that the land was threatened with abandonment.[2] Emigration continued at a rising rate throughout 1533, and the cabildo became even more alarmed. On June 26, 1534, the cabildo made a lengthy and energetic representation to the audiencia that many Spaniards had already left and that every day more were "going to Peru and Spain and other parts by tens and twenties and thirties." Their statement reads like a dirge: Mexico City is come to half the Spanish population it

[1] For notes to chapter ii, see pages 134–138.

once had; Veracruz is less; Coatzacoalcos, almost without people; San Luis, without council or vecino; Oaxaca and Villa Alta have lost many; Zacatula and Colima are far smaller than before; the new city of Puebla is losing settlers so that it is scarcely worth putting so much work upon the Indians "to maintain it against all reason"; the city of Michoacan is diminished. The council had other reasons for its representation since it was trying to ward off a possible royal threat to its jurisdiction over the five-league radius outside the walls of the capital.[3] Nevertheless, it was so sincerely disturbed that it initiated a series of conferences between its members, Cortés, and members of the royal government, to discuss measures for curbing the alarming emigration.[4] In August the audiencia issued an ordinance to meet the situation. Its terms forbade any Spaniard to leave or to send arms or horses out of the realm without a special license. The cabildo received the ordinance with approval and ordered the prohibitions proclaimed a second time through the streets of the city.[5]

How much of this early emigration from Mexico went to Peru cannot be determined. Some of it went west to New Galicia, where Nuño de Guzmán was carving out a new empire in an unusually cruel and bloodthirsty venture. Many of the disappointed returned to Spain and the Antilles; but a considerable number probably moved on to the land that still promised gold and Indians.

Similarly, the route by which these emigrants reached Peru is almost completely conjectural. The first ones may have gone to the Antilles and there have taken ship to the Isthmus for the land trek to the Pacific and the coastal voyage to Peru. Some may have found ships directly on the Pacific shores of Mexico, for, the coastline being known, Central American ships could have sailed to Mexico in search of passengers and freight. There is no evidence on this point. Most of the emigrants probably made their way by land to Guatemala and along the Central American coast to Realejo and the port of La Posesión, a league from the town.[6] At Realejo it was easy to buy passage in one of the many ships carrying recruits and supplies to Peru. A letter of Pedro de Alvarado written in May, 1536, just after his return from Peru, commented that many emigrants were passing through Guatemala on the way to Peru. "Each day they pass in such numbers," he wrote, "that I marvel that Mexico City is left with people."[7]

The first communication between Mexico and Peru in colonial times thus took the form of a southward export of surplus warriors, arms, and horses, and used Central American ports and shipping. It is probable that

Pedro de Alvarado himself transported some of the emigrants, since during 1532 and 1533 he recruited men for the expedition which he took to the coast of Peru in the early months of 1534. When he sailed from the port of La Posesión, he had with him approximately 450 Spanish soldiers, of whom 260 were horsemen, 100 were crossbowmen and arquebusiers, and the rest foot soldiers armed with sword and shield. Some of these men were recruited in Spain, but most of them were recruited in Central America.[8] In all likelihood, warriors from Mexico seeking passage to Peru joined the expedition, since Alvarado's plans were known in Mexico City,[9] and men planning to make the passage would have hurried to join him. Unfortunately, Alvarado's reports to the Crown do not tell where his recruits came from. Virtually all of the men he took with him remained in Peru.

Alvarado's letter of May, 1536, clearly indicated that the movement from Mexico to Peru continued without much regard to the Audiencia of Mexico's prohibition against departure without permission. It was not an easy rule to enforce in the vast spaces of New Spain, and although backed by a royal decree that any man leaving a province without permission forfeited his encomienda and lands,[10] it could have had little effect upon men who were leaving precisely because they had been refused encomiendas or had been given such small allotments that they felt unable to live on the tributes. Only when Peru was filled with Spaniards far beyond the possibility of providing each man with an encomienda did the movement slow down and some of the disappointed begin to return.[11]

The opening of trade rather than immigration between Mexico and Peru came immediately after this first movement. It was the work of Hernán Cortés, who had his finger in so many pies. He was preparing an expedition to Peru as early as 1534. As he tells the story, he became discouraged by the poor results of two voyages of discovery, for which the Crown never reimbursed him. Finding himself burdened with debts, he decided to turn merchant and, with the one sound ship he had, and one then under construction, to send horses and other merchandise to Peru to exchange for money that would pay off his debts and enable him to finance another exploring venture. He bought, for sale in Peru, foodstuffs and other supplies, arms, and more than sixty horses and saddles. Before the trading venture was under way, however, word came to Cortés that his ships exploring the northwest coast of Mexico had discovered land in the Pacific, and that Nuño de Guzmán, hoping to conceal the news, had seized one of the ships. Cortés then hurriedly diverted the ships and supplies destined for Peruvian trade to the preparation of a new expedition to the northwest.[12] He accompanied the expedition to Lower California but only managed to increase his debts.

This tale of a proposed trading venture to Peru may bear more of an air of innocence than it really had, for, as we shall see later, Cortés disguised schemes to explore South Pacific waters with public plans for trade. The excuse was necessary to avoid complaints from Pizarro, Almagro, and others who had exclusive royal concessions to explore the Pacific waters adjacent to the South American coast. Cortés could well have believed, in the light of his Mexican experience, that if he did discover and conquer rich lands, even in violation of express concessions, the Crown would disregard the trespass in its pleasure at obtaining new dominions. One bit of evidence suggesting that Cortés planned to explore southward is a curious aftermath of Alvarado's attempt to force himself into the conquest of Peru: a royal order to Cortés that in his explorations he remain outside the area assigned to Pizarro.[13] At first sight, the cédula appears unnecessary and insulting, since Alvarado had asked Cortés to be his partner in the expedition to Peru and Cortés had refused flatly, even though his refusal meant incurring the enmity of his former companion-in-arms.[14] The explanation for this order may be merely that the Council of the Indies, knowing its conquerors, preferred to take no chances. On the other hand, the later plans of Cortés suggest that the Council, which received a steady stream of detailed reports from informants of all categories, may well have had concrete information convincing it of the need for the cautionary order. Whatever the truth of the conqueror's intentions, there can be no doubt that reports about the pearls of Lower California turned his attention northward in 1534.

Two years later, in 1536, Cortés did begin his ventures in Peruvian trade and, as far as evidence unearthed to date indicates, initiate direct voyages between Mexico and Peru. According to the accounts of Francisco López de Gómara and Antonio de Herrera,[15] he was led to do so by events in the southern realm. In the summer of 1536 a vigorous offensive by Manco Inca Yupanqui placed Cuzco under close siege and threatened to exterminate the Spanish. Francisco Pizarro found himself closely invested in Lima, unable to move by land, with the sea the only channel through which he could send for help. He sent desperate appeals to the Audiencia of Santo Domingo, to Pedro de Alvarado in Guatemala, and to the governors of other Spanish provinces in Central America and northern South America.

According to Herrera, he also sent an appeal to Cortés, but this is unlikely since no ship was sent to New Spain.[16] News of Pizarro's plight reached New Spain through Alvarado, who forwarded a copy of the letter to Mexico City, where Antonio de Mendoza had just arrived as first viceroy. Mendoza, in turn, sent a copy to Acapulco, where Cortés had just returned after his disaster in Lower California. The same messenger brought both the copy of Pizarro's appeal and Mendoza's letter announcing his arrival.

Despite the urgent need to succor the remnant of his own expedition left under Ulloa, Cortés loaded two ships with all the food, arms, men, and presents for Pizarro that he could assemble in haste. The presents included silk clothing, a robe of marten fur, two armchairs of state, velvet cushions, ornamental horses' trappings, and household furnishings that Cortés had used in Lower California.

Although this is the story as Herrera copied it from official reports that probably had as their source letters of Cortés to Mendoza and other royal officials and although this is also the story as López de Gómara probably received it from the lips of Cortés himself, a document in the Cortés records of the Archivo del Hospital de Jesús[17] gives ground for questioning the truth of this version. The document is a contract between Juan Domingo de Espinosa and Hernán Cortés, the former agreeing, for a salary of one hundred pesos of fine gold a year, to go to Peru as business agent, to remain there at least a year, and to render faithful accounting of the proceeds received for merchandise to Cortés, Hernando de Grijalva, or anyone else having proper powers. The contract was executed in Acapulco on April 17, 1536; that is, at least two months before the siege of Lima, which began in July, and at least four or five months before Pizarro's letter could have reached Cortés at Acapulco. The document proves that Cortés almost immediately upon his return from Lower California began to prepare ships for a voyage to Peru; thus, when he received Pizarro's appeal, he merely continued preparations already well under way. In his reports to the Crown and its representatives, he related only part of the truth, wisely pretending that his expedition was diverted from Lower California to go to Pizarro's aid. By this device he avoided unpleasant questions about his plans and gained a further claim upon the somewhat slippery gratitude of the Crown.

The two ships were placed under the command of Hernando de Grijalva, an experienced and trusted captain, already mentioned in the contract with Juan Domingo de Espinosa as head of the expedition. A gentleman named

Alvarado was named lieutenant in charge of the second vessel. The expedition sailed in the last months of 1536 and made a speedy and successful passage, first touching land at or near Piura. This voyage was the first recorded sailing directly between Mexico and Peru that we know of.

In Peru, Grijalva found that the Indians had abandoned the siege of Lima, and that supplies and reinforcements had already come from Panama and Nicaragua, so that Pizarro was no longer in straits, but the conqueror of the Inca empire cordially accepted the presents and gave rich gifts, in return, for Cortés' wife (the Marquesa Doña Juana de Zúñiga). The men who came as reinforcements joined Pizarro's army, and were subsequently used to fight not Indians but their fellow Spaniards of the Almagro faction. One of the men on this voyage was reported to be Francisco de Carbajal, who later earned notoriety as Gonzalo Pizarro's ruthless, but far-sighted and able *mariscal de campo.*[18]

The disposition of the cargo brought in the two vessels is not clear. Much of it was probably turned over to Francisco Pizarro. Some of it was apparently sold to other Spaniards through one or more colonists appointed by Grijalva as business agents, for, on August 1, 1537, Baltasar García, vecino of Puerto Viejo, prepared a sworn list of promises to pay Cortés a sum totaling 4,005 gold *pesos de minas.*[19]

As soon as the ships were unloaded and readied for sea and arrangements completed to care for Cortés' affairs, Grijalva prepared to carry out a second and secret part of his instructions: to explore west in the Pacific along the latitudes of Peru in search of islands rumored to be rich in gold.[20] Early in April, 1537, when the two ships sailed from Paita, that commanded by Grijalva proceeded west and southwest to perhaps lat. 29° S. He then found that he could not return to New Spain against the prevailing winds and was killed in a mutiny. The expedition ended ten months later when a few starving seamen were left enslaved in the Moluccas, to be rescued by the Portuguese governor of Ternate.[21] With the ship were lost Pizarro's sumptuous gifts which Grijalva preferred to keep in his own custody.[22]

The other ship was ordered by Grijalva to return to New Spain with dispatches, and made a successful passage back to Acapulco.[23] It may have brought back specie to be shipped on to Spain, for as early as January, 1538, the Crown complained that Peruvian gold and silver were arriving in Spain via Veracruz with no proof that full taxes had been paid or that the specie had been properly assayed and marked.[24]

En route the pilot and seamen sighted land which they reported on their return to be an island. This may have been a second discovery of the then little known Galápagos Islands, which lie on the most direct sailing route.[25] The news gave fresh impetus to Cortés' hope of a rich discovery in the South Sea.

Meanwhile, before news of the safe arrival of the Grijalva expedition in Peru could reach New Spain, Cortés began to assemble men, arms, and ships for another voyage to Peru. The element of trade was perhaps more pronounced in these preparations than in the Grijalva voyage, for Cortés was ready to furnish transportation to Peru for cash or a promissory note. On March 24, 1537, Gonzalo de Burgos signed an agreement to pay Cortés 138 pesos de minas as fare for himself and his luggage. On October 25, 1537, Blas de Zambrano agreed to pay the same fare fifteen days after he should be landed at Piura. We know these names only because the two men failed to pay on time.[26] There were probably others whose names are not recorded because they met their obligations punctually. Toward the end of 1537 or early in 1538 the second expedition set sail. It may have consisted of only one vessel; at any rate the only record found thus far relates to one. On April 10, 1538, Captain Palacios Rubios turned over cargo, probably what he had not been able to sell in Puerto Viejo, La Puna, and Piura, to Juan Domingo de Espinosa in Lima, who accepted delivery as business agent for Cortés. This was a consignment of arms, save for one item:

56 iron helmets (*cascos*)
4 iron helmets (*celadas*)
10 fowling pieces (*escopetas*)
1 arquebus
60 balls of cord for crossbows
19 molds for casting bullets
46 crossbows
11 pieces of artillery
7 swords
8 barrels of powder
26 coats of mail with sleeves
1 coat of mail without sleeves

Typical of much of the outcome of Cortés' business ventures was the final and non-military item: a promise to pay 962 gold pesos executed before a notary by Lope de Mendoza, one of the early conquerors of Peru.[27]

Like the expedition of Grijalva, the ship or ships of this second voyage had instructions to explore westward on their return voyage to New Spain. Such at least is the inference to be drawn from an obscure letter written to Cortés by Viceroy Mendoza in his own hand and dated February 14, without mention of a year but undoubtedly 1538. Mendoza wrote:

> What I must tell you about the friar is that he assures me that the island that the ships of your lordship are searching for does not exist but that the pilot and seamen made a mistake. It was the coast of Peru itself [which they saw]. This

is very certain from the description that they give. [The friar] verified this with the pilot himself and [urges] that you do not waste time in searching. His fantasy is the land on the other side of the Strait of Magellan for he says that it comes almost as far north as the Tropic [of Capricorn].[28]

The friar was Marcos de Niza, who had been in Peru and Ecuador with Alvarado's expedition and who, in the middle of 1537, arrived in Mexico City, where he came to be on good terms with Zumárraga and Mendoza. Mendoza placed enough confidence in Fray Marcos to send him in 1538-1539 to verify Cabeza de Vaca's report of what lay to the north of the known area of New Spain.[29]

That Cortés would have accepted the unsupported opinion of Fray Marcos is not likely, since he had less confidence in the friar than did Mendoza. Moreover, because of his relations with the pilots of the great centers at Panama and Realejo, he was able to recognize the notions of Fray Marcos about the geography of the South American coast for the fantasies they were. Nevertheless, in 1538 Cortés did not prepare a third expedition to Peru. Probably Palacios Rubios reported that he could find no island of gold or that the islands, if they were the Galápagos, were barren. In the same months rumors of the existence of the Seven Cities of Cíbola and the Gran Quivira diverted Cortés' attention to the north of New Spain. At this time also Cortés was having difficulty in finding enough experienced pilots for all his ships[30] and he may have been forced to restrict himself to what he considered the more important ventures.

Failure to outfit a third Peruvian voyage in 1538 meant not merely changes in plans for exploration but also changes in Cortés' plans for trade to the south. Indeed, one of the reasons for the suspension of Peruvian voyages, whether planned as permanent or temporary, may have been that the bulk of the cargoes Cortés had shipped consisted of arms and munitions. Once Cortés began to plan a new exploring expedition to the north, he had to store these for his own use and had little or none for sale. He was probably short of money, also, after his heavy losses in his marine explorations. Hence, a more important reason for the changes in his trading projects may well have been his hope of selling the surpluses of wheat, biscuit, pork, sugar, and cheese which, by the late 1530's, were beginning to pile up on his estates near Tehuantepec and in the valleys of Oaxaca and Cuernavaca. The main Spanish settlements in Mexico were so far away that cartage on bulky items would have eaten up much or all of the profit. Export, which meant much cheaper water carriage, promised lower freight costs and also opened the possibility of sale in an area with higher price levels and a more abundant supply of specie than New Spain had in those years. At Panama, which was largely dependent on imported food, he could find such a market. In effect, since Panama shipped food and goods to Peru and remitted Peruvian specie to Spain, Cortés was hoping to enter the Peruvian market through the entrance used by Spanish merchants and so spare his ships half the voyage they had formerly undertaken to move cargo from New Spain to Peru, a voyage he was willing to pay for only so long as it embraced exploration. Cortés may have been influenced in his revision of plans at this time by the expansion of trade between New Spain, on the one hand, and between Panama and Central America, on the other, as Central American ships began to undertake more voyages to New Spain.

Whatever the reasons, there can be no doubt that in the second half of 1538 Cortés reorganized his arrangements for trade to the south. He appointed Juan de Segura to act as permanent factor or business agent in the city of Panama, and began to assemble foodstuffs for shipment.[31] He still had substantial sums owing on promissory notes and cargo left for sale in Peru from the voyages of 1536–1537 and 1537–1538 and so had to make arrangements to continue transacting business in Peru. Shortly after his appointment of Segura, therefore, Cortés gave a power of attorney to Alonso de Zamudio, ordering him to proceed via Panama to Peru to become his factor. The instrument of appointment listed some of the debtors: Juan Domingo, Pedro de Ribera, and Gómez de León for merchandise and items manufactured in Tehuantepec for the armada of Peru which they had taken to Peru to sell on behalf of Cortés; Juan Ortiz, who, having collected money due Cortés in Guatemala City without accounting for it, had been imprisoned but had "absented himself from the jail" to flee to Peru; and Juan Balza, who had departed from New Spain without accounting for all of Cortés' cloth and tributes in his care.[32] The appointment of Zamudio may have been made also in the hope that trade with Peru could be resumed in the future either via Panama or by direct shipment with better hope of profit.

The first ship sent to Panama in accordance with Cortés' new plans was the *San Vicente*, loaded with biscuit, flitches of bacon, and cheeses. Segura probably arrived in Panama with this ship toward the end of 1538 or early in 1539. On his arrival he discovered that market conditions were not so favorable as Cortés had hoped, and that the cargo had become so spoiled in transit that much of it could not be sold at any price. "I am offering the biscuit . . . at two pesos and the flitches of bacon at a peso," he reported, "but even though there are no others for sale, no one wants them because of the condition they are in; and as for the cheeses . . . , no one will take them at a low price or as a gift since they are all riddled with wormholes and rotten."[33]

In April, 1539, the *San Lázaro,* piloted by the famous Juan Fernández de Ladrillero, arrived with Alonso de Zamudio and another cargo to be sold in Panama. The inventory of the cargo on April 18, 1539, listed:

184 quintals, 3 arrobas, 19 lbs. of flour
197 quintals, 2 arrobas of biscuit—"white, clean and dry"
61 arrobas, 2 lbs. of white refined sugar
170 sides of bacon
98 varnished wooden shields made at Tehuantepec (for use by Indian allies of the Spanish.)[34]

With the *San Lázaro* arrived an order from Cortés that Segura forward the proceeds from the sale of the first shipment, but his factor was forced to report, with much embarrassment, that there were no proceeds and that he was having trouble preventing the master of the *San Lázaro* from selling the ship's cordage and sails.[35]

The cargo of the *San Lázaro* arrived in good condition with an excellent chance of sale for Pascual de Andagoya, planning his return to Panama after a long absence, was even then outfitting an expedition to explore the Chocó and needed supplies. Segura miscalculated, however, asking too high a price, and lost the opportunity for a sale. In July, 1539, Zamudio reported to Cortés that virtually all of the cargo of the *San Vicente* was a total loss; that some of the food brought on the *San Lázaro* had been sold and unless the rest were sold quickly, it too would spoil. He urged winding up the entire venture.[36]

By the end of the summer of 1539, Cortés' two agents were at odds. Zamudio, hearing reports of the civil war between Francisco Pizarro and Diego de Almagro in Peru, was reluctant to take up his post. His reluctance was based in part, too, upon a sound appreciation that Cortés' plans stood almost no chance of success after the failure to dispose of two cargoes at a profit in Panama. He was also toying with the idea of joining Andagoya's expedition and, accordingly, was not indisposed to take the gloomiest view possible in order to justify abandoning his mission. Segura pressed his fellow agent to move on to Peru, and when Zamudio continued to refuse, asked that he surrender the promissory notes and power of attorney he carried, for the longer collection was delayed, the poorer would be the chances of finding the debtors. In 1539, moreover, many Spaniards, among them some of Cortés' debtors, were returning to Spain from Peru. When Zamudio refused even to turn over the papers he carried, Segura began legal action before the Audiencia of Panama and succeeded in impounding the promissory notes, but Zamudio tore up the power of attorney. All this was reported to Cortés by Segura, who asked that a new agent be sent to go to Peru to collect.[37]

In September, 1539, a third shipment from the Cortés estates arrived in Panama.[38] It was the last, for the unfavorable reports of his agents, who were in agreement on the poor chances of profit in the venture however much they were at loggerheads with each other, persuaded Cortés to suspend shipments to Panama. He decided to send Segura to Peru after disposal of the cargo left in Panama and on September 27, 1539, executed the necessary power of attorney.[39] Forwarding the instrument to Panama was another matter, however; months later the power of attorney had not yet arrived. During that time Zamudio vanished on Andagoya's first expedition. Meantime, on February 15, 1540, Cortés' affairs in Panama met a further reverse. Fire broke out and within half an hour burned down the straw and brush shacks which comprised the city. The unsold cargoes were a complete loss. Segura was able to save only the promissory notes and the funds in his possession. After waiting until April for word from Cortés, he bought wine with whatever money he had, planning to recoup some of the expenses of the venture by trade, and set out for León in Nicaragua. Finding no market for the wine in León, he went on to the port of Acajutla, where Pedro de Alvarado was outfitting a second fleet, the one which was to form his share of the partnership with Viceroy Mendoza. In Acajutla Segura heard that Cortés had gone to Spain. He planned to dispose of his wine either to Alvarado or to men in the fleet and invest the proceeds in cacao, the principal export of the Sonsonate region, for which Acajutla served as port.[40] With the ill luck which plagued Cortés' commercial ventures, Segura found it necessary to lower the price of the wine in order to dispose of it.[41] By November, 1540, he was in Guatemala City where, acting under instructions from Altamirano, the majordomo of Cortés, he turned over to a local resident, Juan de Chaves, the promissory notes due in Peru.

Cortés' southward ventures thus met with little profit. His shipments to Panama were almost total losses. His shipments to Peru can hardly have returned him a profit, even though Juan Domingo and the agents appointed by Palacios Rubios in Peru seem to have handled Cortés' affairs better than his other agents. Juan Domingo in Lima sold the goods entrusted to him to Francisco Pizarro and to a cousin of Jorje de Alvarado, half for gold and half in promissory notes due in four months; these were paid on time. The notes held by Baltasar García in Puerto Viejo, totaling 4,005 pesos, were paid in part, since Segura reported that he had heard that perhaps 2,000 pesos had been collected. Whether Cortés' last agent, Chaves, was able to make his way to Peru and collect the money, however, is doubtful. In 1540–1541 Peru was experiencing another war among the Spanish conquerors, and it was a poor place to collect old debts. The assassination of Francisco Pizarro in 1541, furthermore, put an end to all possibility of payment for the aid sent with Grijalva.[42]

Nevertheless, the voyages of Cortés' ships had opened direct communication with Peru, and the evidence we have, though scanty, indicates that after 1539 a few ships sailed each year between Mexico and Peru. In 1539 Hernando Pizarro, the brother of Francisco, wishing to return to Spain and fearing assassination in Panama at the hands of the elder Almagro's adherents, since he had been directly implicated in the trial and execution of the latter, had the ship carrying him sail to New Spain, where he made his way across the Isthmus of Tehuantepec to Coatzacoalcos. There he was arrested and brought before the viceroy in Mexico City, but since there was no charge against him in New Spain, he was permitted to sail from Veracruz.[43] In November, 1542, a Central American or Peruvian vessel, the *Todos Santos,* was in Huatulco harbor, loading slips of quince, peach, pear, and apple trees for shipment to Peru.[44] That same month Alonso Cano, vecino and encomendero of Villa Alta, was given license to go to Peru to dispose of his horses.[45] In July of the following year Alonso de Arteaga arrived in Mexico City from Peru with silver bars. We know of his arrival because the royal mint in Mexico refused to accept the silver for minting until the viceroy issued an order that any Peruvian silver properly stamped with the mark of the treasury officials in Peru must be accepted.[46]

Later in that same year, 1543, Mendoza himself sent three ships to Peru. The vessels of the Cabrillo expedition had returned from their northward exploration in the middle of 1543. Mendoza planned to use them for a new expedition to the Moluccas, but pending word from Villalobos, who commanded the ships already sent to the Far East, he gave permission to the sailors to take three ships to Peru and agreed to supply enough horses to make up any shortage there might be in cargo.[47] A passenger on these ships may have been Hernando de Villanueva, who had come to Mexico from Peru and was returning in the fall of 1543.[48] The three ships probably made the voyage safely, for they would have left in the winter of 1543–1544 to return in the summer of 1544 in accordance with the seasonal changes in prevailing winds.[49] Mendoza's vessels, strangely enough, may have helped touch off civil war in Peru, for it was partly through private letters from New Spain, arriving in Peru in the winter of 1543–1544, probably on these vessels, that word of the promulgation of the New Laws and the appointment of Blasco Núñez Vela as viceroy of Peru reached the southern realms before the viceroy arrived via Panama with the official notice.[50]

In the year 1544 a ship from New Spain was among the few to encounter trouble because of the civil wars. In December, a well-built galleon from Mexico, owned by Diego de Ocampo, was seized by Bachicao, Gonzalo Pizarro's sea raider, as it lay at anchor off the Island of Puna. The vessel was a fair prize, since it had been requisitioned by the viceroy, Nùñez Vela, to be re-equipped for war use. Mendoza apparently had an interest in this ship, for he later complained that he lost heavily by the seizure.[51] This capture was countered in part by the arrival in New Spain of a Peruvian vessel seized by the royalists it had been taking to exile in Chile by order of Gonzalo Pizarro.[52]

Despite civil war in Peru, at least two ships came to New Spain from Peru in 1545–1546. One ship must have sailed from Peru in August, 1545, arriving in New Spain in late October or early November of the same year, for on November 10, 1545, Lic. Tello de Sandoval in Mexico City was able to send on to the home government an account of Peruvian events up to August.[53] About January 20, 1546, a second vessel sailed from the Island of Puna, carrying some of the men expelled from Peru by Gonzalo Pizarro, and made a direct voyage to Huatulco in approximately two months.[54]

Mendoza let shipping clear from New Spain for Peru even after he knew that the southern colony was in revolt. Early in 1546 a vessel made the voyage, for on June 26, 1546, Gonzalo Pizarro wrote to Mendoza, acknowledging receipt of a letter from the viceroy dated at Mexico City, February 16, 1546. Both letters are models of courtesy between enemies.[55] In the fall of 1546, one of the more curious episodes of the civil wars concerned another ship which was allowed to sail from New Spain to Peru. In October, the ship anchored off the Island of Puna. On board were numerous merchants, bales of clothing, and other merchandise, letters, as well as Iñigo López de Moncibay. This person, a gentleman and yet a merchant, dressed as an Indian and posed as a partisan of Gonzalo Pizarro, but claimed to know Mendoza well. He was regarded by Gonzalo Pizarro's men as a spy.[56] If so, he was a poor choice for such a mission.

Toward the end of 1546 until the defeat and execution of Gonzalo Pizarro, sailings from ports of Mexico to Peru were embargoed by Mendoza,[57] while he readied an army and fleet to assist La Gasca in returning Peru to its allegiance to the Spanish Crown.[58] As soon as the embargo was lifted, communication and trade between the two colonies was resumed on an even greater scale.[59] By the end of the 1540's it is likely that a number of vessels—Mexican, Peruvian, and Central American in ownership—maintained trade in a series of annual sailings.

III. THE PORTS, ROADS, AND ROUTES OF THE MID-CENTURY

MARITIME communication meant ports, roads to connect them with the centers of population, and the selection of sailing routes between ports. Along the coast of Peru, ships sailing to and from Mexico made use of routes, ports, and roads which came into existence primarily to give settlements access to wares coming from the Isthmus of Panama. Hence, trade with Mexico was an unimportant factor in the growth of ports along the coast of South America, the Isthmus, and perhaps even on the coast of Central America. In contrast, along the coast of Mexico, where Isthmian traffic was insignificant, the Peruvian trade was of nearly equal weight with that of Central America and, during the early years, was important in the selection of a harbor to be developed into a port and in the construction of roads connecting the harbor with the major Spanish settlements.

In the middle decades of the sixteenth century, the Mexico-Peru trade was almost entirely confined to the Mexican port of Huatulco. The port took its name from the Indian town of Santa María Huatulco, nearly nine miles inland. Although the town of Huatulco in the sixteenth century was an encomienda until it reverted to the Crown, the port was from the first administered directly by a viceregal appointee. The port is at lat. 15° 44′ N. and long. 96° 08′ W., perhaps thirty miles east by sea from present-day Puerto Angel and forty-five leagues (115 miles) from Oaxaca City by the sixteenth-century road. In the vicinity of Huatulco the coast trends in a southeast–northwest direction; it is the westernmost part of the great curve forming the Gulf of Tehuantepec. The port of Huatulco is the smaller and more sheltered of two neighboring bays, the larger one separated from Port Huatulco by a peninsula jutting out perhaps 800 yards to the sea. (It has been given the name of Santa Cruz Bay by the United States Hydrographic Office, undoubtedly from the name of Santa Cruz Huatulco, the coastal village which served to shelter crews and agents.) Port Huatulco, the smaller bay, is an indentation in a northwestward direction. It is perhaps one to two miles long and about a quarter of a mile wide. The mouth of the bay, at the southeast, is clear of obstructions and easily navigable by sailing craft. Around the bay is a series of peaks which accentuate its landlocked character and give additional protection from wind. The bay is open only to storms from the southeast, which are almost unknown in the dry season, from October to April, and which occur infrequently during the rainy season. It gives excellent protection from the violent northers that blow on occasion from October to April. The bay has a firm bottom affording good anchorage with depths of from five to ten fathoms. The shore is a firm, sandy beach, excellent for landing. Water is obtained from gullies which carry water during the rains but have no surface flow at other times of the year. There is a perennial underground flow which can be tapped by wells. Port Huatulco is probably the best natural harbor on the coast of Mexico from Soconusco as far west as Acapulco.[1]

That Huatulco was the principal Pacific port, between perhaps 1537 and 1575, is little known to writers of Mexican history. Cortés examined a number of bays along the Mexican coast as possible sites for shipbuilding and warehouses, but does not seem to have examined Huatulco harbor. As a result of his investigations, he concentrated his shipbuilding at Tehuantepec and Acapulco. The latter harbor, which is one of the finest natural harbors on the Pacific coast of Mexico and nearest the capital, particularly impressed Cortés. He used it for assembling men and supplies for his expeditions to the north, even though the lack of a road for pack animals through the broken country between Cuernavaca, his country seat, and Acapulco made the use of that harbor almost prohibitively expensive and difficult. All supplies had to be carried from Mexico City on the shoulders of Indians.[2]

Tehuantepec, because water carriage could be used from Verucruz to Coatzacoalcos and from Coatzacoalcos to the continental divide, was a better site for shipbuilding than Acapulco. Moreover, it was the key point of the old Aztec land routes to Central America.[3] Accordingly, Cortés asked for the inclusion of the province of Tehuantepec in his marquisate and established his permanent shipyard there, not at the town of Tehuantepec on the great lagoon but somewhere near it.[4] He envisaged Tehuantepec not merely as a convenient center for shipbuilding but also as the key to sea communication with Central America and areas to the south. His views agreed with those of the Crown representatives in Mexico, who regarded Tehuantepec as too important to be left in the hands of a subject.[5] Their representations to the home government led in 1560 to an agreement with Martín Cortés, the second Marqués del Valle, under which the Crown took back jurisdiction over Tehuantepec and the marquisate was guaranteed the value of the revenues through a permanent grant in maize and specie to be paid from the royal revenues of the province of Chalco.[6] The

[1] For notes to chapter iii, see pages 139–141.

second marqués, although ostensibly giving way gracefully to royal importunities, struck an advantageous bargain, since the tribute from Tehuantepec fell off steadily with the disappearance of the Indian population, whereas the royal settlement stipulated a continuing return at the level of 1560. At the time of the retrocession of Tehuantepec, the major Pacific port was Huatulco, and had been for twenty years. Its rival was not Tehuantepec, which was not to become a major port until the nineteenth century, but Acapulco.[7]

The realization that Tehuantepec was an indifferent harbor came to Hernán Cortés slowly. Through the 1520's and early 1530's he attempted to base shipping on the roadsteads off the Isthmus of Tehuantepec. He probably lost some ships as a result, since the Isthmus, with its low shelving coasts, offers few protected anchorages, and currents and winds are especially treacherous for sailing ships during the storms of the dry season. The only good natural harbor near Tehuantepec is Huatulco, eighty miles by sea to the west.[8] Security from the Tehuantepec gales probably explains in part why Huatulco became the principal harbor on the Pacific coast of the Audiencia of Mexico in the years between 1537 and 1540.

By the late 1530's Cortés was making extensive use of Huatulco. The harbor was nearly as accessible from Oaxaca City as Tehuantepec. The port was also convenient for assembling supplies of foodstuffs, produced on the estates of the marquisate, for distribution along the Pacific coast. Cortés made at least part of his shipments of foodstuffs to Panama from Huatulco.[9] In the fall of 1540, when Pedro de Alvarado brought his fleet north along the coast, he contracted for supplies with Cortés, who had the administrators of his estates bring together an enormous amount of supplies: 1,500 quintals of biscuit, between 2,500 and 3,000 flitches of bacon, many lambs, sheep, pigs, and calves, and quantities of beans and other foodstuffs. All these supplies were sent to Huatulco as the safest and most convenient point at which Alvarado could load his ships. Mendoza, who had not yet come to terms with Alvarado, forbade the latter to land or accept supplies, and so the arrangement fell through—to the loss of Cortés.[10]

By the early 1540's Cortés' vessels were only part of the shipping at Huatulco. The harbor was the point of embarkation for Peru as well as the depot for cacao in the active trade between New Spain and the producing areas of Sonsonate with their outlet at Acajutla. It is likely also that the Nicaraguan ships from Realejo and such Panamanian ships as made their way up the coast used Huatulco. During the middle decades of the sixteenth century Huatulco was listed in viceregal orders as the usual Pacific port of entry and exit from New Spain.[11] The primacy of Huatulco as the Pacific port of New Spain was evident in the fact that a community of artisans, skilled in the various phases of shipbuilding and repair, was established there to service navigation. As early as 1539 Cortés' alcalde mayor of Tehuantepec, when caulkers were needed to caulk one of his master's ships, had to send to Huatulco for two skilled workers, paying for their time on the journey coming and going.[12] In the middle 1540's, it was possible to build substantial ships at Huatulco, using Indians for the rough tasks of cartage, hewing timber, and unskilled labor in general, while European artisans did the skilled work of carpentry, fitting iron, caulking, and rigging. The growth of the port also lured business agents, storekeepers, and others. The community grew so quickly that by 1542 the viceroy appointed a corregidor to administer it.[13] In the latter half of the sixteenth century the town had perhaps a hundred houses. These were of brush and wattle, like almost all other construction on the coast, but they constituted a substantial settlement.[14]

In addition to safe anchorage, a major reason for the rise of Huatulco was the ease with which it could be linked with the highways running from Mexico City through Oaxaca City to Tehuantepec and on through Soconusco to Guatemala. In this fact, nearness to Tehuantepec, and in the production of the valleys and back country of Oaxaca and the Tehuantepec area, lay the early advantage of Huatulco over Acapulco. The latter had a far better natural harbor and lay much nearer the viceregal capital, but building a road through the broken mountain country from the Valley of Cuernavaca to the coast was far more difficult than linking Huatulco to the main route to Central America at Oaxaca. Moreover, the route from Mexico City to Huatulco passes through a series of valleys and basins which are separated by comparatively short stretches of mountainous terrain so that, though longer, it was far easier for travelers than the stretch of broken terrain from Tasco to Acapulco.

The roads of the sixteenth century from Mexico City to Oaxaca City probably followed in major part one of the main routes by which the Aztecs reached the valleys of Oaxaca and crossed to the Pacific shore of the Isthmus of Tehuantepec on their way to Central America. The additional road from Huatulco to Miahuatlán and Oaxaca City branching from this grand invasion and commercial route, probably followed one of the more important trails by which the Zapotecs found their way to the Pacific coast. The

Spanish, upon taking over these routes as heirs in empire, however, were forced to widen and improve the pre-Conquest trails for their own traffic. They needed wider roads and more substantial roadbeds that could take the wear of animal hooves and even cart wheels. Such improvements meant some digging and a good deal of filling in of ruts and holes. Streams too deep to be forded easily had to be spanned with bridges, usually of wood. By twentieth-century standards, these royal highways were still roads only by courtesy. They were unpaved trails, followed custom rather than plan, dusty in the dry season and quagmires in the rains. But horses, mules, donkeys, and the great heavy carts which were used occasionally in the valleys of southern Mexico could pass over them; the deeper streams could be crossed on bridges; and a number of Indian towns maintained rude inns (*mesones*) to provide shelter and food for travelers and, in the process, enrich the community treasuries with the proceeds. The work of building and maintaining the roads was carried out by *corvée* levied on Indian towns near the road. In the Mixteca that meant towns within eight leagues, approximately twenty miles of the road. The Indians often objected both to the labor draft and the seizure of land for the roadbed, but whatever their protests the roads were built and maintained sufficiently well to carry the relatively heavy traffic from the capital to Huatulco.[15]

The accompanying map is an attempt to reconstruct the major roads feeding the port of Huatulco and connecting it with the principal Spanish cities. It should be regarded as schematic, since our information on roads in the sixteenth century is scanty and the exact locations for almost all roads remain to be worked out in detail.

From the map it will be noticed that a traveler leaving Mexico City for embarkation at Huatulco had the choice of two routes. One led him south into the Valley of Cuernavaca, the seat of the Marquisate of the Valley, and from there southeastward through broken country into the Basin of Matamoros to the town of Izúcar (present-day Matamoros). At Izúcar the two southward roads converged.

The other, and probably more widely used, road ran from Mexico City almost due east over the mountains into the Basin of Puebla, running north of the present-day Mexico City–Puebla motor road. In the Basin of Puebla the road passed through the great Indian center of Huejotzingo to Cholula, where the eastward road continued to Puebla and the port of Veracruz. The traveler making for the Pacific coast turned south at Cholula or, farther on, at Puebla, and entered the broad fertile Valley of Atlixco, which in the middle decades of the sixteenth century was being settled rapidly by Spanish farmers. The road ran through the valley, passing through the main valley town of Atlixco, and into the lower, warmer Valley of

SIXTEENTH-CENTURY ROADS TO HUATULCO

Matamoros and so to Izúcar, where the traveler might meet a *recua* that had chosen to go by way of Cuernavaca.

From Izúcar the traveler made his way over another fairly easy mountain barrier to another broad valley, still in *tierra templada.* The main center and administrative seat of this basin was and is Acatlán, the first town of the Mixteca Baja. South of Acatlán the road ran through a series of valleys, each at a higher altitude than the one to the north: the Valley of

Huajuápam with its chief seat, the town of Huajuápam, the last major town in the bishopric of Puebla; the Valley of Tamazulápam, long and narrow, the first of the Mixteca Alta, the higher mountain core of the aboriginal Mixtecapan; the Valley of Teposcolula with its important administration center of Teposcolula; and the Valley of Nochixtlán with its two great towns of Yanhuitlán and Nochixtlán. After leaving the Valley of Nochixtlán the traveler descended the escarpment separating the Valley of Nochixtlán from the central valleys of Oaxaca and reached the border between Mixtec and Zapotec territory as he entered the central valleys at Huajolotitlán, the modern Huitzo, the road running to the south of the modern Pan-American Highway. From Huajolotitlán an easy route along the valley floor led to Etla and the Spanish city of Antequera, present-day Oaxaca, where travelers could rest, replenish supplies and repair equipment, and muleteers remake their animal trains.

Antequera was the hub of a number of roads. One, of some importance, followed by Father Ponce in the 1580's, gave Mexico City and Puebla, especially the latter, another means of reaching Oaxaca. It followed substantially the route of the present railroad from Puebla south through the valleys of Tepeaca and Tecamachalco to the Basin of Tehuacán. From Tehuacán the road led through Cuzcatlán, Tecomavaca, Cuicatlán, and the long canyon of Tomellín to emerge at Sedas in the central valleys and continue via Huajolotitlán and Etla to Antequera. This road was built initially by the city of Antequera at its own cost during the 1540's.

Two other roads leading out of Antequera gave access to Huatulco and Tehuantepec. Travelers making for Tehuantepec turned southwestward to Tlacolula, Tlacochahuaya, Totolapa, Nejapa, Jalapa del Marqués, and Tehuantepec. Those making for the port of Huatulco turned southward along an easy, almost level route through the central valleys to Zimatlán, Ocotlán, Ejutla, and Miahuatlán. This last town was at the end of the central valleys. From there the road entered the Sierra Madre and wound upward to the divide beyond San José del Pacífico, whence it descended through broken difficult terrain to the hot country of Rio Hondo and thence to Santa María Huatulco and the port.

At best the journey by land from Mexico City to Huatulco was long and slow. The traveler who could manage changes of horses probably required several weeks or even a month for the trip. Most freight was carried by pack trains which must have spent several months on the road. The heavy, lumbering oxcarts, which lowered freight costs although they moved as slowly as pack trains, could be used only in the larger valleys such as the central valleys of Oaxaca.

One route which obviated much of the land travel was the water route from Veracruz under the control of the Cortés estates. It was used by officials of the marquisate to reach Tehuantepec and Huatulco from Mexico City because, even though roundabout, it meant easy water transportation for a large part of the distance. It was also used for the transportation of bulky objects such as ships' gear from Veracruz to the shipyards at Tehuantepec and the ships at anchor in the port of Huatulco. Those who wished to use this route from Mexico City had to follow the main road through Puebla to Veracruz, where coastal vessel carried them to Coatzacoalcos on the Caribbean shore of the Isthmus of Tehuantepec, or, if they preferred, they might travel along the coast by land. From Coatzacoalcos, canoes manned by Indian rowers, some of which were kept in readiness for private use by the Cortés estates as late as the 1560's, followed a route up the Coatzacoalcos River which brought them to the head of navigation at Antigua Malpaso, twelve leagues, approximately thirty miles, by land from the town of Tehuantepec.[16] This last route, employing the best highway in New Spain, the Mexico City–Veracruz road, and water transportation, was used by Mendoza to ship his clothing and part of his other luggage to Huatulco for embarkation on the *San Andrés* in 1551, when he went to Peru. Although a semi-invalid, Mendoza, together with most of his retinue, food for his voyage, and the rest of his luggage went by land through the Mixteca and Oaxaca to Huatulco for embarkation.[17]

Once travelers arrived in Huatulco, there still remained the problem of securing passage on a ship sailing to Peru. After 1547 passage was fairly easily obtained, since a number of ships made the voyage each year. These ships, however, sailed during a definite season, hence travelers who arrived at Huatulco during the last weeks of February were likely to have to wait through the spring and the broiling, muggy summer months of rain until late fall or early winter when ships would again sail.[18]

The sailing season was governed by the winds along the Pacific coast from New Spain to Chile. For sailing vessels this is one of the most difficult regions on earth, so much so that during the later years of the colonial period the voyage from New Spain to Manila was generally considered easier than the far shorter one from New Spain to Peru. For most of the year, especially the months from April to September, the central part of the South American coast is under the influence of south winds blowing parallel to the coast, which at a distance from the coast means a prevailing wind from the southeast. The Pacific coast of Central America, southern Mexico, and to a varying extent northermost South America has uncertain winds of low force. Calms are frequent and may last for long periods. Southward travel along the coast in sailing vessels is extremely slow and difficult during the months from April to September or October. If undertaken at the beginning of this season the voyage from Huatulco to a landfall on the coast of one of the realms of Peru took at least seven or eight months.

For ships sailing northward from Peru to New Spain, these same months, especially late summer, were the most favorable. The south winds paralleling the coast sped the vessel northward to the Gulf of Panama. Farther north, it was a matter of luck to pick up a favoring wind, but the chances were better than at other seasons. The months from April to September therefore became the sailing season from Peru to New Spain. The trip from El Callao to Huatulco under most favorable circumstances took from four to six weeks. We are fortunate in having a brief description of the voyage by Father José de Acosta, who sailed from Peru to New Spain in 1586.[10]

> When I sailed from Peru to New Spain, I noticed that all the time that we traveled along the coast of Peru, the voyage, as always happens, was easy and serene because of the south wind that blows there. Because of it one sails before the wind in the return voyage to Spain and New Spain. When we crossed the gulf, since we traveled far at sea and also below the equator, the weather was peaceful and refreshing and we sailed before the wind. When we reached the region of Nicaragua, and during the time that we sailed along all that coast, we encountered adverse winds, clouded skies, and many rain storms. At times the wind howled frighteningly. All this navigation took place within the Torrid Zone, for from 12° S., the latitude of Lima, we sailed to 17° [N.], the latitude of Huatulco, port of New Spain....

The months from October until April, the other part of the year, witness a partial shift in the pattern of winds and currents. The equatorial belt of calms moves southward, so that the Pacific coast of New Spain and Central America is in a belt of light down-coast winds which, in accordance with the configuration of the coast, produce prevailing northeast or northwest winds. In these months there may be storms, caused by outflow from the north of cold continental air, which are called Tehuantepeckers in the Gulf of Tehuantepec and Papagallos along the Central American coast. Along the northern coast of South America, where the zone of equatorial calms is dominant in these months, there is a better chance of picking up a northern wind, especially from December to April. Along the coast of Peru, the prevailing winds continue to come from the south.

Shipping moving from Mexico to Peru used these airs. Travelers awaiting embarkation at Huatulco for Peru would normally take ship at some time between late September and the end of February. Their vessel would hug the coast, taking advantage of down-coast winds, and making a fairly easy voyage, until it reached Guatemala or Nicaragua. Then, it would cut across the Gulf of Panama on a route which might bring it within sight of the Galápagos Islands, to make its South American landfall on the coast of the Audiencia of Quito at Manta, the seaport of Puerto Viejo. Even under favorable circumstances the voyage of perhaps five hundred maritime leagues took a minimum of two months and often three months or longer.

The route followed from New Spain to the realms of Peru during the favorable sailing season was called navigation by the meridian in the later colonial period, for the pilot steered his vessel hugging the coast and, in crossing the Gulf of Panama, tried to maintain a fairly direct southward course, although the vessel sailed through seven to ten degrees of longitude. In contrast to navigation by the meridian, another sailing route was discovered by which vessels could make the voyage from New Spain to the coast of Peru during the months of adverse winds. This route was called navigation by the parallel; that is, by latitude. The vessel followed a gigantic fishhook course, sailing southward into the Pacific as far as 28° or 30° S. sometimes going as far as the Juan Fernández Islands or beyond before turning northeast to catch the prevailing winds and currents for coasting northward until the ship made a landfall on the northern coast of Peru or even as far north as Manta, 0° 57′ S. By use of this course, sailing time could be shortened under the most favorable circumstances to three or four months.[20]

A colonial tradition places the discovery of this route in the 1540's and ascribes it to Diego de Ocampo, the valorous captain and trusted friend of Cortés, whom the latter left as one of the three trustees of his estates when he sailed for Spain in 1526. The earliest written version of this tradition seems to be a passage in the history of Fray Juan de Torquemada.[21]

> In the period of his [Mendoza's] administration, there was discovered the navigation to Peru by way of the Pacific Ocean. Ships were built in the port of Tehuantepec, and sailed to El Callao or Lima. This navigation route was discovered at his own expense by Diego de Ocampo, one of the leading gentlemen, a native of the villa of Cáceres in the kingdoms of Castile, who was one of the conquerors and pacifiers of this New World. Persevering in his worthy plans he carried out this excellent and profitable discovery.

The versions in Humboldt, Pascual de Gayangos' edition of the letters of Cortés, and later writers all derive ultimately from this passage in Torquemada.[22]

The legend presents certain difficulties that require a rather extended discussion. There can be no doubt that Diego de Ocampo built a handsome galleon at Port Huatulco in the 1540's. On November 8, 1542, Antonio de Mendoza issued an order to Cristóbal de Chávez, corregidor of the port of Huatulco, mentioning that Diego de Ocampo was building a ship and ordering that, notwithstanding ordinances against forced Indian labor, the local Indians be compelled to bring to the port timbers cut in the forests of Mazantepec for masts and rudder. A year later the ship was still under construction.[23] On October 30, 1543, the viceroy issued another order, at the petition of Diego de Ocampo, that the corregidor of the port of Huatulco see that local Indians bring to the harbor any additional timber and other items needed, and that the second mate of the vessel, Antón Sánchez de Mecinal, who had sold some gear without permission, be put on trial promptly.[24] Thereafter the vessel was completed, perhaps by the spring of 1544, for late in December, 1544, it was in the Bay of Caraques, off Manta, where it had been detained by the corregidor, Santillana, in the name of Viceroy Blasco Núñez Vela, for overhaul and equipment as a vessel of war. Since the overhaul was well under way by Christmas, 1544, the galleon must have arrived some weeks earlier. The dating indicates a successful voyage that might well have started in the summer of 1544. It was this ship that Hernando Bachicao, then sailing north up the coast to Túmbez, captured for inclusion in the war fleet of Gonzalo Pizarro. In a report to Gonzalo Pizarro the vessel was praised as "buen navío."[25]

Why Diego de Ocampo built this ship we do not know. Possibly, like his friend Cortés, he found a New Spain dominated by Antonio de Mendoza too confining, and sought in Peru a wider, freer field. Yet Mendoza appears to have been his partner in the enterprise[26]—a fact that explains the viceroy's favoring orders. The partnership may well have been the price exacted of Ocampo for freedom to carry out his plans, for Mendoza tended to insist on a share in every enterprise which promised good return.

Thus far the additional evidence jibes with the legend. One difficulty in accepting the legend without revision, however, lies in the simple fact that Diego de Ocampo was a landsman. Great though his services were to Cortés on land, he does not appear to have given either advice or assistance to his chief in the extensive exploration which the latter undertook. Yet one of Cortés' major difficulties in his maritime explorations was precisely lack of skilled men. That a land captain knowing little of the sea should suddenly solve a complex problem in seasons and winds does not make sense. With the wealth gained in the conquest of New Spain, Diego de Ocampo could have had a ship built, but he could not have piloted it himself, much less have thought out a possible solution to the problem of reaching Peru in the months of adverse winds.

A much likelier answer would be that Diego de Ocampo was merely the owner and captain of the vessel, captain in those days implying military commander, whereas the man responsible for conduct of the vessel at sea was the master, who followed a course laid out by the pilot, the latter being the only trained navigator that a vessel normally carried in its crew. Who Ocampo's master and pilot were we do not know, only the name of his rascally second mate is given in the available evidence. It is likely that his sea officers were recruited from the group of trained men developed in the shipping of Nicaragua and Panama, which in the 1530's and 1540's were the sources for most of the pilots. The pilots in these centers became well acquainted with the winds in the Pacific shortly after navigation began. In the 1530's they were directing exploration of the ocean and were searching for more convenient routes for the difficult southward voyage to Peru. The ship on which Fray Tómas de Berlanga sailed from Panama for Puerto Viejo in 1535 ventured beyond the Gulf of Panama and discovered the Galápagos Islands. (At Puerto Viejo Fray Tómas encountered men in a galleon from Nicaragua, who had sailed for Peru in the summer of 1534 and had a difficult passage lasting eight months.)[27] It is likely that Diego de Ocampo employed a pilot, trained in the shipping of Panama or Nicaragua, who was interested in a solution to the problem of a summer passage and directed the successful search. An additional motive for the search, one that would have attracted the interest of a man who had enriched himself in one conquest, might well have been taking up the hunt for rich islands in the South Pacific.

A further difficulty in the legend of the development of navigation by latitude from New Spain to Peru lies in the fact that the earliest version that specifically connects Diego de Ocampo to the long ocean route to 28° or 30° S. occurs in Humboldt, who probably got it from the secretariat attached to the viceroy of New Spain at the turn of the nineteenth century, two and a half centuries after the event. Just what Torquemada meant by the navigation to Peru is far from certain. His statement could even be taken to mean the usual route down the coast of New Spain to Central America and then across the Gulf of Panama, which was used as early as 1536. Torquemada's lack of clarity probably arose from a confusion in his own mind and ignorance of Pacific coast routes. However, another bit of evidence indicates that the story does refer to navigation by parallel. In 1579, Lic. Valverde, president of the Audiencia of Guatemala, reporting on Drake's raid into the Pacific and possible routes by which Drake could return to England, mentioned that in the time of [Gonzalo?] Pizarro, one or two vessels had followed a deep ocean route from the west coast of New Spain to a landfall at Lima or Arequipa. At the time Valverde wrote, no pilot knew the course or just what winds would be encountered. There remained only the legend that men had reached Peru by such a route.[28]

On the whole, the evidence would point to a discovery of navigation by latitude or at least use of the course in the summer and early fall of 1544 by a vessel built and owned by Diego de Ocampo of Mexico. The knowledge and inspiration needed to search for the course probably came from the pilots trained in the shipping of Nicaragua and Panama. The discovery was a triumph of observation and navigational skill. However, it gave too little advantage in time over waiting for the favorable season to be used in the sixteenth century. In the later colonial period, it was again used as a secondary route by a few ships whose owners preferred not to wait until the southward shift of the northern trades and equatorial calms at the end of the northern summer permitted a more direct and easier passage by the meridian.

A vessel sailing during the usual season from Huatulco for passage to Peru by the meridian would leave usually in the late fall or early winter. The voyage would take at the very best two months and usually longer. Landfall on the South American coast would be made in the Audiencia of Quito either at Manta, the Punta de Santa Elena, or the Island of Puna.[29] The customary landfall appears to have been Manta, the port of Puerto Viejo, and the first of the series of settlements along the coast of the realms of Peru. From Manta south the vessels from New Spain entered upon the usual route of the Panamanian vessels.

Manta, a small settlement on the shore of the Bay of Caraques, had a roadstead rather than a port. It offered little possibility of trade even for the supply of Puerto Viejo, a town of seventeen vecinos in the 1570's. Manta did have a precarious supply of fresh water in a well a half league from the settlement, and during the rainy season and for some time afterward had shallow lagoons, from which ships could obtain water.[30]

A short distance south of Manta lay Santa Elena, on the northern shore of the point of the same name, with a large deep bay with alternating beaches and rocky bluffs, which provided excellent anchorage. It also had wells with fresh water, and a short distance inland had springs of asphalt which could be used for caulking ships. It served as one of the ports for Santiago de Guayaquil, which was difficult to reach by ocean-going sailing vessel because of its location at the head of the estuary of the Guayas River, and served also as a port for the Audiencia capital of San Francisco de Quito.[31]

Another of the ports for the cities of the Audiencia of Quito was on the Island of Puna in the Gulf of Guayaquil. The island is large, approximately twenty-nine miles long and from eight to thirteen miles wide. In the sixteenth century the island had a numerous Indian population which raised much maize and sweet manioc. The island had much game. Although the waters around the island were full of shoals, the Bay of Guayaquil offered protection from storms and there were fairly good anchorages near the island. Because of its timber and available food, Puna was favored as a stop on the southward and northward voyages.[32]

At the southern end of the Gulf of Guayaquil lay Túmbez, a hot, low-lying town, then in the Audiencia of Quito. It was one of the first Spanish settlements along the coast, and in the 1540's and 1550's, a port of call for vessels coasting in Peruvian waters. It had no harbor, however, merely an open beach with rough water, so that shipping avoided it. By the 1570's it was used but rarely.[33]

Túmbez was replaced as a port of call by Paita, the port of San Miguel de Piura. Equally hot and low-lying, it was situated on a wide bight in the bay, which could provide good anchorage for a large number of ships. It is probably the least open port on the Peruvian coast. Because of these features it was a port of call for all ships moving along the coast of Peru, and much of the merchandise destined for Santiago de Guayaquil was landed at Paita to be sent on by pack train and cart. Supplies of water and firewood for ships, however, had to be brought by sea on balsa rafts.[34]

From Paita vessels from New Spain, which were less likely to engage in extensive marketing of merchandise along the coast or in coastwise passenger service, generally sailed directly southward for El Callao. The major Spanish settlement on the intervening coast in the mid-sixteenth century was Trujillo, situated on a large unsheltered bay. It was dangerous through much of the year, hence most vessels preferred to avoid it. Moreover, it had no water.[35]

El Callao, the principal port in the realms of Peru, was about two leagues distant by land from the capital city of Los Reyes, present-day Lima, which it served as port. El Callao provided a large, clean, and safe anchorage behind the Island of the Port. It was itself a settlement of considerable size, teeming with sailors from the shipping of the coast. From it an easily traveled road ran the two leagues to Lima, over which passed the pack trains and heavy carts bringing the merchandise destined for the capital. In addition to its function as port for Lima, El Callao also served as entrepôt for the landing and reshipping of merchandise sent by sea to settlements farther south or inland.[36] It seems to have been the final port of call for the vessels from New Spain for which we have records. After discharging the last of their cargo and passengers, these ships waited a few months until the season of favorable winds for their return. They then loaded passengers and such return cargo as they could obtain and began the coastal journey northward to the Audiencia of Quito. From there they struck northwest to the coast of Central America or New Spain and coasted westward until they reached the port of Huatulco, or later in the century the port of Acapulco.

IV. THE TRADING VENTURES OF THE CORTES ESTATE

WHEN Hernán Cortés sailed for Spain in the spring of 1540, he hoped to secure from the emperor redress of his grievances against Viceroy Mendoza and return to continue his explorations in the Pacific. His shipyard near the town of Tehuantepec, then probably the largest and best equipped in the colony, was completing a fine new galleon, the *Santa Cruz*.[1] His fleet in the Pacific was the largest it had ever been; and the trained staff he had brought together in the course of years with much expense was busy assembling soldiers, equipment, and provisions for another expedition.[2]

Cortés met a frigid reception at court. Neither the emperor nor his officers were willing to rebuke Mendoza for his treatment of Cortés, since it corresponded closely to their wishes to reduce the privileges they had been forced to grant as reward to the dangerous conqueror. We do not know when Cortés became aware that he had no chance of obtaining royal assistance for another expedition. To judge by the relatively sound state of the ships in later years, he must have given orders within a year or two after his arrival in Spain to disband preparations for another expedition and take measures for their preservation, otherwise the teredo would have destroyed the hulls. The vessels were assembled near the shipyard and dragged out of the water on rollers to be kept dry, safe from marine pests and northers, but subject to slower disintegration from sun, wind, rain, and land pests on a tropical beach.[3]

In the fall of 1547 the great conqueror died, leaving his estates and titles to a son of fifteen named Martín, born in wedlock of the second marchioness. Control of the estates passed to a council of trustees, comprised of Spanish grandees, until Martín should attain his legal majority at twenty-five.[4] Within four years the supervisory staff of the Estate of the Marquisate of the Valley in New Spain also changed as the aging servants of Cortés sought retirement. Lic. Juan de Altamirano, Cortés' cousin, trusted agent, and formal administrator of his property in the New World, took the less arduous position of accountant-general of the estate for the few remaining years of his life, the title and powers of governor of the estate being conferred upon Pedro de Ahumada Sámano after a brief period of administration by Tristán de Arellano. An enterprising Genoese merchant, Juan Bautista de Marín, who had come to New Spain in the 1540's as agent for

[1] For notes to chapter iv, see pages 142–144.

a fellow Genoese, Leonardo Lomellín, engaged in the exchange of Cortés' sugar for Negro slaves from Africa, became the central treasurer and principal assistant of Ahumada Sámano. Some years later, upon Altamirano's death, Marín was to receive the title of accountant-general. By the middle of 1551 the estate of the marquisate thus came under the direction of new and younger men,[5] who had the vigor and enthusiasm to try to meet the very serious problem of making the resources of the estate cover the charges on it.

The charges on the estate were heavy indeed. Cortés in his will listed a series of encumbrances upon the second marqués' inheritance: generous dowries for Martín's sisters, provision for the dowager marchioness, and for Cortés' children born out of wedlock, restitution to the Indians of the marquisate, many of whom promptly sued and recovered large sums for improper exactions during Cortés' lifetime; bequests to servitors, friends, and executors; and the customary generous endowments for the repose of the conqueror's soul.[6] There were, in addition, the many and complicated lawsuits of Cortés' varied activities. Meeting these charges was to prove a heavy burden upon the estate for the lifetime of the second marqués. For the new administrators in New Spain after 1551, the burden must have seemed almost intolerable. They had not only to secure sufficient revenue from the estate but also to convert the net revenue into gold and silver, the only means by which the large sums needed to pay bequests and the maintenance of the Cortés household could be transmitted to Spain.

Large as were the ordinary revenues of the estate from tributes and from the profits of its farms, houses, and other properties, they were not enough to meet all of the demands. Moreover, the extensive mining ventures of the 1530's had had to be abandoned, except for silver mining in the Tasco area, as gold placering ceased to pay expenses. To secure additional revenue, particularly in the form of specie, Pedro de Ahumada and his resourceful Genoese assistant, Juan Bautista de Marín, tried two major series of ventures. They undertook to replace the loss of revenue in placer mining by investing in silver ventures in the newly opened Zacatecas area; Ahumada personally directed much of the actual prospecting and extraction of ore.[7] His operations contributed materially to the development of the north, the most notable aid coming in 1561 when he was able to utilize the liquid capital of the estate to raise an army and repel a formidable Indian raid at a time when the oidores of the Audiencia of New Galicia found themselves without troops and the royal treasury without funds.[8]

The second series of ventures was an attempt to put to use the shipyard and ships slowly rotting at Tehuantepec. These vessels represented a large outlay and were an unused resource of importance by 1551 as coastal trade between New Spain and Central America and Peru became a fairly regular activity of considerable size. The shipyard could readily repair the more seaworthy vessels, which could then earn freights and perhaps assist in marketing some of the produce of the estate at higher prices than could be obtained in New Spain.

The necessary authority to repair and launch any of the estate's vessels that might be seaworthy and employ them in intercolonial trade, was written into the general power of attorney issued to Pedro de Ahumada at Yanguas, Spain, on October 14, 1551, by the Conde de Aguilar as trustee for Martín Cortés.[9] Two years later on July 15, 1553, the young marqués was able to secure a royal decree declaring him of age and competent to manage his estate, although he was then four years short of the legal majority. By virtue of the royal permission, Martín Cortés, on August 11, 1553, at Soria, executed a new power of attorney to Pedro de Ahumada as governor of his estate, reiterating the permission to put his ships to use. He might put some or all in the water, repair them, employ them in trade or navigation with Nicaragua, Guatemala, and Peru; he could hire sailors, appoint captains, form partnerships or mutual companies, collect freight charges, and sell the ships for cash or promissory notes as he might deem advisable. The power of attorney ratified all such acts in advance.[10] Ahumada could not have received the 1553 power of attorney before the spring of 1554, however, and by then on the basis of the 1551 power of attorney he already had taken measures to salvage the best of the ships.

Two of the largest galleons, the *San Pedro* and *Santa Cruz,* were selected for refitting and launching for the Peru trade. Late in 1552 or early in 1553, the work of replacing timber and recaulking began. For this purpose trees had to be cut and the wood seasoned, and new tools procured for the shipyard—a dozen Vizcayan axes and four shipwright's adzes. By the fall of 1553 the vessels were in good repair and ready for departure.[11] A third vessel, the *San Lázaro,* which had been used by Hernán Cortés in his trade with Panama in 1539–1540, was also repaired and launched for use in transporting supplies between Tehuantepec and Huatulco and probably for coastal trade. The famous Pacific pilot, Juan Fernández de Ladrillero, who had worked for the first marqués, helped in readying the ships.[12]

Meanwhile, Pedro de Ahumada Sámano and Juan Bautista de Marín set about assembling crews and obtaining passengers and cargoes. Hiring of crews probably had to be done in Mexico City. From the records[13] and a later sailing license of the *Santa Cruz,*[14] each crew consisted of a pilot, who also discharged the functions of master; a second mate; a steward; a number of able seamen, perhaps as many as ten; several *grumetes* or apprentice seamen; and several pages or ship's boys. In addition, each vessel had a captain, who was military commander of the vessel to the extent that one was needed, and general overseer for the estate. The names of several of the crew are preserved in the surviving accounts: for the *San Pedro,* the captain was Juan Alvarez de Luna; the pilot and master, Alvaro Muñoz.[15] For the *Santa Cruz,* the captain was Lorenzo Ladrón de Guevara; the pilot and master, Vicente Morera; and the second mate, Juan de Brindes.[16]

The crews were not paid fixed salaries but were to receive their keep and a share in the freight and passenger receipts under a rather intricate plan of division. After deducting all costs of making the vessel seaworthy and keeping it so during the voyage and all costs of alterations necessary to handle cargo and animals, one-third of the receipts, without deduction for costs of food, was divided among the crew in accordance with the usual practice on Spanish merchant ships. In addition, although this does not appear in the records, custom of the sea entitled each crew member to take with him free of charge a quantity of merchandise, the *pacotilla,*[17] which he could sell in Peru. The pilots were to receive part of their pay from the share of the crew and an additional payment from the owners of the vessel, listed as two *soldadas* and one *sesmo,* or two shares and a sixth. The stewards were to receive a half soldada from the owners, probably in addition to a share in the third of the crew. The captains were to receive a share from the two-thirds of the owners, after deduction of costs including food and crew's wages. In the instance of Lorenzo Ladrón de Guevara, captain of the *Santa Cruz,* the share was arranged by the simple expedient of making him part owner of the vessel; that is, selling him a third interest for 2,000 pesos de oro de minas in the form of a promissory note payable from his share of the profits.[18] Juan Alvarez de Luna, captain of the *San Pedro,* was not admitted to partnership in the same manner for some reason unknown.

Since the officers and crew received merely shares in future receipts, the arrangements made it necessary for the officials of the estate to make cash advances to many of the men, payable at the time of the division of the shares. Some of the officers and men used these advances to buy merchandise to sell in Peru. Muñoz, pilot of the *San Pedro,* bought a slave Negress named Iseo with the 300 pesos de oro de minas advanced him.[19] Alvarez de Luna, captain of the *San Pedro,* used 15 pesos of the advance to him to buy 50 pounds of sweetmeats.[20] On the other hand, most of the officers and men were penniless, and without these cash loans could not have made themselves ready for the voyage. Lorenzo Ladrón de Guevara, captain of the *Santa Cruz,* who was singled out for especially favorable treatment, had to borrow 100 pesos from the estate in order to outfit himself for the voyage.[21] Virtually all of the advances were carefully recorded in written promises to pay, which were copied so that a record would remain in New Spain and another go with the ships for collection as soon as the freight and passenger receipts should be divided.

Finding passengers and cargo turned out to be more difficult than the officials of the estate had anticipated. On October 17, 1553, the public crier of Mexico City proclaimed the readiness of the *San Pedro* to provide transportation to Peru, his service costing a half peso de minas. On October 29, 1553, the *San Pedro* and its sister ship, the *Santa Cruz,* were thriftily combined in a second proclamation. In December the readiness of the *Santa Cruz* to accept cargo was cried through the capital twice again.[22] These proclamations produced some passengers and consignments of cargo but hardly enough to fill two ships.

During the fall of 1553 and early winter of 1553–1554, Pedro de Ahumada watched the slow assembling of cargo and passengers from Tehuantepec, where he had gone to superintend the outfitting and dispatching of the ships, although they were to leave from the port of Huatulco, and cargo and passengers assembled at that port. He was determined to send out at least one galleon, even though the estate would have to ship its own goods for sale in Peru. The sharply defined season for sailing, ending in the last week of February, set a firm limit to the time he could wait. When the *Santa Cruz* also was ready to leave, Ahumada decided to dispatch both ships, filling out the cargo from produce of the estate.[23]

His decision forced a new arrangement, since the estate would need a business agent to handle sales in Peru, a function which none of the officers and crews of its ships were trained to discharge. The man selected to act as factor in the realms of Peru was Nicolás Ortiz de Ybargüen, who agreed to go to Peru for five years, at the end of which he was to return to render a final accounting in person. He was to receive cargoes sent by the estate to Peru, store and sell them, and remit the net proceeds to New Spain at least once a year if vessels were making the sailing. He was also to administer passenger and cargo receipts, paying expenses, dividing the shares of the officers and crews among them in accordance with prevailing custom in the Pacific, and remitting the share of the estate. For his services the new factor was to receive 300 pesos de minas a year for wages and subsistence, lodging at the expense of the estate, and 2½ per cent commission on the proceeds of the cargoes sent him for sale. That this appointment was a later arrangement not in the original plans but made necessary by the decision to ship produce of the estate is evident from the fact that the necessary power of attorney for Ortiz was only issued by Ahumada on the day the two vessels sailed.[24]

In February, 1554, passengers, cargoes, and crews were finally assembled. The records for the *San Pedro* found to date relate only to the cargo it carried for the account of the estate: 51 mules and 1 horse valued at 30 pesos each at the time of sailing, or 1,560 pesos de oro de minas in all.[25] The *Santa Cruz* carried a more varied cargo for the estate:

Tallow	621 arrobas
Dried quince, peaches and jam	504 arrobas, 2 lb.
Whole quince	96 arrobas, 21 lb.
Sugar	45 arrobas
Pitch and tar	261 arrobas, 11 lb.
Sackcloth and coarse frieze: 2,138 varas weighing	100 arrobas, 18 lb.
Mules	30
Cheeses—aged, of which 10 were the property of Ortiz	120

These listings do not include the containers, which brought the gross weight of the shipment by the estate, exclusive of livestock, to 2,461 arrobas, 10 pounds, or approximately 28 long tons at 88 arrobas to the long ton.

The accounts of the *Santa Cruz* show it as carrying the following list of passengers and cargo, exclusive of the bundles each crew member was entitled to take without charge:

Clothing and other merchandise of the marquisate	2,461 arrobas, 10 lb.
Mules	30
Merchandise of Pedro Del Río, merchant	248 arrobas, 20 lb.
1 saddle, style jineta de Durana	
5 passengers and 1 slave Negress	

For food the two ships each carried some 70 odd sheep, probably as dried meat; half of 14 steers and 5 calves made into jerky; and quantities of biscuit, 43 quintals on the *San Pedro* and 50 quintals on the *Santa Cruz*. In addition, the *Santa Cruz* was supplied with 50 cheeses and both ships divided 6 strings of garlic and 6 of onions, 1 arroba of rice, 1 of chickpeas, 2 pounds of assorted spices, 2 arrobas of dried quince and peaches, 2 arrobas of sweetmeats, 10 arrobas of carrots, and 3 arrobas of wine.[26] It was a relatively varied provision, probably far more generous than that customary on European ships in the Atlantic.

The two vessels submitted to the required inspection and registry of persons and cargo to insure that they carried no contraband and that no passengers were being carried without license. Then, on February 22, 1554, they sailed from Huatulco, following the customary route, hugging the coast southeastward to take advantage of the favorable winds of the season. During this part of the journey five of the mules on the *Santa Cruz* died; probably losses on the *San Pedro* were proportionate. The two vessels proceeded farther along the coast than was customary, past Acajutla to the coast of Nicaragua. Then they turned south or perhaps even southwest to cut across the Gulf of Panama. They passed near Cocos Island, where they were becalmed and the *Santa Cruz* lost eight more of its mules.[27] As they proceeded southward, they ran into storms. The *Santa Cruz,* the only ship for which records are available, sustained severe damage to its main mast and bowsprit, and the rough seas broke the containers of much of the tallow, dried fruit, and jam. The worst damage was to the pitch and tar, a third of which was lost.

Early in the spring of 1554 the two vessels arrived at the coast of South America somewhere near the Gulf of Guayaquil. They sailed to the Island of Puna, where the *Santa Cruz* was remasted at a cost of 65 pesos de minas. This was apparently an emergency repair, for the *Santa Cruz* required further extensive repair and replacement of gear, which was done later. After the remasting of the *Santa Cruz,* the two ships sailed to Túmbez, where the *Santa Cruz* bought two pigs to provide fresh meat for the crew, and Nicolás Ortiz began the sale of the cargo. Two casks of quincemeat weighing ten arrobas were sold for 80 pesos de minas in specie, and one mule was sold to a secular priest of Trujillo for 340 pesos, 98 pesos in the form of a promissory note and the remainder in specie. The other mules of the *Santa Cruz*, and probably those of the *San Pedro,* were landed to be driven overland along the coast to Lima under the care of Nicolás Ortiz, while the ships proceeded southward to the capital, touching at the major ports en route. One mule of the *Santa Cruz* died in the landing.

Ortiz got as far as San Miguel de Piura, where he fell ill. He soon became aware that his illness was mortal and executed a formal transfer of the power of attorney he carried as factor of the marquisate in Peru to Lorenzo Ladrón de Guevara.[28] He also seems to have made arrangements to have the mules driven south to Lima. May 24, 1554, Ortiz died, leaving to Ladrón de Guevara the task of selling the cargo, paying expenses and seamen's shares, and keeping records of transactions. It was to prove a difficult problem for a man inexperienced in business affairs.

The first consequence of Ortiz' death was that, despite the vesting of power in Ladrón de Guevara, the captain of the *San Pedro* kept control over the livestock brought on his ship and kept the proceeds in his possession. After May, 1554, the records of the *Santa Cruz* contain no further disbursement or receipt for the *San Pedro*. The *San Pedro* never returned to New Spain and as late as 1566 no accounting of its operations had been rendered to the administrators of the marquisate.[29]

After landing Ortiz and the mules at Túmbez, the *Santa Cruz* made its way southward against the coastal winds and shore currents. Its next stop was Paita, the port for Piura, where the damaged bowsprit was replaced, more ship's gear acquired, and fresh food bought for the crew at a total cost of 85 pesos de minas. The iron hoops of some of the empty water casks, five quintals by weight, were sold at 16 pesos a quintal. At Paita also the *Santa Cruz* was able to pick up some coastal cargo for delivery in Lima—57 arrobas, 15 pounds of textiles and clothing.

Sometime in the spring of 1554 the *Santa Cruz* arrived at El Callao. The cargo was registered at the customs house and paid duties of 514 pesos de minas, 4 tomines, an assessment that can only be explained as a decision of the local treasury officers, since merchandise shipped between New Spain and Peru was not legally subject to levy in these years.[30] The next problem was moving the cargo to Lima, two leagues from the port. Hiring carts proved impossible until Ladrón de Guevara presented Abendano, the secretary of the audiencia, with a barrel of conserves. Carters and carts were then made available, and the merchandise was moved to Lima at a cost, exclusive of the conserve, of 179 pesos.

Once the cargo was landed, Lorenzo Ladrón de Guevara had the *Santa Cruz* readied for the return voyage to Huatulco to be undertaken under the command of Morera while he remained behind to sell the cargo. The crew was lodged at the inn of Jorge Griego (probably equivalent to George the Greek) in El Callao, and was paid their shares of the freight and passenger receipts as soon as the money was collected, a process which probably took two or three months. The *Santa Cruz* was recaulked and provided with fresh provisions and water. On July 17, 1554, the license of the audiencia was obtained for the return voyage. Shortly thereafter the ship underwent the customary inspection and registration of crew, passengers, and cargo by Diego de Porras, alguacil mayor, at a cost of 20 pesos de minas and entertainment at the inn of Jorge Griego. At the end of July or early in August, the *Santa Cruz* set sail for the return voyage. It carried few passengers and little cargo; total receipts for the return voyage coming to but 263 pesos, no more than three or four passengers and a few arrobas of personal luggage. The crew, disgusted with the small return they could expect, seized a third of the receipts without waiting for the end of the voyage and deduction of costs which would come to more than the receipts.

The *Santa Cruz* must have made a rapid voyage since it arrived safely at Huatulco, discharged its cargo and passengers, was recaulked and repaired, and by the fall of 1554 again began to load passengers and freight. There were more of both than the year before. A number of merchants sent textiles and other merchandise probably on consignment to agents in Lima, the proceeds to be remitted with the return of the *Santa Cruz* or some other ship. The accounts list twenty-two passengers, of whom one was a slave Negress accompanying her mistress. Three passengers booked passage only as far as Acajutla. Perhaps because of the relative abundance of passengers and cargo and the reports of difficulties with cargo in the previous voyage, the administrators of the marquisate sent out far less of the produce of the estate on this voyage for sale in Peru. Tar and pitch, which in view of the availability of natural asphalt at Santa Elena on the Gulf of Guayaquil, could hardly be a profitable export, were not shipped. Only one mule, a bay, was sent for the account of the estate. For the rest, the estate shipped 423½ arrobas of quince, whole and preserved, and 101 arrobas of tallow. The ship carried 54 quintals of biscuit as food. It undoubtedly also carried jerked meat and pot herbs, hidden in the accounts under general expenses of outfitting.

The *Santa Cruz* was not ready for departure until the end of the sailing season. Its license to make the voyage was issued only on March 5 or 6, 1555,[31] so that the galleon must have left Huatulco port about the middle of March, when the adverse season of contrary winds and currents was dangerously close. The ship sailed with a relatively full complement. Vicente Morera was master and pilot. With him went a new second mate, Mateo Fernández, a steward, the indispensable notary, ten able-bodied seamen, four *grumetes,* and five ship's boys. The number of ship's boys seems large but so many may have been needed to take care of the larger number of passengers.

Once out of Huatulco harbor, the *Santa Cruz* followed the usual course. It proceeded southeastward along the coast of the Gulf of Tehuantepec and northern Central America to Acajutla, where, anchoring in the shallows off the dangerous shore, it landed three of its passengers and some cargo. Morera took advantage of the stop to buy more jerked beef and load fresh water. Then the galleon began the crossing of the Gulf of Panama. Because of the lateness of the season, it encountered stormier weather than usual and suffered considerable damage to its sails and cables; it was also slowed down by calms. When it finally reached the South American coast at Manta, Morera offered an unusually good dinner to the crew; the accounts list four pesos de minas as the cost of the one meal. The *Santa Cruz* then took on fish for the crew and started southward.

The final run of the voyage to El Callao in calmer South American coastal waters was slow but uneventful. The *Santa Cruz* stopped at Santa Elena Point to pick up more fish, and then skirting the point, made for the Island of Puna in the Gulf of Guayaquil for the repairs it badly needed. It must have spent some days or even weeks at Puna while it replaced lost gear. A main sail and other canvas, probably second-hand, came to 18 pesos de minas, 7 tomines; a cable weighing six hundredweight, 72 pesos; and miscellaneous gear, 30 pesos. Recaulking used up 31 arrobas of the cargo of tallow and some of 27 quintals of tar brought from Huatulco. Again, fresh food consisting of 42 pigs, cheese, fish, a quintal and a half of biscuit, farinaceous paste, and *guarme* (?) and water and wood were loaded for the southward voyage.

From the Island of Puna the *Santa Cruz* sailed to Paita, where the only passenger, a married man, marital state carefully specified in the accounts, but without his wife booked passage to Lima for 20 pesos de minas. The galleon picked up additional firewood and fresh water and then made directly for Lima, where it arrived on August 11, 1555, nearly five months after leaving Huatulco. Passengers and cargo were disembarked, the crew lodged in El Callao, the freight shipped by the estate passed through customs, where it paid 414 pesos de minas, 4 tomines in duty, and was hauled by cart to Lima for storage and sale.

When the *Santa Cruz* reëntered El Callao, it had been gone for almost exactly a year. During that time, from the summer of 1554 to the summer of 1555, Lorenzo Ladrón de Guevara sold the cargo which had been brought on the first voyage. Shortly after the galleon left the harbor for its return to New Spain in 1554, he moved to Lima and rented a house to serve the triple function of lodging for himself, warehouse for the goods, and display booth for sales. The cost of this came to 250 pesos de minas, but he was able to rent out two shops for 135 pesos, bringing the net cost to 115 pesos. He bought scales to weigh silver to be received in payment, wood and canvas for a display booth, hired two assistants, and prepared to sell the cargo at retail.

The preserved quince and peaches had come through the voyage with considerable damage so that it was necessary to hire a confectioner to recook them with the 45 arrobas of sugar in the cargo. When the whole quince proved unattractive to the Limeños and sold slowly, the confectioner was ordered to remake the bulk of that item into packets of fruit confit for sale at a special shop set up for this purpose. This sold fairly readily at a varying price, reached by bargaining with each purchaser. Relations with the confectioner were marked by the same strain that characterized so many of the dealings of the estate. Ladrón de Guevara accused him of damaging the conserves he was to remake and brought suit for damages. The suit cost the estate 106 pesos, 5 tomines but, apparently, failed to recover any money from the confectioner. The wages of the confectioner and the cost of small boxes for the confits came to 467 pesos, 2 tomines, or with the costs of suit added, 573 pesos, 7 tomines.

The remainder of the cargo sold more easily. The tallow was sold in five lots at a uniform price of 12 pesos, 4 tomines the arroba. A further item in connection with the tallow was the iron hoops of the barrels and pipes in which the tallow had been packed. These brought 37 pesos, 6 tomines. The tar and pitch was disposed of without difficulty in fifteen lots, at varying prices. The total received came to 590 pesos, 4 tomines for 169 arrobas, 9 pounds, a price which represented little increase over the cost of the pitch and tar in New Spain. The large deposits of tar and asphalt at Santa Elena, which provided an excellent, readily accessible local supply, are almost certainly the explanation.

Most of the mules and the remaining cargo were sold to one buyer in the late summer or early fall of 1554. Bernaldino del Campo had brought thirteen mules to Lima, one having died and two more having been sold on the road. Lorenzo Ladrón de Guevara sold one more to a private purchaser and was thus left with eleven. He suddenly found a purchaser in the audiencia, which was desperately raising and equipping troops to suppress the revolt of Francisco Hernández Girón, whose attack on Lima in March, 1554, had failed but who still held much of Peru in the summer of 1554. Girón's faction represented a ready rallying center for the discontent which had kept the realms of Peru in war and turmoil since 1537.[12] The officials charged with raising the army, took the eleven unsold mules, all of the 120 aged cheeses at a half peso each, 1,560 varas of the frieze and sackcloth at a peso the vara, and, in addition, six saddles and four blankets which apparently were part of the crew's equipment, rather than cargo for sale, at 90 pesos de minas. The sale had both the characteristics of condemnation under eminent domain and of a sought sale. Three and a half arrobas of tallow worth 48 pesos de minas passed to the royal contador as a gift; on the other hand, at least part of the price received was set by official valuation. Payment was in the form of a promissory note against the royal treasury in Lima.

The remaining 424 varas of cloth were sold to private purchasers at a peso de minas the vara, and by the late fall of 1554 or early winter of 1554–1555 Lorenzo Ladrón de Guevara was free of the cares of sale.

He used some of his newly found waiting time to reëxamine and rearrange accounts for clearance when he should present them in Huatulco. It was not until December 12, 1554, that Guevara formally accepted the transfer of power of attorney for the marquisate in Peru that Nicolás Ortiz had signed on May 24, 1554.[13] In the six-month delay in acceptance lay a legal justification for the refusal or failure of Juan Alvarez de Luna to turn over to Ladrón de Guevara his accounts and receipts. On February 22, 1555, Ladrón de Guevara prepared yet another document which would be needed in New Spain: a *probanza* to prove that the death of thirteen mules on the voyage from New Spain to Peru could not be ascribed to any neglect on his part. Four passengers testified he had given the mules the best possible care, keeping them clean and seeking vinegar, wine, and other medicines among the passengers to treat the animals when they fell sick.[21] The probanza completed, Ladrón de Guevara had nothing to do but wait until the *Santa Cruz* arrived in August, 1555, with new cargo for sale.

The sale of the second cargo presented fewer difficulties than that of the first, since its contents had been selected according to firsthand knowledge of market conditions in Lima. Then, too, Ladrón de Guevara had undoubtedly gained considerable experience in retail selling. The dried quince meat and quince conserves sold readily, the best quality at 11 pesos the arroba, and that which showed signs of deterioration at 7 and 7½ pesos.

Final sales of seven arrobas at 9 and 10 pesos probably represented the closing out of the remaining stock. The tallow sold quickly but at no more than 21 and 22 pesos the quintal of four arrobas—a sharp drop from the 12/4 the arroba received in 1554. The decrease in price reflected the increase in Peruvian livestock and the general peace obtaining after the defeat and execution of Hernández Girón. The one animal brought in 1555, the bay mule, sold for 170 pesos.

While the cargo of the second voyage was being sold, the *Santa Cruz* was readied for the return voyage. It needed extensive repairs to its planking and timbers, which could not be made at Lima, where wood was scarce. Instead, the nails necessary were bought at Lima—a quintal of ordinary ones, 500 for the sides, 30 for the scuppers, and 300 very large ones, at a cost for all of 107 pesos de minas. A cauldron for tar cost 41 pesos, and three large augers 12 pesos. Hatchets, jars, and *manteles reserbilletes* (some kind of napkins?) were also bought. The ship was recaulked, reprovisioned with water, pork, and biscuit, and was ready to depart. As on the previous return in 1554, there were few passengers and little cargo for the return voyage. Receipts on this account were only 192 pesos de minas. Again the crew seized a third without waiting for an accounting. In Lima Lorenzo Ladrón de Guevara concluded his affairs, sold what articles of furniture he could, paid his bills, and boarded the galleon. Inspection and registry again came to 20 pesos. On October 20, 1555, the *Santa Cruz* sailed from El Callao.

The return voyage was complicated by the need for repairs. Early in November the ship was at the Island of Puna, where it could get timber. Planking and other timber came to the heavy sum of 103 pesos de minas. Tearing out and replacing rotten and damaged timber, and recaulking must have taken weeks. Ladrón de Guevara took advantage of the delay to have pigs and beans for food on the voyage rafted to the island from Guayaquil by balsa.[85] He also bought some chickens locally. Long after the usual sailing season was over, perhaps as late as December, the *Santa Cruz* finally began the crossing of the Gulf of Panama. It must have had a trying voyage against contrary winds. Early in 1556 the *Santa Cruz* cast anchor in the port of Huatulco. Lorenzo Ladrón de Guevara paid off the crew, including a handsome bonus to Morera as required by the customs of the sea;[86] and burdened with his books of accounts set out in company with his accountant for Mexico City to report to the administrators of the marquisate.

Accounting for the two voyages turned out to be a long process, replete with painful surprises for all parties. When Ladrón de Guevara arrived in Mexico City, he found Juan Bautista de Marín there but Pedro de Ahumada Sámano in Zacatecas, where he had gone to administer the marquisate's mining enterprises. Accordingly, Ladrón de Guevara and his accountant took the overland trail to the little settlement of Apozol, where Ahumada was easing a tumor in his groin, which already disposed him to ill-humor. When Ahumada saw how poorly the books of accounts had been kept, he almost exploded with anger. The cargo of the marquisate had not been weighed on landing in Lima, so that the net weight to be accounted for had to be reconstructed from the sales. Losses for the first voyage in the dried quince and peaches ran at first glance to 86 arrobas in the 504 shipped, so large an amount that Ahumada refused to accept it although eventually he was forced to allow even a slightly higher quantity. The whole quince in which there had been no loss showed an unexplained disappearance of nearly 58 arrobas, almost two-thirds. In paying the crew, Ladrón de Guevara had used the record of lading at Huatulco rather than the amount landed in Peru—an overpayment on more than 300 arrobas. He had failed to deduct from the share of the crew, their proportionate share of expense for stalls and slings for livestock, legal expenses, and some of the repairs, thus overpayments had been made to the crew with little chance of recovery. Ladrón de Guevara had also paid large sums to Vicente Morera for repairs on simple statement without authorization from any of the officials of the marquisate in New Spain and without any audit of accounts. The annoyance of Ahumada was all the greater in that he had expected large amounts of specie from the voyages and instead Ladrón de Guevara appeared with several thousand silver pesos and a number of promissory notes as the net proceeds of the voyages. "I fully believe that he has not erred through malice," commented Ahumada to Marín, "but I am so irritated by the errors of his ignorance that I should have been less upset had another man taken a larger amount by straight theft." The luckless Ladrón de Guevara was sent back to Mexico City with his books and accountant for a remaking of accounts by Juan Bautista de Marín and the aged Juan de Altamirano, while Ahumada nursed his irritation and tumor in the soothing waters of Apozol.[37]

Between March and September, 1556, the parties finally arrived at a settlement of accounts. The officials of the marquisate accepted most of Ladrón de Guevara's errors of judgment under the formula that if the money could be recovered, it was to be paid to the estate. An overpayment to the crew of 150 pesos de minas was compensated by a scribe's error in addition which counterbalanced the 100 pesos that Ladrón de Guevara had to make good to the marquisate. An allowance of 968 pesos, 2 tomines for the loss in turning Peruvian small change into *plata ensayada,* the equivalent of pesos de minas, substantially eased the captain's indebtedness. The auditors also accepted all the accounts for repairs. They even accepted the fact that somehow the 4,000 pesos the captain had with him in Apozol diminished to 2,848 pesos, the sum that the raging Ahumada found by actual count, as against the 2,954 claimed for discharge in the accounts. In the final reckoning, however, Ladrón de Guevara had to sign over to the estate ownership of a slave Negress and her son whom he had bought for sale in Peru and sign, in addition, a promissory note for 1,770 pesos, 6 tomines, payable in eighteen months.[88] If his poor accounts were the result of inexperience, as the trained administrators of the estate decided, and as seems likely, he lost heavily in his nearly three years of service. He received only room and board and emerged deeply in debt, for besides the promissory note of September, 1556, he still owed 2,000 pesos de minas for his third of the ship.

The final accounting between the parties restated as far as possible in present-day terms is presented in tables 1–4. From them it is plain that the Cortés estate suffered no actual loss, although it failed to make as substantial a profit as had been expected. Its share of freight and passenger receipts, that is, its net income from the operation of the galleon, came to 2,400 pesos, 2 tomines on an investment valued at 4,000 pesos, after very substantial repairs. Return on investment was thus 20 per cent a year for the three years from the fall of 1553 to the fall of 1556. This figure makes no allowance for depreciation. In terms of the risks of sinking and the rapid disintegration of wooden ships in the tropical Pacific, a reasonable rate of return should have been perhaps 50 per cent a year.

On the merchandise shipments, the net receipts of the estate came to 5,514 pesos, 5 tomines, but since at most the records give only clues to the original cost of merchandise, there is no accurate basis for estimating the cost of the goods and hence the rate of return. Any possibility of reaching a profit and loss statement on the merchandise is further diminished by the fact that all of it was produce of the estate and therefore cost less than similar merchandise in Mexico City. The estate, moreover, saved a substantial sum in costs through movement by the short land haul to Huatulco rather than by the long and costly carriage by pack train to the Spanish

TABLE 1

MERCHANDISE ACCOUNT OF THE *Santa Cruz* VOYAGES: GROSS PROCEEDS

Item	Quantity shipped	Losses	Quantity landed	Price received (in pesos de minas)
FIRST VOYAGE				
Tallow	621@	59@17#[a]	560@8#	1,757/1
Dried quinces, peaches, jam	504@2#	88@12#	415@15#	4,519/5
Whole quinces	96@21#	....	96@21#	439/[b]
Sugar	45@	....	45@[c]	....
Pitch and tar	261@11#	91@16#[d]	169@9#	590/4
Sackcloth and coarse frieze	2,138 varas	....	2,008 varas[e]	1,984/[f]
Mules	30	15	15	2,520/[g]
Cheeses	120[h]	....	120	60/
Sub-total	....	....	....	11,870/2
Equipment sold:				
Hoops of tallow barrels	37/			....
Six saddles and four blankets	90/	....	....	127/6
Total	....	....	....	11,998/
SECOND VOYAGE				
Quince, whole and conserves	423@12#	94@24#[i]	328@13#	3,498/
Tallow	101@	31@[j] 6@	64@	506/4
Mules	1	....	1	170/
Total	....	....	....	4,174/4
TOTAL BOTH VOYAGES	....	....	....	16,172/4

[a] Account is 1 arroba short.

[b] Price received for 38@ 11#. 57@ 14# left charged to Ladrón de Guevara to be accounted for. The reckoning of the marquisate accountants still came to only 96@, a further 21# being ignored. The missing quince probably was reworked into confits and sold as such.

[c] Used in recooking the dried quince and peach meat for sale as fruit confit.

[d] Reckoning is 11# short.

[e] Of this quantity, 130 varas turned over to Juan Alvarez de Luna for trappings of mules brought on the *San Pedro*.

[f] Proceeds of sale of 1,984 varas. The reckoning does not account for 100 varas, which were probably used as trappings for the mules of the *Santa Cruz*.

[g] Price of fourteen mules. One sold by Juan Alvarez de Luna in Túmbez was charged to him for accounting.

[h] Ten of these were the property of Nicolás Ortiz.

[i] The adjustments for taxes and losses actually come to 4 pounds more.

[j] 31@ used on galleon.

TABLE 2

MERCHANDISE ACCOUNTS OF THE *Santa Cruz* VOYAGES: EXPENSES OF TRANSPORTATION AND SALES
(in pesos de minas)

FIRST VOYAGE	
Freight charges	4,697/
Customs	514/4
Cartage to Lima	179/
Supplies for mules	136/6
Wages of drover	60/
Costs of recooking conserves, incl. suit	574/7
Total	6,162/1
SECOND VOYAGE	
Freight charges	1,128/
Customs	414/4
Cartage	40/6
Total	1,583/2
BOTH VOYAGES	
Sale in Lima and maintenance of Ladrón de Guevara	
Cost of setting up and equipping shop	40/4
Town crier (*corretaje*)	4/
Wages, two salesmen	478/
Food expense account, June 11, 1554–November 21, 1555	941/7
Rent and domestic service (incl. warehouse and shops)	229/4
Losses on exchange of Peruvian small change into *plata ensayada*	968/2
Bad debt	10/
Bribes	53/
Legal costs	52/4
Miscellaneous	34/7
Total	2,812/4
Error of accountant in copying	+100/
TOTAL COSTS	10,657/7
TOTAL RECEIPTS (see table 1)	16,172/4
NET PROCEEDS FROM MERCHANDISE	5,514/5

TABLE 3

FREIGHT AND PASSENGER RECEIPTS
(in pesos de minas)

GROSS RECEIPTS		
First Voyage		6,955/4/6[a]
Sale of iron hoops of water barrels on First Voyage		144/1
Second Voyage		5,759/5
Total receipts		12,859/2/6
EXPENSES		
Wages on First Voyage		
Crew	2,468/4/2	2,940/6/6
Pilot	472/2/4	
Wages on Second Voyage		
Crew	1,850/	2,299/2/
Pilot	324/6/8	
Bonus to pilot	50/	
Steward	74/4	
Total wages		5,204/0/6
Food for crew, incl. maintenance in El Callao		2,062/0
Repairs and gear for galleon		1,976/4
Costs of licenses, inspection, and registry		48/3[b]
Stalls and slings for mules		74/[c]
Hire of horses in Peru on First Voyage		8/
Total expenses		9,408/7/6
NET PROFIT TO PARTNERS		
Share of the partners		3,450/3/0
Marquisate (2/3)		2,300/2[d]
Ladrón de Guevara (1/3)		1,150/1/

[a] Adjusted by deduction of overcharge on merchandise shipped by marquisate: 450/.
[b] Does not include 5/4 which the crew were supposed to pay from their share.
[c] Includes third which the crew were supposed to pay from their share but which was not collected at the time they were paid because Ladrón de Guevara had no records of the item.
[d] Adjustment on overcharge in freights left Ladrón de Guevara responsible for the overpayment of the crew's salary. Of this the marquisate's share was 100/ so that share of the marquisate in profits of freight was charged as 2,400/2.

TABLE 4

BALANCE
(in pesos de minas)

DEBITS		
Notes collected		
Gil Ramírez de Avalos	96/7	699/1
Alvaro Muñoz	300/	
Crew	260/	
Vicente Morera	42/2	
Advances for expenses		1,293/2
Profit on merchandise		5,514/5
Profit on freights—share of marquisate		2,400/2[a]
		9,907/2

CREDITS		
Balance against Nicolás Ortiz		99/2
Bills paid for the marquisate		
Back bill of caulker	35/	142/
Advance to Alvarez de Luna of the *San Pedro* for expenses	107/	
Note of royal treasury in Lima		1,869/2
Note of Francisco Sanchez of Trujillo		98/
Note of Juan Diez		213/
Payment to Juan de Termino on behalf of Ahumada		2,411/
Slave Negress and son assigned by Ladrón de Guevara to marquisate		456/
Specie delivered to estate		2,848/
Promissory note of Ladrón de Guevara		1,770/6
		9,907/2

[a] See table 3, note [d].

centers in New Spain. The mules cost 30 pesos at the beach in Huatulco and netted a substantial profit. The tar and pitch were worth little more in Peru than in New Spain and were sold at a loss. The quince and peach preserves, sugar, and tallow sold for substantially more than they could have brought in New Spain but did not do well because large amounts spoiled. Table 5 summarizes the available data on average costs and sale price for the fruit preserves and tallow shipped on the first voyage. The figures do not take into account any charge for overhead.[39]

Perhaps the most disturbing result of the two voyages was that so much of the proceeds came in the form of promissory notes collectable in Peru. The net proceeds realized in September, 1556, came to one note of 2,411 pesos owing by Ahumada paid in Peru and 2,848 pesos de minas in silver. Disappointing as these results were, the *Santa Cruz* and Lorenzo Ladrón de Guevara had still done far better than the *San Pedro* and its captain who had sent no accounting and represented a total loss to the marquisate.

TABLE 5

AVERAGE COSTS AND PRICES PERCEIVED PER ARROBA FOR FRUIT PRESERVES AND TALLOW SHIPPED ON FIRST VOYAGE OF THE *Santa Cruz*
(in pesos de minas)

	Fruit preserves incl. whole quince	Tallow
Market value in Mexico City	3/2/9	1/2/0
Packing and hauling to Huatulco	1/0/1	5/5
Freight to Peru	2/0/0	2/0/0
Sugar for recooking in Lima	2/4	
Conversion into confits	7/4	
Total cost of merchandise	7/4/6	3/7/5
Price in Lima[a]	8/0/10	2/6/4
Profit or loss, not allowing for overhead	+0/4/4	−1/1/1

[a] Calculated by dividing money received by original quantity shipped. Losses on preserves ran about a seventh and on tallow a tenth.

The results of the voyages were so poor, and made all the worse by the high hopes of 1553–1554, that Pedro de Ahumada decided upon retrenchment. The more profitable part of the venture had been the operation of the galleon as a common carrier; the less profitable part and the one in which the most difficulties in accounting had arisen, had been the shipment of merchandise by the estate. Accordingly Ahumada decided to send no more of the estate's produce on the galleon but to operate it for such silver as it might earn by carrying passengers and freight.[40] He still had high hopes of profit if we may judge by the comment at the end of an inventory of the estate dated December 12, 1556: "The other assets of the marqués are his ordinary revenues and tributes and whatever return God may grant from the Peruvian trade, which is off to a good start and should yield great profit if some rebel does not interrupt it. . . ."[41]

During the summer and fall of 1556 the *Santa Cruz* was repaired and made ready for its third voyage. Again, it sailed nearly at the end of the season, on February 22, 1557.[42] It carried 21 lots of merchandise totaling 4,616 arrobas, approximately 52 long tons. The largest shipment, by Enrique Garcés, a merchant, was 880 arrobas or nearly 10 long tons of assorted merchandise. The second largest shipment was made by Lorenzo Ladrón de Guevara: some 633 arrobas in conserves, tallow, and other merchandise. Vicente Morera shipped 63 arrobas in partnership with Juan Jiménez, alcalde mayor of Tehuantepec, and Juan de Urrea, a notary. Most of the shipments consisted of assorted merchandise—textiles, trinkets, household articles,—shipped by merchants or carried by passengers. The number of passengers came to twelve or fourteen, half of whom were married men, half bachelors.[43] The galleon carried far more cargo and passengers on this third voyage than it had on the previous two, and the administrators of the estate, seeing the manifest, must have felt hope that at last the shipping venture would bring a good profit.

The decision of Pedro de Ahumada that the estate would ship no more merchandise with Ladrón de Guevara did not mean that the marquisate would confine itself to trade in the Pacific. At the time the *Santa Cruz* sailed in February, 1557, the marquisate was already engaged in another venture to Peru, a straight merchant partnership. The associate in the venture was Pedro del Río, a merchant who had shipped cargo on the first voyage of the *Santa Cruz* in 1554. The terms of the partnership were embodied in a formal contract signed at Mexico City on February 4, 1556,[44] which must have been made shortly after the *Santa Cruz* returned to Huatulco from its second voyage. Under the agreement, Juan Bautista de Marín acting for the marquisate agreed that the estate would supply goods and money to the value of 6,000 silver pesos and Pedro del Río agreed to invest 4,000 silver pesos to make up a partnership capital of 10,000 pesos. Of this sum, 1,200 pesos was earmarked for payment of freight on the merchandise from Mexico City to Huatulco, payment to be made by Juan Gómez Zorita, the estate's majordomo in Oaxaca; 7,053 pesos was spent for an assortment of merchandise listed in the contract; the value of a Negro slave, Pedro, from the Grand Canary, to be sold in Peru, was assessed at 430 pesos, 1 real. The remainder of the capital sum was to be spent in Oaxaca on tallow, conserves, and hides produced by the estate at the prices current in that province. Del Río was to go to Peru with the merchandise, and be in charge of sale. He agreed to keep books and settle accounts within two years from the date of the agreement or earlier if he disposed of the merchandise more quickly. He was to receive his expenses from the proceeds and pledged that they would be moderate and confined to customary items. The proceeds of the sales were to be divided in the following manner: expenses and the capital sums were first to be paid; the remainder, that is, the profit, was to be divided equally between the partners. Del Río's only recompense over costs was to be his receipt of half of the profits, although he contributed only a third of the capital.

The contract is especially interesting because the list of merchandise in it affords a much clearer idea of what was meant by assorted merchandise. The largest single category in the list consisted of sugar, dried fruit, and the expenses of turning it into 248 arrobas of quince and peach conserves, 102 arrobas of whole quince, and 18 arrobas of rose-flavored sugar. Evidently the Peruvian sweet tooth still afforded the surest and most profitable market. The remaining items covered almost the entire range of religious objects, textiles, saddles, household furnishings, clothing, medical supplies, paper and school texts, metal tools, spices, toilet articles, and the like. Much of the merchandise was of Spanish manufacture, transshipped to Peru because the higher Peruvian price levels made the transshipment profitable. A considerable part of the merchandise consisted of European-style wares manufactured by Spanish or Indian artisans in New Spain. A third category, and perhaps the most interesting, consisted of Indian-style wares for which there was a demand in Peru. Among them were Huaxteca mirrors, perhaps of polished obsidian; lacquered gourds from Michoacán for drinking chocolate; an Indian-style guitar, and Indian feather headdresses. Yet another category represented the use of Indian techniques and materials for European-style wares, such as saints' images in featherwork. The merchandise clearly was meant for sale in a rather small Spanish community with a good deal of specie at its disposal, but with little local industry, and an avidity for consumers' goods. It was also carefully balanced so that no glut of any one or several items from Spain, still the largest supplier, could bring disaster to the trading venture.

Pedro del Río must have completed his cargo in the spring of 1556. He did not wait for the *Santa Cruz* to sail but took an earlier ship, and the estate did not press him to use its galleon. He arrived in Peru at the end of 1556 or early in 1557 and sold his wares without serious difficulty. He was ready to return to New Spain after a few months, before the close of the return sailing season, and arrived in New Spain toward the end of 1557, the whole venture having taken approximately a year. The accounting took place in the last days of 1557. After deduction of expenses and repayment of capital, the partners found themselves with net profits of 4,308 silver pesos, which on being divided equally left the estate with 2,154 pesos as its profit on 6,000 pesos, or approximately 36 per cent. The capital and profit, or 8,154 pesos, actually 967 marks, 1 ounce, 2 reales of silver of varying fineness brought by Del Río from Peru, was shipped to Seville at the earliest opportunity, in July, 1558.[45]

The year 1558 appears to have been a profitable one for the marquisate's Pacific shipping. The *Santa Cruz* returned and apparently made satisfactory accounting for freight and passenger receipts. Although the accounts for this voyage have not been found, the profit was satisfactory enough for the administrators of the estate to continue operation of the vessel. Even though Lorenzo Ladrón de Guevara had not collected any of the promissory notes due in Peru for the sale of cargo of the first two voyages and could not make any payment on the sums he owed the marquisate, the administrators continued him in his position as captain of the galleon and sold him 300 arrobas of refined sugar worth 1,200 silver pesos against two promissory notes due in eight months. The second of these notes was executed on March 10, 1559, so that the *Santa Cruz* again sailed for Peru on its fourth voyage at the end of the season or indeed a few weeks after the end of the season.[46]

This fourth voyage of the *Santa Cruz* was its last. In 1559 the galleon was twenty years old. It may have reached Peru in such condition of rot and teredo that it could not be used further, or it may have been wrecked near the coast of South America, for Lorenzo Ladrón de Guevara arrived in Peru, but the galleon disappeared from the reckoning without the marquisate's demanding accounting for its share in the vessel. His vessel gone, Lorenzo Ladrón de Guevara gave up the sea and retired to Cuzco with such money as he had been able to make on his voyages.[47] He was heavily in debt to the marquisate, but New Spain was a long remove from Peru, and Cuzco a considerable distance from Lima so that he could have virtual certainty that he could not be committed to debtor's prison during his remaining years.

News of the fate of the *Santa Cruz* and Lorenzo Ladrón de Guevara's departure for Cuzco probably did not reach Pedro de Ahumada in New Spain until 1560 or 1561. He apparently decided to throw the good money of the second marqués after bad, for he gave orders that another vessel, the

Santispiritus, be repaired and readied for Peru. On July 14, 1562, he issued an appointment to Alonso Ruiz de Alarcón as captain, empowering him to hire a crew, outfit the ship, contract to provide freight and passage for Peru and other parts, and make all necessary payments. The new captain set about finding a crew and cargo, and on October 29, 1562, signed an agreement with Marcos Borjes de Acosta, who had shipped merchandise on the *Santa Cruz* on its second voyage, to carry all of the cargo the merchant could provide at the low rate the arroba of 1 peso, 4 reales, 6 granos in silver, payable in three months. Ruiz de Alarcón agreed that the galleon would leave in January or not later than February 5, 1563. If the ship sailed at a later date, Borjes had the option of paying a half peso less an arroba or of shipping his merchandise in another vessel, the marquisate reimbursing him for whatever sum he might have to pay for passage and for any other damages. Borjes, for his part, agreed to have his freight on the beach at Huatulco not later than January 25, 1563, under penalty of a half silver peso an arroba additional charge.

The *Santispiritus* was not ready at the agreed time, but, nevertheless, Borjes, who was acting as business agent for a group of merchant shippers, underwrote promissory notes signed by Ruiz de Alarcón for 830 silver pesos in money and supplies during December, 1562, and the spring and summer of 1563. When he finally became convinced that the galleon would not sail, Borjes and his associates contracted with Jácome Vasallo, master of *Nuestra Señora de la Concepción,* engaged in the cacao trade with Central America, to make the voyage. The 630 arrobas of cargo assembled had to be moved to Acapulco for shipment and freight for the voyage paid at the rate of 2 pesos de minas, 2 tomines the arroba, nearly three times the rate agreed with Ruiz de Alarcón. The damage suffered by Borjes was further aggravated in Peru when in March, 1565, he was forced to pay the notes he had endorsed for Ruiz de Alarcón. On his return to New Spain in 1567, Marcos Borjes de Acosta presented a claim for damages and on February 13, 1568, brought suit against the second marqués before the Audiencia of Mexico. In August, 1569, seventeen months after the suit was begun and six years after the failure of the *Santispiritus* to sail, Borjes collected 1,830 silver pesos in payment of judgment against the marquisate.[48]

Why the *Santispiritus* never sailed remains a minor mystery. Any attempt at an explanation is straight guess. It was an old ship, hardly fit to make the voyage, so that the administrators of the estate may have decided not to take the risk. It is also true that in 1562 a new factor entered the affairs of the estate: Martín Cortés, second Marqués del Valle, arrived in New Spain[49] and took over the personal direction of his estates. He can hardly have been satisfied with the results of the Peruvian ventures through the nine years since 1553 and may well have issued orders to disengage the marquisate from any further voyages. At any rate, after his arrival the marquisate outfitted no more ships and entered into no more trading ventures to Peru.

Cessation of shipping and trade still left large sums owing to the marquisate in Peru, for the promissory notes resulting from the voyages of the *Santa Cruz* were still unpaid. For collection, Martín Cortés hired Diego López de Toledo to go to Peru with a power of attorney and certified copies of the promissory notes signed by Ladrón de Guevara, by royal treasury officials of Lima, and others. It may be symptomatic of his judgment on the results of the Peruvian trade that the power of attorney was carefully worded to give authority merely for the collection of the notes which were equally carefully listed in the body of the power.[50] Diego López was also empowered to ask for an accounting of the cargo and expenses of the *San Pedro* on its voyage of 1554.

In April, 1566, Diego López was ready to sail from Huatulco as instructed, but with many misgivings. He wrote to Juan Gómez de Zorita, the marqués' majordomo in Oaxaca, that the power of attorney was hardly full enough to allow the necessary discretion and that his own knowledge of Peru did not extend beyond the vicinity of Lima; Cuzco where Ladrón de Guevara had taken up residence was unknown to him. He pledged himself, however, to find out how best to go about collection and to consult the president of the audiencia as the marqués commanded. In a final clause which may explain why the marquisate was so unfortunate in its commercial ventures, he promised that he would see to it if any collection could be made that Zorita's claim against Ladrón de Guevara was paid first.[51]

Diego López arrived in Lima in the summer of 1566 and began his attempts to collect. He apparently was able to secure payment from the royal treasury and all others but Ladrón de Guevara, for their notes disappear from the later lists of outstanding debts owing the estate. He may even have secured some kind of accounting for the voyage of the *San Pedro*. Ladrón de Guevara, however, proved far more difficult to bind. In August, 1566, Diego López appealed to the Audiencia of Lima for orders to pay, but he either could not enforce the writ in Cuzco or the ex-captain had nothing on which payment could be levied.[52] The debts of Ladrón de

Guevara probably never were paid, for they appear as still outstanding in an inventory of the marquisate dated January 10, 1570. In the inventory they follow hard upon a listing of debts owed by Pedro de Ahumada Sámano, deceased.[53] The last reminder of the marquisate's Peruvian ventures disappeared during the 1570's when the herd of *ovejas del Perú*—llamas or related species—brought to the Peñol de Xico for domestication in New Spain reached a maximum of sixty head and then died out.[54]

The marquisate's trading and shipping ventures to Peru thus formed an unhappy recapitulation of the unprofitable Peruvian ventures of Hernán Cortés, the founder of the estate. It is unlikely that the earnings from freight and passenger receipts and the slender returns from trade actually realized in specie repaid the cost of the ships, goods, and expenses. The management of the estate was too unwieldy, its procedures too much like those of the Crown, for it to handle small-scale and greatly varied business ventures. The most profitable, least complicated, and best managed of the marquisate's Peruvian ventures was the trading company with Pedro del Río, in which the estate furnished capital and left all management to an experienced trader who could carry out the varied operations of retail trade with a minimum of expense.

V. THE EARLY TRADE AT MATURITY 1550–1585

The years from 1550 to perhaps 1585 marked the full development of early trade and navigation between Mexico and Peru. For, after 1550, when the Spanish Crown succeeded in quelling the worst of the civil disorders in Peru, the southern colonies began a long period of orderly, prosperous settlement which encouraged trade and navigation with the Audiencia of Mexico and other colonies even more than had the scarcity brought about by the earlier disorders. The trade was actively encouraged by the Spanish authorities in the hope that by providing the turbulent citizens of the southern realms with goods, it would help to keep them content. An end came to this high period of the early trade in the 1580's not as decline but as a great expansion when the trade in Chinese goods swamped the exchange of local and Spanish products. By good fortune enough documentary evidence has survived, especially in Mexico, to permit a fairly intensive analysis of the nature of Mexico-Peru trade and navigation during this relatively stable period from 1550 to about 1585.

SHIPS AND THEIR CREWS

After 1550 sailings between the two viceroyalties became sufficiently regular and rapid so that transmission of news between Peru and Spain was sometimes faster via Mexico and Veracruz than via Panama and the galleons calling at Nombre de Dios. In 1555 the Audiencia of Lima asked the Viceroy of New Spain, Luis de Velasco I, to send news of the defeat and execution of Girón to Philip II in Spain because there was no ship available at Panama.[1] Again, in 1559, news of the death of the Emperor Charles V was brought to Lima by a group of Augustinian friars arriving from Mexico. The cabildo of Lima, thus forewarned, was able to make preparations for the purchase of mourning and the celebration of funeral honors before official notification came via Panama.[2] On the other hand, the Mexico-Peru navigation was not invariably so efficient, and the restriction of communication to sailings at the favorable periods of winds sometimes meant long delays in the transmission of mail. On May 5, 1554, Luis de Velasco wrote to the Audiencia of Lima, offering help to suppress the Girón rebellion if any was needed. His letter, arriving at the coast after all ships had sailed, had to wait nearly a year. It was delivered to the Audi-

[1] For notes to chapter v, see pages 145–151.

encia of Lima only on March 26, 1555,[3] long after Girón had been executed and only a few weeks before Velasco, in turn, received the audiencia's letter to that effect. The Mexico-Peru navigation was at best a supplement to the usual Peruvian communication with Spain, to be used in off seasons, emergencies, in the absence of a fast ship at Panama, or when war closed the normal shipping lanes.

The number of vessels engaged in the traffic cannot have been large at any time. The only surviving licenses to sail—those in Mexico—indicate that in the season of 1554–1555, four ships were licensed to sail from Mexico to Peru. On November 23, 1554, the galleon *San Jerónimo,* owned by Francisco de Valenzuela and Antonio del Campo, which had been sent from Peru to pick up wares in Mexico because of the great shortage occasioned by the Girón rebellion and the attendant interruption of the Panama trade, was given formal permission to leave from Huatulco.[4] On the same day a license was issued to the *nao La Concepción,* which also was to leave from Huatulco.[5] On January 8, 1555, a much smaller ship, the *Santiago,* anchored in Huatulco harbor, received its license;[6] and early in March, 1555, the *Santa Cruz,* owned by the second Marqués del Valle, was licensed to make its second voyage to Peru,[7] which has already been described. For the 1555–1556 sailing season from New Spain, the viceregal records show only three licenses extant: to *La Magdalena,*[8] *Nuestra Señora de Loreto,*[9] and *Nuestra Señora de la Concepción,* the same ship which made the voyage in 1563.[10] For the sailing season of 1556–1557, there survive only two licenses: to the *Nuestra Señora de la Concepción,*[11] apparently another vessel of the same name as the one sailing in 1555–1556, since the names of officers and crew are different, and to the *Santa Cruz* of the Cortés estate,[12] sailing on its third voyage. For the sailing season of 1560–1561 from the Audiencia of Mexico, there survive three licenses: to the *San Lorenzo,*[13] *La Concepción,*[14] and the *San Juan de los Frailes.*[15] The primacy of Huatulco as the Mexican port for this trade is apparent in the fact that all of these vessels sailed from it.

These licenses serve at best merely as an indication of the minimum number of vessels engaged in the Mexico-Peru run, since only fragments of the viceregal records survive, and they are so broken for the decades of the 1560's, 1570's, and 1580's that they give little clue to the number of vessels sailing in those years. It seems likely on the basis of this inconclusive evidence, that a minimum of perhaps four to six vessels sailed each year on the round trip, which would have kept them engaged for from nine months to a year, and that this number was rarely extended by more than two or three. It seems unlikely that the number of vessels in the trade ever reached ten in any year until the late 1580's. The ships involved in this navigation, therefore, cannot have been more than a fraction of the number sailing between the ports of Peru and Panama, or between Peru and Central America, or even in the cacao trade between Sonsonate and New Spain.

The surviving licenses suggest also that few vessels were engaged exclusively in Mexico-Peru navigation. The ships of the marquesado's ventures in the 1550's, salvaged from Hernán Cortés' projects for exploration, were indeed used almost entirely in the Peruvian trade. A number of other vessels may have been used exclusively in the Mexico-Peru run. The *San Jerónimo* of El Callao was licensed in 1554 and again in 1565[16] to return to Peru from Mexico. It may have made only these two voyages or perhaps have been used fairly regularly to bring merchandise from New Spain to the southern realms. The *San Lorenzo* of Juan López de Azpia was licensed in 1560 and again in 1564[17] to sail to Peru. It also may have been engaged in regular sailings. Since neither license mentioned return to Peru, presumably the ship was either Central American or Huatulco was its home port. The *Nuestra Señora de la Concepción* which made voyages in 1556 and 1563, was engaged primarily in the cacao trade between Central American and New Spain. The fact that the names of so few vessels appear more than once in the surviving viceregal licenses issued in Mexico suggests that instead of using a ship exclusively for the Mexico-Peru navigation, the more usual practice of shipowners was to detach a vessel from the cacao trade between Central America and New Spain or the Peru-Panama or Peru–Central America run whenever enough cargo accumulated at a port or a group of merchants and passengers were willing to guarantee enough fares and freight charges to make the voyage profitable. Such was the case of the *Nuestra Señora de la Concepción* in 1563.[18]

Our information on the construction and outfitting of the vessels taking part in the Mexico-Peru navigation is too scanty to permit more than a series of conjectures. The ships were built in yards which were placed to be near an adequate supply of timber. By the middle of the century, the yards on the Bay of Guayaquil were the most important and built the largest and best vessels. Those at Realejo were second in importance. New Spain, despite its promising beginning in the 1530's and 1540's, became relatively unimportant in shipbuilding. The Tehuantepec yard of the Cortés family fell into decay and its staff of trained artisans was allowed to disperse. An occasional vessel was built at Huatulco by shipwrights at that port, but they were primarily concerned with repair and no permanent yard developed there. A royal shipyard was established at La Navidad in the jurisdiction of Michoacan. It existed primarily for the Far Eastern trade. Here were built the vessels of Legazpi's expedition. The yard was closed on the death of Luis de Velasco I, but then reopened and built a number of the Manila galleons. However, it remained a small yard to the end of the century.[19] At least two of the larger vessels on the Phillippine run, the *San Martín* and the ill-fated *Santa Ana,* a ship of seven hundred tons seized by Cavendish in 1587, were built at Realejo in Nicaragua.[20] This information suggests, beyond the indications in the sailing licenses, that the bulk of the vessels entering the Mexico-Peru navigation were of Central American and Peruvian construction and perhaps ownership.

Metal fittings for ships on the Pacific coast, in general, still had to be brought from Europe, and must have been so costly that they were used as little as possible. Cables and sails used on vessels outfitted on the coast of New Spain were brought from the Atlantic. They were almost invariably old and in poor condition, discards from the Atlantic shipping at Veracruz, but deemed still salable for use in the Pacific. Contemporaries were agreed that they gave wretched service indeed.[21] The shipping outfitted in Central and South America had a considerable advantage in that cables and sails were manufactured near Realejo, on the Island of Puna, and at a number of other points, using local fibers, especially *pita* and *cabuya.* Both of these fibers proved excellent and became the basis for a considerable production.[22] In 1560, when Luis de Velasco was attempting to bring together the cables and rigging needed for the ships of the projected expedition to the Far East, he was forced to send to Nicaragua to have the cables and other gear manufactured there from pita.[23]

Vessels built in Pacific yards probably differed little in type from those used in the Atlantic. By the middle of the sixteenth century, the caravel type, which had given such good service to earlier navigators, apparently became obsolete, although a modified form, described as a *carabelón,* appeared in a license of 1550.[24] It was owned by Francisco Pilo and was based on the port of La Navidad in New Spain. It was probably built there for exploration, but in default of a promising opportunity, was sent on a trading voyage to Peru. Some of the sailing licenses and accounts describe vessels as *naos,* but by the middle of the sixteenth century, nomenclature was too loose to permit any reliable judgment on the basis of this word. It may have been applied, in general, to smaller vessels. A number of the licenses describe vessels as *navíos,* and it seems likely that this term was applied to galleons: well-built, three-masted long vessels with high sides, especially seaworthy and good sailers. The *Santa Cruz* and *San Pedro* of the marquesado's ventures, described indiscriminately as galleons and navíos, were of this type. In rigging, steering gear, and the like, they probably conformed to patterns of the Atlantic vessels.

Contemporaries were agreed that ships built in the Pacific were smaller than those used in the Atlantic.[25] Such evidence as we have bears out their judgment. A list of vessels at El Callao, prepared in the summer of 1589, showed that those privately owned and used in private trade ranged from about 35 to 180 tons; most of them were between 50 and 135 tons. The three royal galleons in the harbor ranged from 200 to 365 tons, but they were treasure ships not used in trading voyages. Two vessels in El Callao harbor when the list was made were engaged in the Mexico trade: the *San Francisco de Buena Esperanza,* 135 tons, Bernal Bueno master; and the *Buen Jesús,* 90 tons, Pedro Cerrado master, which arrived the very day of the count.[26] The reports on vessels captured by Sir Francis Drake during his memorable cruise along the Pacific coast in 1578–1579 agreed fairly well with the 1589 survey at El Callao. Drake captured a number of barks of 12 to 15 tons engaged in short-distance coastal navigation; the rest of the vessels ranged from 60 to 120 tons. The ship of Francisco de Zárate laden with textiles and Chinese wares taken off the Central American coast en route from Mexico to Peru was of 60 tons burden. Another vessel surprised in Huatulco harbor was of 100 tons. It was loaded with Rouen linens and other kinds of textiles. Cavendish's expedition in 1587–1588 reported a few merchant vessels of larger size, one as large as 300 tons, but otherwise agreed with reports of Drake's men and with the listing made at El Callao. The absence of these larger vessels at the time of the listing is explained by the fact that Cavendish destroyed them.[27] The vessels of the marquesado, since they were built for exploration, probably reached 200 to 250 tons and were among the largest ships engaged in the Mexico-Peru run. Their very size and consequent expense of operation and repair may help to explain the losses suffered by the Cortés estate.

A further clue to the size of the vessels may be found in the number and composition of the crews. The largest crew was carried by the *San Jerónimo* when sent from Peru in 1554. It carried, in addition to its owners and their servants, a master, pilot, notary, second mate, caulker, carpenter, steward, nine able-bodied seamen, and eleven apprentice seamen, of whom three were Negroes—twenty-seven men in all.[28] From the size of the crew, it may be guessed that the *San Jerónimo* was a galleon of perhaps 200–250 tons. The *Santa Cruz* on its 1555 voyage southward carried a master-pilot, second mate, steward, notary, ten able-bodied seamen, four apprentice seamen, and five pages.[29] A less lavishly manned vessel, such as *Nuestra Señora de la Concepción* of Jácome Vasallo and Bautista Natarén on its 1563 voyage to Peru, carried a master, pilot, second mate, carpenter, caulker, notary, steward, four able-bodied seamen, and two apprentice seamen.[30] This was probably a vessel of 60–100 tons. Another of the larger vessels was *La Concepción* licensed in 1566 to go to Peru. It carried a master-pilot, second mate, notary, caulker, carpenter, nine able-bodied seamen, two apprentice seamen, and one page.[31] Some of the larger vessels were under the command of a captain, but most sailed under the sole command of a master, who was in charge of sailing in any case.

These larger vessels often carried more men than they really needed. The *San Jerónimo* on its voyage of 1565 sailed with a master-pilot, notary, second mate, caulker, and four sailors—fewer than a third of the crew it carried in 1554. It may have had trouble finding crewmen, for the license noted that it might recruit two more seamen.[32]

Smaller vessels carried far smaller crews. The carabelón *San Mateo,* which sailed in 1550, carried only a master-pilot, notary, and three sailors, one of whom was the owner's Negro slave.[33] This must have been a small vessel of no more than 30 tons. A vessel of more usual size, such as the *San Lorenzo,* of 60–100 tons at a guess, carried in 1560 master, pilot, second mate, notary, carpenter, caulker, three able-bodied seamen, two apprentice seamen, and two more seamen of unnamed category—thirteen in all.[34] The same ship in 1564 carried master, pilot, notary, six able-bodied seamen, and two apprentices—a crew of eleven.[35] Although practice varied widely, the size of crew of the *San Lorenzo* must have been more nearly the usual complement of the vessels that comprised the bulk of those on the Mexico-Peru run; that is, ships of 60–100 tons burden.

The evidence on the crewmen on the vessels also permits a comment on their national origins and racial composition. They do not seem to have differed greatly from those employed in the Atlantic navigations, and probably were recruited to a great extent from seamen in the Atlantic. The bulk of the men were Spanish, from Castile, León, and Aragon. But there were also a considerable number of seamen of foreign origin if we can judge by surnames for an age when these were still adopted *ad hoc* and very often indicated the holder's place of birth or nationality. One seamen on a ship licensed in 1554, was named Francisco Portugués.[36] This would indicate that some Portuguese seamen drifted into the navigation even before the union of the Crown of Portugal with those of Castile and Aragon under Philip II made them subjects of a common monarch. A fairly large number of the foreign seamen were Italians, particularly from Genoa and other towns of the north as is indicated by such names as Juan de Niza,[37] Antonio de Niza,[38] Sebastián Genovés,[39] Francisco Genovés,[40] Bernal Genovés,[41] and Gaspar Toscano.[42] A number of seamen came farther eastward from the Christian areas of the Levant. A license of 1560 listed a Nicolás Griego. *La Resurrección* of El Callao, which cast anchor in Acapulco harbor on December 29, 1581, carried three Levantine seamen in its crew, probably Greeks.[44] A few seamen also found their way to far Pacific shores from the Low Countries, for the *Espíritu Santo,* which arrived at Acapulco from Peru on February 27, 1587, had as its one foreign crewman a Fleming. One of the most skillful pilots on the Pacific coast was a Marseillais with the un-French name of Miguel Sánchez.[45] Foreign seamen were probably a small proportion of the total number of sailors, but this use of foreign-born sailors continued even after 1572, when Philip II ordered that no foreigners be employed on ships sailing the South Sea.[46]

The navigation appears to have been almost exclusively a European affair (European including mestizos and mulattoes counted as Spanish). After the 1540's no Indians appear to have entered it as seamen, whether slave or free, perhaps because of the laws forbidding moving Indians from their lands of origin.[47] Although such laws were often evaded or directly breached, this unwonted obedience may have been due to an abundance of European sailors. Moreover, slaves or men held in involuntary service would find many opportunities to jump ship.[48] A few Negroes were used as seamen, perhaps more in the earlier decades than later. The carabelón *San Mateo* mentioned above had among its crew in 1550, Blasillo, a Negro slave of the owner. The *San Jerónimo,* on its perhaps overstaffed voyage of 1554, carried at least three Negro apprentice seamen: Juan Biafra, Bartolomé Xilof, and Cinamari Congo—all *bozales* or born in Africa.[49] *La Concepción* in 1554 carried Francisco, a Negro apprentice seaman.[50] Licenses issued in later years did not mention Negro seamen, a circumstance which suggests that few, if any, were used who were reputed to be Negroes. On the other hand, by the 1560's, 1570's, and 1580's, many of the sailors with European surnames, although reputed to be Spanish, must have been of European blood mixed with Indian or Negro or both. During these later years use of Negro slaves, such as that on the *San Mateo,* probably was not attempted. It must have proved too costly, since they would have had the same chance to jump ship as Indians or other men under forced service.

The evidence does not indicate conclusively how crew members were paid. The custom of the sea included at least two methods. Seamen might be paid a straight wage, as were those employed by Hernán Cortés in his voyages of the 1530's.[51] This method must have been used on vessels engaged in other than trade, such as royal ships and those sent on voyages of exploration. A second method of payment involved division of the freight and passenger receipts. After deduction of the costs of maintenance and repair of the ship from the gross receipts, part of the remainder went to the owners of the vessel and part to the crew, to be divided among them in accordance with an allotment of shares based on function. Officers received in addition to their shares as crewmen a further payment from the owners of the vessel. Under this system, the shipowner provided food for the crew, but its cost might not be deducted from gross receipts. In addition, each crew member had the right to carry, free of freight charges, a stipulated quantity of merchandise, the *pacotilla,* for sale in the ports of destination. The profit from it must have been a substantial supplement to the payments received as shares in the freight and passenger receipts.

This second system of dividing the ship's receipts was used by the marquesado to pay the crewmen of the *Santa Cruz* on its voyages of the 1550's. The division in this instance was two-thirds of net receipts to the owners, and one-third to the crew. This was the customary medieval proportion. It was undoubtedly the usual proportion in both the Atlantic and Pacific, since the marquesado would hardly have been able to impose a less favorable division on the mariners or have been willing to accept one less advantageous to itself. The arrangement was especially well adapted to trading voyages in that it freed the shipowner from an obligation to meet fixed charges for wages which might have brought bankruptcy should the voyage prove barren of cargo and passengers. Such flexibility must have been necessary for continued operation of the medium-sized vessels which comprised the bulk of those on the Mexico-Peru run after the 1540's, since they were maintained upon current freight and passenger receipts. The officers and crew, for their part, became partners with the owner for the voyage, in effect, sharing in his failure or success. In general, they probably preferred this arrangement, since it promised better returns from any successful voyage and the pacotilla made them merchant-adventurers themselves on a small scale.[52]

However, when the crews were paid in shares, a peculiarly uneven movement of freight and passengers, which was characteristic of the Mexico-Peru trade, caused some trouble. The disappointing receipts for northward sailings of the marquesado's *Santa Cruz* on the two voyages in the 1550's for which we have detailed records, led the crews to seize all the money. The difficulty lay in the small bulk of the items shipped northward by Peru and the smaller number of passengers moving from Peru to Mexico. A partial solution was worked out by having the vessels touch at Acajutla, which lay near the usual landfall of vessels crossing the Gulf of Panama on the northward run. Acajutla, although a dangerously exposed roadstead, was the outlet for the prized cacao of Sonsonate, and the center of an active trade between Central America and New Spain.[53] Cargo and passengers could easily be found for carriage to Huatulco and Acapulco. The freight and passenger receipts were less than those on the Mexico-Peru voyage, since the Sonsonate trade involved a far shorter voyage and brisk competition kept down rates, but at least some receipts could be found to meet part of the costs of the northward voyage and supplement the crew's share. In March, 1587, for example, a ship of Diego López de Toledo, a Peruvian merchant, entered Acapulco harbor with a cargo of Central American cacao; its sole freight from Peru was silver. It also carried a few passengers, some of whom may have come from Peru rather than Acajutla.[54] Such Central American traffic, of course, was merely supplementary. The Mexico-Peru run furnished the bulk of receipts and had to cover most of the expenses and profits for the round trip. That there were sufficient receipts is evident, since ships and crews did appear for the annual round of sailings.

In this period 1550–1585 the pattern of ownership of vessels underwent distinct change. Most of the early ships were built essentially for exploration and conquest, and were sent to Peru to keep them occupied between voyages into the unknown. Such was the case with Cortés' Peruvian enterprises of the 1530's, those of Mendoza in the 1540's, and a number of others including Francisco Pilo and his carabelón as late as 1550. These men were encomenderos and administrators, who gained their capital and met any losses from holdings other than shipping. Others of the men who sent vessels to Peru in the 1540's were conquerors and settlers, fleeing before a stiffening royal control in New Spain, who planned to move to Peru with arms and a ship which could be used for further conquest. Ships operated for straight profit formed only a small proportion of those engaged in the Mexico-Peru traffic before 1550.

In contrast to the earlier situation, from 1550 on vessels were owned by merchants or the masters and pilots and were operated for profit. The trading enterprises of the marquesado, using vessels built for exploration and conquest but aiming at profit from navigation, formed a curious link between the older pattern of ownership and the new. The *San Jerónimo*, a galleon already mentioned as coming to Mexico from Peru in 1554, was owned by two Peruvian merchants, Francisco de Valenzuela and Antonio del Campo.[55] In 1566 another Peruvian merchant, Cristóbal de León, brought a ship owned by him to Mexico in association with a group of other Peruvian merchants; unfortunately for them, the vessel was commandeered by the viceroy of New Spain to send assistance to Miguel Legazpi in the Far East.[56] It must have been large and well-built to have been selected for trans-Pacific sailing. *La Resurrección*, which entered Acapulco harbor in December, 1581, was owned, two-thirds by Jerónimo Guenico of Lima and one-third by Felipe Corzo of El Callao.[57] *Nuestra Señora de la Concepción*, already mentioned a number of times, was owned by its master, Jácome Vasallo, in partnership with Bautista Natarén, who was also a ship's master.[58] A ship hired in 1580 by a newly appointed *oidor* of the Audiencia of Lima, Dr. Bades Carcano, to take him to his post, was owned by its pilot, Juan Díaz.[59]

To the extent that we can judge from the fragmentary evidence of the sailing licenses, supplemented by some records of Inquisition inspections, most of the vessels making the Mexico-Peru run in the 1550's, 1560's, and 1570's were owned by the masters or in some instances, by the pilots. A number of ships, usually the larger and probably better built ones, were owned by Peruvian merchants and were sent north for merchandise from Mexico. They usually carried a captain—an official who would have been superfluous in any vessel owned by the mate or pilot. These vessels could be used in the Panama trade whenever the Mexico-Peru trade seemed less promising, or may have been withdrawn from the Panama trade for an occasional Mexican venture.

Few of the wealthier merchants resident in the Audiencia of Mexico found the Pacific trade attractive enough to own ships. Their reluctance had good reason in that the lack of good shipbuilding facilities on the Pacific coast of New Spain certainly made vessels built there more expensive, and they did not have a profitable Pacific coast alternative to the Peruvian trade as did the Peruvians in the Panama–El Callao run. The cacao trade was probably difficult as an alternative because it was handled by smaller vessels operating on narrow margins. The unprofitable experience of the marquesado in its Peruvian ventures must have been discouraging to Mexico City people of means in any event. As far as the evidence now available shows, it was only in the 1570's and 1580's, when the opening of the China trade via Manila brought the possibility of profitable employment of larger capital and higher rates of return, that wealthy Mexico City people began to engage in Pacific shipping. Francisco de Zárate, whose ship and its cargo of Chinese wares were seized by Drake, was a nobleman of means, although a newcomer to Mexico.[60] In the 1580's Baltasar Rodríguez and Captain Juan de Chapoyán, powerful and wealthy enough to secure a royal *cédula* of protection, placed a vessel in the Pacific trade.[61] Their entrance into the navigation and trade may have meant that because of the entrepôt trade in Chinese wares, for the first time the Mexico-Peru trade could offer as much or more profit than the Veracruz trade with Spain.

THE PASSENGER TRAFFIC

The Mexico-Peru run carried a considerable number of passengers. Presumably all of them bore licenses authorizing them to make the voyage, but most of such records have been lost. Those surviving, found in Mexico and consisting therefore entirely of licenses granted by the viceroy and Audiencia of Mexico, represent at most a fraction of the permits which must have been issued, but they do give an idea of the reasons why people traveled and the size and composition of groups moving from New Spain to South America. They even include a substantial number of Peruvians returning home. The licenses have been tabulated in table 6 by year, by nature of business, and by number and racial composition of the people involved. The tabulation unavoidably contains no clue to one group of passengers; namely, people migrating from Peru to settle in the Audiencia of Mexico since such people would have needed no further license once they reached New Spain.

The licenses indicate that relatively few of the passengers went from Mexico to Peru on official state or Church business, and that almost none of the people returning to Peru had come to Mexico on such affairs. This

TABLE 6

PASSENGERS FROM MEXICO TO PERU AS SHOWN BY LICENSES ISSUED IN MEXICO

Years	Official and Church affairs		Trade and business		Settlement		Joining relatives		Continuing voyage Spain to Peru		Unstated		Return to Peru			
													Trade and business		Unstated	
	Lic.	People	Lic.	People	Lic.	People	Lic.	People	Lic.	People	Lic.	People	Lic.	People	Lic.	People
1550–51	3	8 S 7 N 1 IP														
1554–56			5	6 S 3 N	5	12 S	1	1 S					6	6 S	7	24 S 10 N 1 PI
1560–61			7	10 S 2 N	5	8 S 1 N	4	6 S 3 M	1	1 S						
1563–66			9	12 S	4	12 S 1 N	4	4 S 2 N	1	3 S			11	16 S	7	8 S 1 M 3 N
1575–76			6	9 S	3	5 S	7	27 S 3 N	1	1 S			7	15 S 1N	9	12 S 1 M 1 N
1579–83	8	59 S[a] 1 M 11 N	9	17 S 2 N	4	9 S 1 N	15	48 S 2 N	1	2 S	2	2 S	4	4 S 2 N	6	10 S 1 N
TOTALS	11	67 S 1 M 18 N 1 IP	36	54 S 7 N	21	46 S 3 N	31	86 S 3 M 7 N	4	6 S	2	2 S	28	41 S 3 N	29	54 S 2 M 15 N 1 PI

S = Spaniard; M = Mestizo; N = Negro; IP = Indio de la India de Portugal; PI = Peruvian Indian.

[a] Includes Oidor Bades Carcano but not his party.

fact is not surprising, since both areas were colonies subject to a central administration in Spain which sent almost all officials to the colonies directly from the home country. The major reason for movement of officials from one colony to another was transfer to new posts, and that occurred primarily from Mexico to Peru, since in the sixteenth century service in the wealthier realms of the south was considered more advantageous.

The two major movements, reflected only by stray licenses, involved the transfer of viceroys. In 1551 Antonio de Mendoza went to Peru with a very large cortège of followers, servants, and slaves.[62] His transfer meant not so much promotion as the Crown's need for a trained and firm administrator to govern its unruly subjects in Peru. In 1581, Martín Enríquez was rewarded for excellent service in Mexico by transfer to Peru. His retinue of followers, servants, slaves, and the servants and slaves of his followers was so large that his successor had to requisition two vessels to transport the viceregal party from Acapulco to El Callao.[63] The surviving license pertaining to the Enríquez party sheds light on viceregal administration. It was issued to Francisco López de Segura, a *criado* or retainer of Enríquez, who remained in New Spain eighteen months after his master's departure to finish out an appointment as *juez repartidor* of the Valley of Atlixco. Once his appointment expired, he requested a license to follow his master and secured it without difficulty from the Conde de Coruña,[64] who had his own followers to provide with posts.

The two other officials of importance for whom licenses exist also took with them retinues of considerable size. In 1580 Dr. Bades Carcano, on his way to Lima to take up a post as oidor, chartered a ship to carry himself and his party.[65] That same year, Alonso Granero de Avalos, who had served in the Inquisition of Mexico and was on his way to the see of Charcas as bishop, took along a household of relatives, priests, and servants numbering almost thirty free persons and ten slaves.[66]

In addition to these grander personages, there was some movement of lesser figures, one such being Jerónimo de Eugín, who had served the Inquisition in Mexico for years and in 1583 went to Lima as secretary of the Inquisition there.[67] Some of the passenger movement comprised unattached notaries, scribes, and gentlemen in search of official posts. Don Hernando Cortés, a grandson of Cortés through La Malinche and her son, Martín, came to New Spain from Quito *ca.* 1590 to secure government employment in the land his grandfather had conquered for the Crown. He was unusually successful in securing posts and in 1605 was alcalde mayor of the old city of Veracruz.[68] As might be expected, the licenses contain some indication of the movement of friars from one colony to the other.[69]

One of the most important reasons why people went from Mexico to Peru or vice versa was, of course, trade and other private business. This category embraced approximately a third of the surviving licenses issued to people to go from Mexico to Peru as a first voyage and half of those issued to people returning to the southern realms. The number of people involved was less than in other licenses, since merchants and businessmen in general normally took smaller parties. The most typical instances involved merchants who took merchandise valued at several thousand pesos. They might travel alone or be accompanied by a Spanish relative or servant and a Negro slave or two.[70] In a number of instances, merchants from New Spain took their wives and families.[71] Doubtless in such cases the men went to Peru prepared to settle if they found conditions there more attractive. It may well be that a number of those listed as merchants were emigrants and took merchandise to qualify for the license and to transport their funds in a form that might be carried without interference and could, moreover, be converted into cash in Peru at a considerable profit.

Trade implies credit, and credit in turn collection. A number of the passengers traveled between the colonies to secure payment for debts. In 1580, for example, Bernardino Martínez, a *vecino* and bookdealer of Mexico City, secured a license to go to Peru to collect for shipments of books sent during past years.[72] One of the most interesting instances of travel for debt collection involved Pedro Martínez Aguado, who had come to the Audiencia of Mexico from Spain in search of Captain Hernán Sánchez Morillo, his debtor in the sum of two thousand ducats, and in 1576 secured license to continue to Peru since he had discovered that the captain was living in Quito.[73]

A number of licenses bore out the legend of Peruvian wealth. They involved vecinos of the Audiencia of Mexico who went to Peru to claim the estates of deceased relatives. In 1579, for example, Diego Delicana secured a license to go to Peru to collect the estate of his dead brother. Delicana thriftily improved the opportunity by taking along merchandise valued at 3,050 silver pesos. He also took his wife, and so was prepared to settle in Peru.[74]

Two instances involved the transfer of industrial processes from New Spain to Peru. In 1566 Guillén de Almas, a vecino and old settler of Mexico City, secured a license to go to Peru to establish a glass factory in Lima.

He had already shipped dyes and iron machinery imported from Spain, but found that he and his partner had to go to the southern colony to set up the factory in person. Almas specifically wanted to return to Mexico, where he had grown old and had his house.[75] In 1579 Juan Francisco de Ojeda secured a license to go to Peru to introduce a new invention for sifting ores. He was in partnership with the Jesuit College of San Pablo, which financed his voyage. He took his entire family, presumably planning to remain in Peru.[76] These two instances cannot have been unique. To cite only one other, the techniques of the patio process were brought to Peru from New Spain by men whose licenses to travel have not been found.

The most important reason for travel from New Spain to the realms of Peru was migration, listed in table 6 under two categories, settlement and joining relatives. The licenses listed under settlement concerned families who declared that their intention was to take up residence. A typical license of this kind was issued in 1563 to Lucas Ruíz, a stockingmaker, his wife, and two sons aged six and four. For such a family, the only legal proof needed to secure the license was that the couple had been married in church.[77] It was migration of this type that brought the first printing press to Lima in 1579, when the Italian printer, Antonio Ricardo, who had operated a press in Mexico City from 1577 to 1579, moved to Peru.[78] Another case was that of Juan Esdocurio (probably Ezcurdio), a Basque, who had become crippled in arms and legs. Having spent all his money fruitlessly seeking relief in New Spain, he wished to go to Guayaquil, which was famous for its medicinal baths.[79]

The group of migrants singled out in table 6 as those joining relatives formed a category the complexity of which is masked by a simple heading. A few instances will show their variety. A number of passengers were searching for their fathers or husbands. In 1554 Juan Camacho, a lad of twenty, was sent to Peru by his mother to seek his father who had deserted her and her children a decade before and was reported to be leading a prosperous life *"en ofensa del matrimonio."*[80] Less represensible instances involved, in 1560, Lázaro de Rosales, a lad of twenty-two, who wished to go from New Spain to join his father in Peru;[81] and, in 1576, Juan López de Vergara, eighteen years of age, who had come to Mexico City from Spain, looking for his father, only to find that he had migrated to Cuzco fifteen years earlier.[82] Apparently the father had not written to his family in Spain during the entire period, or, if he had, as is unlikely, the letters had never been delivered.

Another group of licenses was issued to older people who were searching for sons to support them. In 1564, Doño Elvira de la Cueva, widow of the treasurer of the port of Acla, who had come to New Spain, secured leave to migrate to Peru to join a son resident there.[83] The next year Alonso Rodríguez Lucero, one of the early settlers of Mexico, was given license to join a son, who was a conquistador with an encomienda in Peru. The old settler was blind and could no longer support himself.[84] The reverse of the profligate male, in the form of the dutiful son, occurred in the same year 1565 when Martín Fernández Castaño was granted license to seek his impoverished mother and two sisters in Peru. Since he was a priest, he had to have the license of the Archbishop of Mexico.[85] In 1579, the person in flight was the wife. Ana López, wife of a tanner of Mexico City, secured license to go to Peru, taking her daughter and son-in-law with her. When her tanner husband denounced the project, orders were issued to the justices at the ports to halt the voyagers.[86]

Many of the people who migrated to Peru to join relatives were Spanish families who had not been able to secure what they regarded as an adequate standard of living in Mexico and wished to join relatives in Peru who were able to assist or even support them. In 1576, Francisco Díaz Cortés, born in Madrid but a vecino of Mexico City, went to Peru with his wife to join a half-brother, a prosperous hatmaker.[87] That same year Lucas Hernández, a native of Simancas who had come to New Spain four years before, went to Peru with a pregnant wife, their three-year-old son, and a Negro slave in the hope that a maternal uncle would support them.[88] In 1576 Francisca Nueva, a widow who had come from Spain the year before hunting for a relative to support her, a seventeen-year-old son, and three daughters, went on to Peru.[89] Some of the families thus searching for relatives to maintain them represented sizable numbers of mouths. In the fall of 1576 license to sail from Mexico was issued to Manuel Rodríguez, vecino of Mexico, to his wife, ten children, and two slaves. The children ranged in age from sons of thirty and twenty-six down to a *niño de teta.* The brother who had sent for them, an *abogado* of the Audiencia of Quito,[90] more than remedied his childless condition. Another family of generous size moved to Peru in 1579 when Diego de Castañeda took out license for himself, his wife, and their six children to join a wealthy uncle in Lima. Castañeda was thirty-four and his wife thirty-one so that the family was probably merely at the midpoint of its eventual number.[91] The Spanish authorities, far from discouraging such migration, approved of it as caring for people who otherwise might not be supported in the state to which they were entitled. The official attitude was manifest in a license granted in 1583 to Doña María de Silva, a gentlewoman of thirty who lacked the means to maintain herself in the state befitting her quality in Mexico and so wished to proceed to Peru, where rich relatives promised to provide for her. She traveled with two widows and a number of slaves.[92] A year earlier, in 1582, license was granted to Diego Hurtado de Mendoza, a bachelor of twenty-seven born in Seville, who came to New Spain in 1581 and had planned to return to Spain until he received news that a close relative, Rodrigo Hurtado de Cueva, had been appointed secretary of the Audiencia of La Plata. Hurtado de Mendoza at once changed his plans in order to share in the possible benefits of the post.[93] Occasionally the migrants were searching for friends. In 1580 Sebastián Negrón, a blind man, and his wife, who had come to New Spain from Peru about 1574, wished to return because they knew no people in the northern colony who would help them.[94]

As the instances listed show, there must have been a churning movement of Spanish across the Atlantic and through the colonies in the New World in search of relatives, friends, chances to find a means of livelihood. This same movement sent numbers of people on the Pacific voyage from one colony to another.

People returning to Peru from New Spain made the voyage for reasons as diverse as those given. The licenses clearly indicate that about half were issued to Peruvian merchants who came to New Spain to buy merchandise. A number of the Peruvians came on business of other kinds, also unspecified, since they came with proper certification from the southern authorities. Some must have come merely on visits—to relatives or to see friends in the northern Audiencia, such as the party of Doña María de la Cueva, which returned to Peru in 1556. The party included a number of dependent Spaniards, white servants, and free and slave people of color, as well as a Peruvian Indian woman named Catalina, one of the very few Indians of any kind who made the ocean voyage between Mexico and Peru.[95] In another instance of visiting, in 1575, Jerónimo de Macuecos, who had come from Peru to see his brother, a resident in the mines of Pachuca, secured a license to return home.[96]

One of the licenses in this category points to a trickle of migration northward. Diego de Alfaro, a harnessmaker, came to New Spain from Peru as a bachelor in 1566. He married, but finding that he could not earn a living at his trade, secured license in 1576 to migrate with his wife to Peru, where trade brought better returns.[97]

In general, the licenses suggest that most of the people who made the voyage from Peru to Mexico came on trade and business and that relatively few made the voyage to settle in the northern colonies. In contrast, of those going from New Spain to Peru who were not returning residents of the southern colonies, many were merchants or sailed to transact business; however, the largest number were those who planned to settle in the southern realms. A few licenses involved people who were en route from Spain to Peru and because of shipwreck or the need to transact business in the Audiencia of Mexico as well, went via Mexico City rather than Panama.

The passenger movement concerned Europeans primarily. A few people listed as mestizos, but thoroughly Europeanized, traveled as servants or the children of families. Almost no pure Indians were involved. A number of Negroes and mulattoes appear in the licenses as servants, free or slave; with one exception, a free woman of color who made the round trip on her own initiative.[98] As we shall see later, a fairly large number of Negroes, who did not appear in the licenses, made the voyage as slaves for sale, and presumably were considered merchandise.

THE TRADE

Trade between Mexico and Peru in the generation and a half after 1550 continued to follow a basic pattern set in the 1540's. Indeed, that pattern probably lasted for a century and a half. The civil wars in Peru in the 1530's, 1540's, and 1550's meant high prices for manufactures, horses, and European foodstuffs, all of which had to be imported. They not only kept prices much higher than even normal conditions of initial scarcity and large finds of specie would have made them, but also prolonged the period of scarcity. In 1549 La Gasca cited prices for Lima and Potosí that indicated a bitter dearth of imports.[99] As the Crown was able to impose order on its tumultuous subjects by axe, rope, lash, and exile, conditions became more favorable for the development of local production of European foodstuffs, local breeding of horses and other livestock, and local development of craft guilds to manufacture cloth, shoes, furniture, swords, and the hundreds of other items a European community of considerable wealth required. This imposition of order came slowly through the decade of the 1550's. Only in 1560 was the Marqués de Cañete, a sadistic and brutal viceroy but one who had the force to stamp out disorder, at last able to report to Philip II that the southern realms were completely at peace, crafts were flourishing, and foodstuffs had become so cheap that all scarcity was ended.[100] His comparison was relative to previous conditions in Peru, for even in the new era prices remained much higher than those in New Spain. In 1567 Licenciado Castro complained bitterly that prices in Peru were so high relative to the northern viceroyalty that official salaries which were ample in New Spain could not support the holders at a decent standard of living in the Peruvian realms.[101] Fourteen years later, in 1581, Viceroy Enríques was forced to object to any attempt to fix costs for the new royal mint on the basis of the experience of New Spain because Peruvian wages and costs were far higher.[102]

This disparity in price levels between Peru and New Spain was probably a constant condition throughout the sixteenth and seventeenth centuries. It arose from a number of factors. In the first place, Peru had a far greater production of specie. Scholars are in flat disagreement on amounts, but are in fair agreement on the trend—an initial outpouring from hoards at the time of the Conquest; a vast output from mining, especially at the Cerro de Potosí, from 1545 to the middle 1560's; decline in the last years of the 1560's and the first years of the 1570's until introduction of the patio process unlocked lower grade ores and thus initiated a remarkable rise in yield that was to make the name of Peru proverbial in Europe. During the same period, output of specie in New Spain ran a more erratic course until the introduction of mercury amalgamation in 1553. Thereafter silver production rose steadily, but at its peak, in the 1580's and 1590's, it probably amounted to no more than a third or a quarter of the wealth in specie that was pouring out of Peru.[103] New Spain's production, moreover, took place among a much larger European population so that its production of specie proportionate to the size of the European community was perhaps a sixth to a tenth that of Peru.

A second factor raising price levels in Peru was the difficulty of importing goods from Spain. Whereas the Audiencia of Mexico had direct communication across merely one ocean, with only one transshipment by cart or pack animal at the port of Veracruz, Peru had the far greater expense of a haul across the Atlantic, transshipment and carriage across the Isthmus of Panama, storage in a tropical climate, reshipment down the coast, and eventual landing in El Callao for further transportation by land or by a series of sea and land hauls to the Spanish centers in the southern colonies. Each of these stages meant substantial additional middlemen's charges and a compounding of costs. Licenciado Castro estimated in 1567 that four-fifths of the added cost of goods in Peru over Seville arose in the various carriages and transshipments from Nombre de Dios to Lima.[104] Savings in middlemen's charges were so great in movements via the Audiencia of Mexico that Spanish wares imported there could pay all the costs of carriage across the breadth of New Spain, including sale and resale in Mexico City or Veracruz or both, and costs of shipment down the Pacific coast to El Callao, and notwithstanding could still be sold at a considerable profit in Peru.[105]

A third factor in the trade relations and differences in price levels between Mexico and Peru arose from the far larger Spanish population of the northern colony, which had passed through a much shorter "time of troubles" some years earlier and had a considerable headstart in the development of European agriculture and crafts. For, if the 1550's and 1560's were a period of rapid development of European crops, livestock, and craft guilds in Peru, New Spain began its economic development in the 1520's, and through the 1540's, 1550's, and 1560's was experiencing a virtual boom in the rapid expansion of European agriculture and the rapid growth of manufacturing. Its development, moreover, involved a much larger Spanish population with far more farmers and craftsmen, and brought more of the Indian population into European-type production, especially in raising sheep and silk, weaving of textiles, and manufacture of furniture and clothing. Relatively small though New Spain's production of European-type crops and manufactures was, it met much of the local demand, helping to keep prices lower by its competition with many of the imports from Spain. There was even some exportable margin in the output of sugar, textiles, clothing, furniture, household and toilet articles, books, and other items of manufacture.[106]

The pattern which was set in the 1540's and continued through the sixteenth century was thus one of movement of manufactures and luxury items from New Spain to Peru. A market developed at Lima and other centers, especially Potosí, which became famous for its extravagance, and was starved for goods. The trickle of Spanish wares to Peru via the Isthmus of Panama, and the slowly rising production of Peruvian guilds of European craftsmen could not meet its demands. Nor could the Indians, who furnished the labor and raised most of the foodstuffs, since they did not produce European-style manufactures and luxury items. Almost automatically, the southern colonies reached out to the other colonies on the Pacific to drain them of all goods that they would release in return for specie. The movement of exports to Peru was hardly a Mexican phenomenon alone. Central America's share in this trade, especially in the export of cacao, was probably far larger than that of the Audiencia of Mexico.[107] The northern colony, on the other hand, relative to other colonies was especially well-provided with European textiles and manufactures, either imported or manufactured by the new guilds in the Spanish cities, all of which were in eager demand in the markets to the south.

The long-term pattern of trade which developed upon this basis scarcely meant that New Spain sold a surplus of manufactured goods which it was unable to consume under the economic conditions prevailing within its borders, but rather that it deliberately permitted export of merchandise which, although more abundant in New Spain than in most other colonies, yet was in fairly short supply even in Mexico City. For shipments to Peru meant removal of goods of local manufacture and of Spanish imports acquired with considerable difficulty. All such wares could easily have been consumed in the Audiencia of Mexico and the Audiencias of Guatemala and Guadalajara—the territories which New Spain was bound to supply even at the cost of scarcity to its own vecinos. Peru, supplied by a separate fleet, could hardly be held to fall within this obligation except in years of unusual events like 1554 and 1555, when the Girón rebellion cut off imports via Panama.

The acceptance of what sixteenth-century authorities and vecinos of New Spain must have regarded as a drain rather than export of a surplus—and acceptance it was since the shipments could easily have been stopped by refusing permits to buy or ship—came from the surprising fact that New Spain, despite its own substantial output of precious metals, was perennially short of specie. The Spanish fiscal system and economic and political arrangements seem to have been unusually efficient in stripping the colony of precious metals. Enormous sums were remitted to Europe as the share of the Crown in mining, the profits from various state monopolies, and balances from taxes not spent within the colony. Impressive sums were remitted by officials, who after a period of years in the colony building up fortunes, retired with their gains to enjoy life in the home country. A class of new rich of the Indies also returned with their funds to live in Spain: the famous *Indianos* caricatured by sixteenth- and seventeenth-century Spanish writers. Those from the Audiencia of Mexico were fewer than the *Peruleros,* but must still have been a substantial number. The remission of the revenues of the Marquesado del Valle alone involved enormous sums. Payments for goods, pensions, and other items also drained specie, for practically all of these remissions were made in precious metal, essentially silver.[108]

As a result of these shipments, very little specie was left in New Spain, and the colony, for all its wealth of mining, faced the twin problems of keeping a medium of exchange within its borders at a time when bills of exchange and banknotes were little used, and of finding yet more specie to meet its payments to Spain. As early as the middle 1550's representations were made to the Crown urging that half the precious metals mined be coined and kept in the colony; but the Crown, although ordering the usual report,[109] was unwilling to take any step that would have diminished shipments of specie. In 1569 a series of general inquiries into conditions in New Spain, carried out by the city of Mexico as the prelude to a petition to the Crown, showed general agreement among the officials and old settlers testifying that the drainage of specie was so complete that the colony found itself desperately short even of small coins. The royal treasurer, Fernando de Portugal, agreed that the complaints were justified.[110] Peru, on the other hand, although subject to the same drain, produced so much precious metal that it was able to keep somewhat more of it. Furthermore, even after the establishment of a royal mint in 1568, trade in Peru continued to use unminted pieces of silver and ore, weighed and assayed crudely by traders at the time of any transaction,[111] which were probably less subject to acquisition or seizure for remission than coin. Trade with Peru, then, opened for New Spain another source of specie. For only in the later development of mercury exports did Peru during these years produce a commodity in demand in New Spain.

Within the basic pattern of trade, there were continual shifts and adjustments and a continuing change in the types of goods shipped by New Spain. Textiles, clothing, and other manufactures probably formed the bulk of exports from the earliest voyages of the 1530's to the end of the sixteenth century, but throughout the 1530's and 1540's Peru was a land in the process of being conquered, and its requirements were those of a new settlement. In the first years of communication, therefore, New Spain also shipped armor, crossbows, swords, arquebuses, shot, powder, and other military supplies. Horses were an eagerly bought-up export as were European-type provisions such as meat and sugar. As the conquest of Peru progressed to the point at which the Spanish could begin to develop farming and ranching, New Spain shipped slips of fruit trees, sugarcane stock, and probably cattle and donkeys as well as horses for breeding. Much of the earliest trade thus involved a stocking of a land which was still empty of European crops and livestock. When Peru built up its farming and ranching to a point at which it could supply its own needs, there was no market for further shipments of livestock and foodstuffs. Thereupon, the trade concentrated almost entirely upon manufactures and such luxury items as could not be raised in the southern kingdoms. This phase was reached during the 1550's;[112] the shipments of mules by the marquesado on the first voyage of the *Santa Cruz* must have been one of the last of livestock.

The last foodstuff to be eliminated from the trade as Peru developed its own production was sugar, about which there are a number of legends. New Spain together with Spain (really the islands of the Caribbean and Atlantic) shipped sufficiently large amounts of sugar to be listed as the principal source of supply for Peru. In the late 1540's, Peruvian production began at a number of places on the coast, in at least some instances using cane stock and equipment brought from Mexico. Legend associates the name of Captain Diego de Mora of Trujillo and the Valley of Chicama as the beginning of this development,[113] and it is true that by 1554 Mora was producing and shipping enough sugar to Lima to need a *solar* in El Callao for storage.[114] However, as early as 1549 La Gasca reported that there were five *trapiches* pressing cane,[115] hence more probably sugar cultivation began as a series of isolated developments, of which Mora's plantation was merely one.

The Inca Garcilaso de la Vega, who passed his adolescence in the region of Cuzco in the 1550's, reported yet another story of the beginnings of sugar that throws some light on Mexico-Peru trade. According to him, the first sugar mill in Peru was built at Huánuco, but it did not prosper because of the competition of sugar from Mexico. On the advice of a servant, the owner loaded a ship with his own sugar which he sent to New Spain as a sign that Peru was overstocked. Merchants of New Spain, understanding the hint, shipped no more sugar, and Peruvian mills entered upon a period of great prosperity.[116] The story is improbable if for no other reason than that the Peruvian sweet tooth kept sugar prices high at all times. As late as 1561, despite sizable local production, sugar still brought eight pesos the arroba in Lima or approximately two and a half times its price in Mexico.[117]

Mexican shipments of sugar stopped because merchants found that Peruvian prices, high though they remained, had dropped too low to pay the heavy costs of shipment and still yield a profit. Again, the experience of the marquesado in its ventures came at the turning point. The sugar shipped in the *Santa Cruz* could no longer be sold when it arrived but had to be turned into sweetmeats. In 1556–1557 Pedro del Río, in partnership with the Marqués del Valle, could sell at a profit in Peru quince and peach preserves and rose sugar; that is, processed forms. In the next years sugar, even in the form of candy and jams, ceased to figure as an item of Mexico-Peru trade.[118]

The years from 1555 to 1560, then, mark the end of the stocking of Peru with European plants and animals in any quantity. Presumably thereafter seeds, slips, or new stock were sent on occasion, but these were isolated introductions. The movement of merchandise from New Spain to Peru thereafter concentrated upon manufactures, and luxury products which could not be produced in Peru either in sufficient quantity to meet local demand or at all.

What were these commodities? The surviving export licenses and a few other bits of evidence indicate the nature of the wares.[119] Of the manufactures, the most important group was textiles, including Rouen cloth, sackcloth, baize, broadcloth, damasks, taffetas, and all the variety of woollens and silks woven in Spain and Mexico. Yarns of various kinds, tapes then so important in clothing, ribbons, thread, towels, napkins, blankets, and quilts dyed with cochineal—all appear in the lists. Large amounts of clothing were sent: shoes, a special form of cowhide boot made in Mexico, hats, doublets and jackets, cloaks, gloves, and woollen drawers for children. An item of particular interest was hats for Indians mentioned by Henry Hawks. A permit of 1580 listed 150 of these costing three reales each. New Spain sent dyes for use in Peru: brazilwood (black), red (presumably cochineal), and assorted pigments. Household furniture and wares were another prominent group. Surprisingly enough, beds were shipped the long distances to Peru, as were writing desks manufactured in Tlaxcala and Granada. Among other household articles there were small Michoacán chests, probably of lacquered wood, *jícaras* from Michoacán (lacquered gourds) for drinking chocolate, small gilded jars, snuffers and scissors for candles, wooden and ivory clocks. Important items, catering directly to the luxury market, were toilet articles, such as rose water, quince water, soaps of Mexican and European manufacture, combs and brushes of rosebay, root, and ivory; gold and silver hairnets, razors, some of them specifically named as "de la tierra," of Mexican manufacture. Wealthy Peruvians were interested in many kinds of jewelry: earrings of jet, glass, and trimmed with silver; garnets, and other semiprecious stones; necklaces, jet rings, assorted trinkets, and looking glasses. New Spain supplied the new guilds of Peru with many of their necessities such as shoemakers' knives and awls; goldleaf; knives of various descriptions including a forerunner of the machete and butchers' knives; barbers' scissors and lancets for letting blood; augers and gimlets for carpenters; silversmiths' files; needles, thimbles, pins, and assorted buttons for tailors; weights for scales to weigh gold. Leather goods, most of which must have originated in New Spain, included saddles, reins, saddlebags, prepared sheepskins, and dressed lambskins. Some of the saddlebags were listed as "of Tlaxcala." The complement of the riding equipment was apothecary's salve for piles. The religious urges of wealthy Peruvians were catered to by substantial shipments of devotional objects and church articles: retables, altar stones, bells, large saints' images for churches and chapels, small ones for private use, devotiónal pictures of saints in Aztec feather work and in painting, crucifixes, and rosaries. Some of the rosaries, listed as "of Michoacán" may have been of lacquered wood. Many books were shipped; the greater number were ponderous tomes of the Church Fathers, devotional works, catechisms, and breviaries. Some classical works such as Ovid, Quintilian, and Virgil were included, but, if we may judge from the one list we have, Peru depended for its lighter reading on direct shipment from Spain. Peruvian learning was further assisted by shipments of pencils, paper, letterbooks for children; and amusement was furthered by Indian and Spanish guitars, Indian feather headdresses, and dolls for children. The headdresses may have been for a market among the Indian caciques in Peru; the shipment of cheaper hats for Indians also indicates some sort of market among the lower-class Peruvian Indians, perhaps the miners of Potosí. The practice of merchants seems to have been to make general assortments and offer a wide range of goods, so that they would not suffer loss through the failure to sell any one type of item. They really engaged in long-range peddling.

One item of export from New Spain remains to be mentioned: slaves. Peru received many Negroes directly via Panama, but the market was so great that all slaves sent from the Audiencia of Mexico could be sold. A Negress and her children or a slave couple (the latter costing perhaps 600–650 gold pesos in Mexico City) figure in some of the licenses and lists of merchandise. The number of slaves sent to Peru was relatively small in any given year, but in the 1570's importations of Negroes from New Spain were mentioned in the deliberations of the cabildo of Lima as important enough to be bracketed with shipments from Panama.[120] Since the adult Negroes shipped had to be born in Africa,[121] the sale meant that the Audiencia of Mexico gave up some of its limited supply of slaves in its need for specie.

Return shipments from Peru to Mexico to pay for the imposing list of merchandise sent included very few items. First and foremost was specie, mostly silver. It came at first in bars bearing the mark of the royal treasuries in Peru;[122] after the establishment of a mint in Peru, much must have come in the form of coined money. Large amounts were probably brought to Mexico clandestinely, thus avoiding the quinto or marking charges.

Peru could have shipped some stocks of plants and animals, since it had a number that might have been adapted usefully to Mexican conditions. It did send one species of animal. We have already mentioned that the marquesado tried to acclimatize a number of "obejas del Perú," llamas or related species, on a ranch at Peñol de Xico.[123] They probably were not so useful as donkeys and mules for transport or cattle for meat at the lower altitudes of New Spain.

The most surprising omission in the Mexico-Peru trade is that there was no northward transfer of the cultivated potato.[124] The most probable explanation is that it was regarded as food fit only for poor people and Indians and so did not interest the Spanish in Mexico. The Mexican Indians, who found maize adequate to their needs, would not have been inclined to shift to a new crop even if an attempt at introduction had been made. The potato was to be planted in Europe as a food for the poor, undergo considerable modification, and come to Mexico much later as an item of European diet. Today it is eaten by people of social position, and shares some of the prestige of wheat bread as compared to the lower-class tortilla of maize.

In the 1560's the second major item of shipment from Peru to Mexico made its appearance: mercury. In 1555 the mercury process of amalgamation was introduced successfully in New Spain, where it spread very rapidly. Since there was no source of mercury in Mexico, the miners were dependent on shipments from Almadén in Spain, but the supply proved too small to meet their needs, even though the Crown made special efforts to send all that could be set aside from home needs and finally agreed to ship the full output of Almadén.[125] It occurred to the Crown officials in Spain, perhaps as a result of reports that the Peruvian Indians used a substance resembling cinnebar for personal adornment, that mercury might be found in Peru. In 1555–1556 the Marqués de Cañete was ordered to have searches made for possible sources. About 1558 Enríque Garcés discovered a small cinnabar mine. He thereupon went to New Spain to study the patio process with a view to introducing it into Peru. He made the acquaintance of a young miner from Sanlúcar, Pedro de Contreras, and persuaded him to come to Peru. Early in 1559 the two set out for Guayaquil and Lima with some mercury from New Spain for experimentation. En route they added to their company a Portuguese, Pedro Pinto de Sousa, who knew metallurgy. The three did locate a number of small mercury mines; the first to be exploited was at Tomac. The yield from all of their finds was slight, nor were they able to apply mercury to the silver ores of Peru by using the methods which gave such success in Mexico. The reports were so discouraging that the Crown decided to have whatever mercury could be mined in Peru, beyond the very small needs of the colony, sent on to New Spain, where the miners and vecinos of the cities were petitioning for larger supplies of mercury at lower prices. Peruvian mercury, it was hoped, would prove cheaper than that sent from Almadén.[126] Some was probably sent under this arrangement, but the amount was disappointingly small.

The hopes of the home administration became reality in 1563 when Amador de Cabrera discovered the famous mine of Huancavelica. Thereafter Peru produced thousands of quintals a year. The first export took place in the summer of 1567 when a substantial quantity was sent to New Spain. It arrived in the fall of 1567, but was promptly embargoed by the royal treasury officials in a dispute over customs duty, since the owners insisted that having paid quinto in Peru, it was exempt from customs levies.[127] In the summer of 1568 a full shipload of mercury was sent from Peru to New Spain. It remained unloaded for some time while the treasury officials and consignees disputed over taxes. The cabildo of Mexico City in some exasperation begged the audiencia to intervene, for the mercury was badly needed.[128] Despite these difficulties, the market for mercury in New Spain was so good that merchants moving from Peru to New Spain carried quantities with them for sale. It was worth 100 silver pesos the quintal in Mexico City.[129]

The news that mercury was being shipped in some quantity from Peru to Mexico quickly brought visions of possible revenue to the perennially poverty-stricken home government. As early as 1559 exports of mercury from Almadén to New Spain had been declared a state monopoly.[130] Sometime late in the 1560's or in the opening years of the 1570's the decision was reached to make the shipment of mercury from Peru to Mexico also a Crown monopoly. The decision was embodied in a secret letter of instruction to the viceroy of Peru, but when Viceroy Enríquez attempted to confiscate Peruvian mercury the audiencia, holding with admirable and rigorous justice that a private instruction could not be held binding upon subjects who in all good faith would have had no means of knowing the royal will, and who, moreover, had carefully complied with all publicly known requirements, ordered the mercury returned to its importers. This set of suits at once led to another over the question whether the same mercury barely emerged from the earlier litigation could be held to pay customs duties since it had paid the quinto in Peru. The king, in some annoyance at his too upright judges, ordered that regardless of any decision to the contrary, the treasury officials were to collect the duty.[131] Finally, in 1572 the king decided to make all traffic in mercury a Crown monopoly, whether the mining or shipment. The decision was embodied in a series of orders in 1572–1573 and proclaimed in New Spain and Peru in 1573–1574.[132] It was the first time in seven years that the law was clear.

During 1573–1574 Francisco de Toledo in Peru took over the Huancavelica mines as part of the royal monopoly but promptly leased them to concessionnaires.[133] Meantime, between 1571 and 1573, Toledo was encouraging a series of experiments by Pero Fernández de Velasco to adapt the patio process to Peruvian ores. Velasco successfully worked out a modified process for the vast quantities of low-grade ore in Peru. When Toledo, then in Cuzco, convinced himself in 1573 that the process worked, he at once set out for Potosí, stating that he was hastening to the most important wedding in the world: that between the peaks of Potosí and Huancavelica. Thereafter Potosí absorbed the bulk of Peruvian mercury, but the output was so large that there was still a substantial surplus available for shipment to New Spain.[134]

The royal monopoly, which went into effect as far as actual shipments to New Spain were concerned at the end of 1574, was administered in two ways. The first, used in the 1570's and 1580's, was to sell licenses to private parties, who, upon suitable payment, then had the right to buy mercury from the Crown concessionnaires in Peru and ship it to New Spain for sale. Among the surviving licenses for travel issued in Mexico are two of the late summer of 1576 which illustrate the system. At that time Diego Díaz and his family were ready to return. They had come to New Spain with a quantity of mercury, which could have been brought only under special license.[135] Another license to return to Peru was issued to Juan de la Torre, a merchant, who had brought a very substantial quantity of mercury. With the proceeds of the sale, he was able to buy merchandise to the value of 80,000 pesos for export to Peru.[136] At the going price of 100 silver pesos the quintal, he must have brought 800 quintals of mercury. This system of handling the monopoly meant merely an additional tax upon the trade in the charges for the royal licenses. It had one further effect, arising out of the need for more capital and the preference of the viceregal authorities for disposing of Crown mercury in as large lots as possible: it froze smaller merchants out of the trade and concentrated it in the hands of the few men who could command such enormous sums as the 30,000 to 50,000 silver pesos that the mercury and freight must have cost Juan de la Torre. In 1591, when Juan Pérez de las Cuentas was given the concession to bring 2,000 quintals of mercury to New Spain to make up the loss of the Spanish shipment seized by English privateers,[137] the capital involved must have been around 100,000 silver pesos. Few men had such sums at their disposal; in 1592 only one man could be found in Lima who was willing to take up the concession to export 1,500 quintals of mercury to Mexico and his terms were too onerous for the viceroy to accept.[138]

The second method of handling the royal monopoly of mercury shipments between Peru and New Spain was direct operation by the Crown. The viceregal officials in Peru assembled mercury for shipment, either by purchase or from the Crown's share of the output. It was sent at royal expense to New Spain, where it was delivered against receipt to royal treasury officials there. It was stored in warehouses, sent to distributing points, and sold as a purely Crown enterprise, the proceeds being entered in the receipts of the royal treasuries in New Spain.[139] This method of administration was already in use after 1559 for shipments of mercury from Spain. Luis de Velasco II when viceroy of New Spain urged that it be used for any shipments from Peru. His advice reached the Marqués de Cañete, then viceroy of Peru, just as the latter was finding it impossible to sell the concession to export 2,000 quintals of mercury to Mexico. With this encouragement, the Peruvian viceroy decided upon shipment on Crown account.[140] For some years after 1593 this system was used to the exclusion of any other.

Imposition of the royal monopoly in 1574 enabled the Crown to control the movement of mercury from Peru to Mexico and thus to limit sharply competition with shipments from Spain. Such competition was clearly evident in 1573 when Enríquez reported that a new shipment of mercury from Europe arrived at a time when substantial stocks were held by merchants who had imported them from Peru. Enríquez put the royal mercury in storage until the private stocks should be sold. His report to the Crown showed some impatience since he threatened to set a time limit for the sale of Peruvian mercury.[141]

By the middle 1570's there was a clear Spanish policy. Exports of mercury from the home country were given preference in the Mexican market. Peruvian mercury was shipped only when Spanish exports could not meet Mexican mining demand, a contingency which arose when the yield of Almadén was low, or when the mercury ships could not sail on schedule or were captured or sunk en route. As a result of the policy, substantial surpluses of mercury were built up in Peru, for even the large needs of Potosí and other mines proved insufficient to consume the whole of Peruvian production. The excess mercury was stored in leather containers, which rotted under action of the metal with substantial losses. The viceroys of Peru pleaded that some of the surplus be disposed of by shipment to New Spain, but such export was authorized only to make up deficits in Spanish shipments.[142] This policy continued in the 1590's when direct royal administration of the monopoly meant that all Peruvian mercury entered a general stock in Mexico controlled by the Crown so that there could be no possible lowering of royal profits. The larger shipments from Peru in the 1590's[143] were made not to dispose of the Peruvian surplus, but because wars in Europe made it necessary to build up a reserve stock in Mexico against failure of European shipments.

Mercury export from Peru to Mexico thus ran an erratic course. From the first shipments in 1567 until perhaps 1572 or 1573, almost all the production of Huancavelica was sent to Mexico. We do not have reliable figures either for production or export, but the amount may well have averaged around 1,500 quintals a year. From perhaps 1574 to 1590, the viceregal authorities, using the control given by the Crown monopoly of both mining and export, kept shipments to Mexico to a minimum. Exports made only at fairly long intervals cannot have averaged more than a few hundred quintals a year. They had a plausible excuse in the needs of Peru once the patio process had been adapted to the ores of Potosí, but mercury output was rising so sharply in those years that Huancavelica could have supplied both colonies had the home country been willing to sanction the export. From 1591 to 1595 Peruvian mercury was again shipped in quantity to Mexico, perhaps 1,500 quintals annually. These shipments were in response to war conditions in Europe that had resulted in the capture of some of the ships bearing Almadén mercury to Mexico and made it too risky to send more.

For a few years, mercury was of considerable importance in the balance of payments of the Mexico-Peru trade. The first shipments of mercury came at a time when Peruvian production of specie was falling off sharply. There may well have been difficulty in assembling the silver needed to pay for shipments of goods from Mexico. Mercury provided a commodity eagerly bought in Mexico; hence there was less urgency to ship precious metal. Mercury shipments thus carried the trade through the period just before adaptation of the patio process to Potosí's ores when specie became relatively scarce in Peru. After 1574, when the viceregal officials, obeying official policy, drastically reduced mercury exports, silver production, rising sharply at Potosí, again could provide precious metal to pay for goods. The final step in the development of the Crown monopoly in the sixteenth century, direct administration, removed mercury as a factor in the balance of payments in the intercolonial trade, for such exports did not help pay for Mexican shipments to Peru as had the earlier shipments on private account. The one effect of Crown shipments on private trade was some assistance in maintaining the navigation, since shipments were usually made in private vessels and the royal government paid freight like any merchant. As a result of direct administration of the mercury monopoly, private trade between Mexico and Peru returned to the form that it had had before the discovery of mercury at Huancavelica: a straight exchange of merchandise from Mexico for specie from Peru.

Toward the end of the sixteenth century or early in the seventeenth century, Peruvian merchants finally found another commodity which was in demand in Mexico and could be shipped in payment: wine. By the early decades of the seventeenth century, wine exports to pay for Central American cacao and manufactures from Mexico became a factor of considerable importance, and served as an acceptable, though only partial, substitute for payment in silver.[114]

The size of the Mexico-Peru trade in the years 1550–1585 is not easy to ascertain, since most of the records have vanished. There must have been considerable variation from year to year. In 1564 Dr. Villanueva of the Audiencia of Mexico reported to the king that exports from the Audiencia of Mexico to Central America, Panama, and Peru via the Pacific were worth about 200,000 silver pesos a year.[143] If we assume that the share of Peru in this trade was as large or larger than that of Central America and Panama, the value of exports from Mexico to Peru around 1564 would have run from 100,000 to 120,000 silver pesos. Another indication is the quantity of mercury shipped. We have estimated an average for the period 1567–1573 of perhaps 1,500 quintals a year. This would have fetched 150,000 pesos in Mexico. Presumably all the money was converted into merchandise for shipment to Peru. It seems unlikely that the value of the goods shipped from Mexico, in terms of prices paid in Mexico, often exceeded 200,000 pesos in the 1560's and early 1570's. Landed in Peru, the shipments were worth at least double the original price. From the late 1570's on, as the Manila trade built up stocks of Chinese silks, porcelains, lacquered wares, and other luxury goods at Acapulco, the Mexico-Peru trade began to handle very much greater quantities of goods. In the early 1590's when failure of fleets to arrive at Nombre de Dios forced Peruvian merchants to look north for additional stocks, the trade may have risen to two million silver pesos or more.[146]

The manner in which the trade was carried on can only be guessed at. For the most part it was handled by merchants who traveled in person to invest their funds. If from Peru, they came north to select an assortment of wares and return with them. If residents of New Spain, they journeyed south with an assortment of merchandise and returned with specie or mercury. In only rare instances was the trade set up on a fairly permanent basis by appointing a factor. One of the major Mexico City dealers in books, however, seems to have handled his shipments in this way.[147] His experience and that of a number of others who used agents suggests that this system proved unsuccessful because so many of the agents refused to transmit payments, and the distance between the two viceroyalties made collection difficult and expensive.

The earlier merchants were essentially peddlers. The majority of those who figure in the licenses issued at Mexico City carried assortments worth 2,000–8,000 silver pesos at the time of purchase; these were substantial sums for the times but hardly equal to the sums involved in the Atlantic trade. A partnership in 1565 between two Mexico City merchants, Alonso Ortega and Luis Villarroel, which involved wares valued at 20,000 pesos,[148] was a large enterprise among much smaller ones. The ventures of the marquesado were probably the largest in terms of capital involved during the 1550's and 1560's. Some of the Peruvian merchants traveled in associations, but these meant mutual assistance in chartering vessels and moving goods rather than partnerships of any size or the merging of funds to form a company.[149]

The sums needed to handle mercury exports during the period from 1574 to 1591, when the Crown monopoly was administered by selling export licenses, meant the entrance into the trade of much wealthier men and, at times, much of Mexico's export trade to Peru was concentrated in a few hands. In 1576 Juan de la Torre's merchandise valued at 80,000 pesos was a substantial part of the exports of that year even though by that date the sale of Chinese goods was appreciably raising the total of the trade.

In the last two decades of the century, much more capital was invested in the trade. The availability of Chinese wares diverted a substantial amount of Peruvian capital from the Panama trade to Acapulco.[150] The chance of much greater profit and parallel suspension of fleet sailings from Spain to Veracruz brought in also numbers of wealthier merchants of New Spain.[151] Part of the much greater capital may have come from accumulation of profit in the trade itself. Such was the case of Diego López de Toledo, a merchant resident in Lima, who in 1565 was a fairly small figure in the trade.[152] Twenty years later he was the owner of a large ship making annual voyages that meant the turnover of sums upward of 100,000 silver pesos.[153] His prosperity suggests that the viceroy of Peru was truthfully summing up the experience of Peruvian merchants in 1592 when he reported that those persons trading with Spain were being ruined by the difficulties of securing shipments as well as by the long periods they had to wait for returns on their capital, whereas those trading in local products or importing wares from New Spain were enjoying quick turnover and steady prosperity.[154]

VI. REGULATION AND TAXATION, 1535–1585

THROUGHOUT the sixteenth century, Spanish trade and navigation along the Pacific coast of America were free, that is, permitted. Initially, this freedom came from the lack of any kind of legislation. But, in an age when the only unassailable basis for an activity was specific royal license, the lack of legislation permitted and indeed encouraged provincial governors to institute local systems of licensing and control, either to concentrate shipbuilding and trading in their own hands or in those of their associates or to derive revenue from the sale of permits. Within a few years, therefore, the Crown was forced, probably as a result of complaints and petitions, to issue a series of orders, writing into legislation its intent that trade and navigation in the Pacific be free to all its subjects. In 1535 a royal cédula gave general license to all inhabitants of the province of Guatemala to build ships in the ports of the Pacific.[1] Although issued specifically for Guatemala, the order seems to have served as a rule for the other colonies on the Pacific coast. In 1543 another royal cédula ordered that there be complete freedom of movement for ships in the Panama-Peru navigation; royal officials were not to interfere so long as any taxes owing the Crown were paid.[2] This order was amplified and extended to the entire Pacific coast of America on March 9, 1551, and again on April 2, 1560, in a royal cédula that constituted a charter for Pacific shipping. Under it, all merchants and traders in the South Sea might ship their wares in large or small ships as they pleased, and such ships, regardless of their size, might load freely so long as they had adequate provision for defense.[3] Since at that time and for some years following, no enemies appeared in the Pacific nor were any expected, few ships were required to carry, or carried, artillery or other defensive equipment. The restrictive clause at first thus meant nothing. As part of the Pacific traffic, the Mexico-Peru navigation and trade shared in these general permissions.

Crown permission, of course, did not mean the absence of careful inspection and control. Freedom in that sense was unthinkable to the sixteenth-century administrator. The royal authorities were under clear obligation to extend to the traffic in the Pacific, and to enforce, the long series of regulations and customary requirements obtaining in Europe and the Atlantic. The government was supposed to see to it that ships were seaworthy; that they carried proper provision of rigging, sails, anchors, and

[1] For notes to chapter vi, see pages 152–156.

other gear; that they had food and water, not only adequate for the length of the voyage contemplated but with margin for storms and delays; that the ship was not overloaded and the cargo was properly stowed; that the crews were sufficient; and that the pilot was properly trained and duly examined.[4] From the first voyage of Columbus, Spanish administrative practice further insisted upon detailed, formal registry of all cargoes and passengers, an obvious and necessary requirement that facilitated collection of taxes and became indispensable in the event of dispute between shipowners and merchants.[5] Furthermore, as the Crown issued a series of regulations establishing categories of wares and persons forbidden passage to the Indies, registry became essential for enforcement of these rules.

Registration was so customary that a careful man like Cortés had a notary prepare sworn statements of cargoes and passengers[6] before there was any formal machinery set up in New Spain to regulate movement by ship in the South Sea. Ships sailing from Peru to New Spain in the first years probably observed the same rule of registry at the insistence of authorities in Peru and as a precaution against demand at the end of the voyage. The only exceptions must have occurred during the civil wars when some ships left the coast of Peru in such haste that they had no time for notarial certification.

In the course of the sixteenth century, the requirements for registry and inspection were written into royal legislation, which eventually was incorporated into the *Recopilación*. In 1552 a royal cédula ordered that any article of merchandise shipped from one port to another in the Indies, whether in the Atlantic or the Pacific, must be registered in a sworn statement before a notary, a copy to be left with the notary and another to go with the ship for presentation at destination.[7] In 1558 this rule was reinforced by another: that all ships sailing from the Indies to Europe or to any other port of the Indies carry a register, executed before a notary, of whatever they had on board.[8] In 1575 yet another cédula ordered that all rules for registry of passengers established for the Atlantic navigation be enforced in the Pacific.[9] That same year royal officials in ports of the Indies were ordered to inspect all vessels of whatever kind entering or clearing those ports even if they were merely bound for another port in the Indies. The officials charged with inspection were to be the first to board any vessel entering harbor.[10] These regulations testify to laxity in the enforcement of inspection and registration and to royal annoyance at it rather than to the absence of such requirements before the regulations were issued. Local evidence makes it abundantly clear that the rules issued for the Atlantic and customary requirements originating in the medieval Mediterranean and Atlantic trades were very early applied to navigation and trade in the Pacific.

In addition to the general reasons for imposition of government controls on the Pacific navigation, there were a number of problems, present in the Pacific and in the Mexico-Peru trade, which furnished special reasons for control. Some of the problems centered about the movement of persons. One concerned the appearance of foreign seamen and pilots in Spanish navigation in the Pacific. In general, foreigners were forbidden to enter the navigation to, or in, the Indies at all, but there were special reasons for attempting to keep them out of the South Sea. That ocean was a Spanish preserve, the detailed knowledge necessary for its navigation to be kept a jealously guarded secret.[11] The rules on exclusion of foreigners were hardly well kept,[12] but they did constitute a policy which royal officers were bound to enforce.

A second series of problems arose out of the migration of Spanish subjects. Under a royal cédula of 1480 all subjects might fix their residence where they wished within the realms of the common Crown.[13] At first, this freedom of movement was conceded to Spanish subjects wishing to remove to the New World or from one part of the New World to another, subject only to a requirement of registry.[14] But freedom of movement became impossible to maintain, for the lure of Peru threatened to depopulate all other colonies and to fill that colony with fortune-seeking hordes who fed the fires of crime and rebellion. In 1534, therefore, the Crown decreed that no man might leave the province where he was a vecino without express license of the governor under penalty of loss of any office or encomienda he might hold and perpetual disability to hold any in the future.[15] Thereafter the cédula of 1480 was restricted by interpretation to a general permission to Spanish in the New World to remove from town to town or to change residence at will within the same province. In this sense it was reaffirmed in 1544 and 1548.[16]

The need to impose rigid controls on Spanish movement to Peru, which was manifest as early as 1534, became critical by the 1540's when the Crown lost control of the colony for a number of years. In 1548 La Gasca, after having crushed the rebellion of Gonzalo Pizarro, tried to establish the basis for a more enduring royal peace in the colony by asking the governors of Panama, Nicaragua, and New Spain to refuse to permit any person not a bona fide merchant or seaman to go from their colonies to Peru.[17] His letters amounted to a demand that permanent migration be halted. In his retirement as Bishop of Palencia, he repeated his suggestions in even stronger terms. Peru, he commented, was overrun with thieves and wastrels who not only robbed and plundered the Indians but also were ready to revolt on any pretext against the Crown.[18] The basic difficulty was put succinctly by the Marqués de Cañete in a report to the Crown in 1555. There were in Peru, he estimated, more than eight thousand Spanish adult males. To provide employment and maintenance for them, there were but 480 encomiendas, which together with government offices and appointments of one kind and another, could provide berths for perhaps a thousand. There were thus more than seven thousand Spaniards who scorned occupation as artisans or farmers and upon failing to receive an income from the Crown were ready to follow any adventurer who promised a new distribution of encomiendas and offices.[19] The solution of Cañete was to urge once again that only bona fide merchants be permitted to come to Peru—in effect, a halt to further settlement—and that all unemployed Spaniards be expelled from the colony.[20] Complaints of restless Spaniards who threatened the royal government with the possibility of rebellion continued to occur in the correspondence of later viceroys throughout the sixteenth century. The solution urged was always the same: to put all movement of passengers to Peru under strict control.[21]

The advice of La Gasca and subsequent administrators in Peru led to a series of royal orders forbidding all people to go to Peru without express royal license. In May, 1549, the first general order to this effect was communicated to Antonio de Mendoza in Mexico and to the audiencia there. The only categories of persons exempt from the prohibition were married men taking their wives with them and merchants or their factors. The viceroy and audiencia were given special warning that Spaniards seeking to evade the regulation went to Mexico and from there made their way to Peru. They were further instructed to see to it that the justices at the ports were stringently enjoined to enforce the royal order.[22] This cédula presumably was one of a series sent to all provinces in the New World. To make sure that the viceroy and audiencia in New Spain understood the seriousness of the instruction, it was repeated in another royal cédula issued in October of the same year.[23] A complementary royal order of September, 1549, ordered the Audiencia of Lima to return to Spain as prisoners all Spaniards who were in Peru without express royal license.[24] The royal intent that license to go to Peru as a settler be issued only by the Crown directly was reaffirmed in 1561 when a royal cédula ordered the expulsion of all who had migrated to Peru with licenses issued by the Conde de Nieva as president of the Audiencia of Panama.[25] In 1566 the insistence that licenses to migrate to Peru must be issued by the Crown in Madrid was repeated in an order that all in Peru without such licenses be expelled even though they might have come with formal licenses issued by the viceroys and governors of other colonies.[26] In 1569 the requirement for an express royal license was extended to married couples.[27]

This legislation was enforced from time to time by special examinations of the licenses under which settlers were in Peru and the expulsion of any who could not show royal authorization to remain in the colony. The fear of excess Spanish settlers in Peru was manifest in a savage instruction to Martín Enríquez in 1580, requiring him to expel from Peru any Spaniards who had settled there without proper license since the Girón revolt of 1554; that is, during the twenty-seven years preceding Enríquez' arrival.[28] A similar clause was incorporated in the instruction to the next viceroy, the Conde del Villar, in 1584.[29] Even so conscientious a royal servant as Enríquez found it inexpedient to enforce this order to the letter. In this matter as in others, the Spanish principle of "Obedezco pero no cumplo" must have led to a sensible accommodation on the basis of official blindness in exchange for cash. Nevertheless, a royal policy of sharply restricting movement to Peru was embodied in the series of instructions and orders which could not be ignored even though in the case of deserving people it might be modified by the dictates of common sense.[30]

Closely linked to the problem of vagabonds and footloose bachelors was that of married men living away from their wives. To the Spanish authorities, with their conception of the well-ordered Christian state, the idea that a man might live away from his wife except for a short period and under a special license to be granted only with the consent of the wife, was an abomination, a violation of the obligation of the king to enforce decency and Christian morality. Such men, moreover, tended to swell the ranks of adventurers and the lawless who complicated the enforcement of order and justice in the Indies. There seems to have been a substantial number of refugees from matrimony in the Indies, especially in New Spain and Peru in the earlier decades of the sixteenth century. In 1550 the Crown administrators estimated that there were more than seven hundred in New Spain alone.[31] The solution to this problem presented no difficulty in theory, although enforcement presented many difficulties in fact. In 1544 a long and stern royal cédula ordered officials in the Indies to search out married men living away from their wives and send them back without delay. The order included those who had crossed the sea without license and those who, having crossed with license, had stayed in the Indies after the allowable two years had expired.[32] The prelates of the Indies were to make special inquiry, each in his jurisdiction, to report offenders.[33] The orders were repeated at intervals during the sixteenth century in further instructions which enjoined rigid enforcement of the earlier cédulas.[34] The orders were almost impossible to enforce fully in the vast spaces of the New World, but derived as they were from a deeply held sense of obligation and morality, they could not be ignored.

Another policy of the Spanish Crown which meant an enforcement problem in the Pacific navigations involved the moving of Indians. The ghastly devastation wrought by slaving expeditions among the Indians of the Antilles, Central America, and the Caribbean coast of New Spain, a devastation which brought only a dubious economic profit to the Spaniards since Indian slaves died off rapidly, led in 1528 to a stringent clause in the ordinances for the government of New Spain forbidding the moving of Indians from one province to another even if they were slaves.[35] In 1541 the prohibition was reinforced by a quaint cédula forbidding Spaniards to take with them Indian women, whether by land or sea, because of the offense against morality.[36] The order is associated with the administration of Fray García de Loaisa, and thus may bear a flavor of special clerical concern. Two years later, in 1543, Philip II as prince regent made the ordinance of 1528 general for the Indies. Indians whether slave or free, might not be removed to another province, even if they were willing to go.[37] That there was need for such an order in the Peruvian traffic cannot be doubted, since many of the Indians enslaved in Nicaragua and Honduras were shipped to Peru. Pedro de Alvarado in 1534 took with him several thousand Guatemalan Indians, almost none of whom returned. Had there not been such a prohibition, a thriving trade in Indian slaves might well have grown up between New Spain, where there was at first a substantial number, and Peru with its demand for personal servants and laborers.

Another series of enactments which greatly affected government control of the Mexico-Peru navigation arose from attempts of the Crown to ensure payment of taxes and other dues. As early as 1521 a cédula of the emperor forbade any settler to leave the locality where he was resident without proving to the governor or justice that he had discharged all obligations to pay tithes.[38] Oddly enough, this requirement seems to have been ignored in subsequent provisions for enforcement of fiscal obligations. It may have occurred because the tithes, having been regranted to the dioceses, concerned the clergy rather than the Crown. The legislation which was enforced concerned civil fiscal obligations. In 1535, Charles V ordered that no person might be given a license to leave the city or province where he was resident until he presented an affidavit that he owed nothing to the Crown as trustee for *bienes de difuntos* (the property of people deceased intestate or without executors in the Indies), that there was no suit pending against him for money, and that he owed no accounting as the guardian of a minor.[39] The requirement for affidavits was extended in 1537 to include certification that the traveler owed nothing to the royal treasury.[40] This requirement of an affidavit on bienes de difuntos was reënacted a number of times during the sixteenth century. In 1550 it was incorporated in a general ordinance on the subject and became part of the ordinances of the House of Trade.[41]

In addition to these charges to prevent evasion of depts and taxes, Crown officials in the Indies were also under a series of general obligations, inherent in their offices, to prevent the flight of criminals from justice and to enforce prohibitions on movement of precious metals, and certain wares such as weapons. The obligation regarding precious metals was made explicit in 1538 when the viceregal government in New Spain was enjoined to put an end to surreptitious export of Peruvian silver via Veracruz which evaded payment of the quinto and other royal dues.[42] At that early date in Mexico-Peru communication of any kind, the amount that might have reached New Spain by way of Central America or on Cortés' returning vessel could not have been great, but the Crown was intent on closing every gap.

All these restrictions on movement of persons and wares; requirements for affidavits, inspections, and registry; and general Crown policy considerations made rigorous control of Mexico-Peru navigation indispensable. The means by which control was to be imposed were clearly indicated by custom and the new rules as they were issued.

The enforcement of government requirements for licenses, ship registry, and ship inspection came within a few years of the opening of Mexico-Peru navigation. For New Spain, sufficient records survive to give clear indication of the development of these controls. On August 24, 1539, Antonio de Mendoza issued a general ordinance for the Pacific coast of his viceroyalty which established a general system of registry. In the preamble to the ordinance, the viceroy complained that the masters and captains of some of the ships sailing from Pacific ports for Peru and other areas were not preparing and filing registers. Under cover of this neglect, they had shipped many things forbidden export by royal regulations and were secretly carrying off stolen Indian and Negro slaves. The ordinance decreed that henceforth masters and captains must make formal registry of their vessels, cargo, and passengers before the justice of the port from which the ship was to sail. Penalties for failure to register included forfeiture of the ship and half of any other property involved, a quarter of the proceeds to go to the informer.[43]

Although the ordinance dealt only with registry of vessels clearing west coast ports for other colonies, it obviously meant as well implementing all other controls and regulations then in effect. For an official to whom application was made for registry could hardly fail to demand that any passengers on the register show their licenses to leave the province, that proof be presented that all items of cargo were carried with proper clearance, and finally that the vessel met the customary requirements of seaworthiness, provisioning, and crew.

Proclaimed in Mexico City on August 25, 1539, the day following the viceroy's signature, the ordinance was enforced as quickly as word could be sent to the justices of the Pacific ports. Its speedy enforcement served Mendoza's personal ends in his attempts either to cripple his rivals in the race for the Gran Quivira or to force them into partnership with him. A few years later, Hernán Cortés complained that Mendoza not only had forbidden any person to leave New Spain without viceregal license but also used this prohibition and his new control over the departure of shipping to seize Cortés' ships and supplies.[44] But Mendoza's ordinance was consistent with his duty to extend royal control over traffic in the Pacific. Nor does he seem to have departed from the custom of Spain and the Atlantic navigation or royal regulations already issued by 1539. The approval of his measure by the home government was apparent in the scant attention it paid Cortés' complaint.

The ordinance of 1539 necessarily underwent modification and clarification in the first years following its promulgation. In 1542 an order of the viceroy to the alcalde mayor of Tehuantepec made it clear that the ordinance was intended to require registry of vessels, cargoes, and passengers arriving at west coast ports as well as sailing from them.[45] This interpretation was reinforced in 1550 by orders to the alcaldes mayores of the ports of Huatulco and Acapulco to seize all persons not on the registers of arriving ships, their goods even if registered, and any unlisted goods. All persons arrested were to be questioned, and if guilty of any crime, were to be sent with copies of their testimony to Mexico City for decision as to trial. This order specially mentioned that people were arriving in New Spain from Peru and Nicaragua.[46]

The major adjustment in the system of controls as extended to the Pacific in 1539 involved not the Peruvian trade but the Sonsonate navigation. By the early 1540's a number of small vessels were carrying on an active traffic in Mexican foodstuffs and other wares sent south for the provinces of Guatemala and in cacao shipped north. Shipowners and masters in this trade complained that the requirement of a specific viceregal license for each voyage meant long delays and heavy expense. During 1542 the viceroy attempted to solve these grievances by issuing general licenses for sailing at will to specific masters and shipowners engaged in the Sonsonate trade, provided they made formal registery at the port on leaving and arriving and went only to the Guatemala coast.[47] The following year, in 1543, perhaps under pressure from Mexico City merchants interested in the cacao trade, Mendoza granted general permission to all ships engaged in it to sail freely. They were still required to register at the beginning and end of each voyage and were forbidden to carry passengers, wares normally prohibited from export or import, and Indians whether slave or free, unless the viceroy by express license had given permission.[48] The fact that Mendoza was willing to make these modifications, as well as the language of one of the special licenses issued in 1542, suggests that the imposition of controls was aimed chiefly at regulating traffic with Nicaragua and Peru, in which there was much more likely to be illegal movement of persons, evasion of royal taxes, and smuggling of prohibited goods.

The machinery to enforce the system of controls was so simple that it cost the royal treasury little. It cannot have differed much from the arrangement at Veracruz. The official charged with enforcing registration of vessels was the alcalde mayor or justice of the port.[49] Customarily such a justice was assisted by an alguacil.[50] The act of registration had to be carried out before a notary. In ports with little traffic, the notary was undoubtedly the customary one attached to each justice. In a large port, the right to prepare the acts of registry and inspection and to levy the fees attached to performance of that function became an attractive plum. Wherever performed in New Spain, the function seems to have been attached to the office of the *escribano mayor de minas, relaciones y registros* of the viceroyalty. Since the escribano mayor was the chief notary of the realm and head of the viceregal secretariat in Mexico City, he obviously could discharge his functions on the west coast only through a lieutenant. In 1556 Juan de Cuevas, escribano mayor of New Spain, successfully asserting his claim, secured a formal order from Luis de Velasco I that registry and inspection at the port of Huatulco must take place before a notary appointed by Cuevas and acting for him. Fees were to be charged in accordance with the schedule established for Veracruz.[51] The inspection of vessels was customarily carried out by the alcalde mayor or other local justice in the smaller ports, but in a large port, such as Huatulco early became, an attempt was made to set up a special post. The arrangement perhaps paralleled that at Veracruz but also reflected the need of the viceroy to find as many positions as possible for deserving Spaniards. The first inspector of shipping appointed for Huatulco was Hernando Díaz, who may have been given the post in 1542 or early 1543. Since he was unable for an unspecified reason to discharge the function, Mendoza appointed Pedro Pantoya to replace him in May, 1543. For his services as inspector, Pantoya was to collect two pesos de minas from the master of each ship visited. Lest there be any doubt of the requirement that each ship be checked for seaworthiness and supplies, Mendoza formally reënacted the requirement in the order of appointment.[52] This institution of the post at Huatulco by Mendoza was admittedly an experiment, the success of which depended upon whether or not the volume of shipping would be large enough to support an official through fees. In the later decades of the century, the function of inspection reverted to the alcalde mayor. By then Acapulco was an important center, but its alcalde mayor was given the charge to inspect shipping under an additional title of *veedor* attached to the office.[53]

Imposition of controls on the Mexico-Peru traffic and the creation of machinery to enforce it took place in Peru in the same years as these developments in New Spain. In the southern colonies, the process was simplified by the fact that there was but one coast and the controls and administering machinery established for the Panama navigation could apply to the New Spain run. Indeed, it would have been a resented anomaly to have permitted the Mexico navigation to remain free from controls required of all other traffic. The evidence in the Mexican archives shows that by the early 1540's authorities in Peru were issuing licenses for people and vessels to go to New Spain.[54] During the first years, such licenses were issued by the governors of the various towns. After the establishment of royal control by La Gasca toward the close of the 1540's and the creation of an effective central government, licenses to go to New Spain were issued by the viceroy in Lima, or in his absence by the audiencia there, and for the district of Quito by the audiencia resident in that city. Licenses for vessels were issued by the same authorities.[55]

The other requirements of registry and inspection were enforced in the Peruvian realms as fully as any other rules, since these were required by custom and law.[56] In the smaller ports, control formalities were probably carried out by local justices and their notaries. For El Callao, the principal Pacific port of Spanish South America in these years, there were as at Huatulco certain special officers. In 1556 the Marqués de Cañete created a special post of *alcalde de la mar* with criminal and civil jurisdiction over ships, sailors, merchants, and passengers at the port.[57] El Callao also had a special escribano de registro, before whom all records of registry had to be made. Just when this office came into existence is not certain, although it may well have been an early creation. At some time in the 1570's Francisco de Toledo on royal instruction sold the post to Jerónimo de Andrada.[58] Inspection at El Callao was handled by an official with the title of alguacil mayor, who also enforced requirements of registry.[59] At smaller ports on the South American coast, these functions were discharged by the local justice.

The effectiveness of the system of controls and the machinery for administering it in enforcing the various requirements and regulations is difficult to determine. The controls operated over vast areas only sparsely populated by Spaniards. Enforcement was in the hands of officials dependent for their livelihood on collection of fees and therefore unusually prone, even in an age of venal administrators, to connive at evasions. There can be little doubt that there must have been much evasion, as the complaints about Spaniards moving to Peru in defiance of repeated royal prohibitions demonstrate clearly. On the other hand, the licenses issued to vessels and passengers in New Spain suggest that there was substantial enforcement of the rules. In 1542 Alonso Cano, an encomendero of San Ildefonso de los Zapotecas (present-day Villa Alta) received license to go to Peru only after posting bond to return within a year and a half after sailing. If he failed to return on time, his bondsmen were to make good to the Crown all tributes and services received from the encomienda from the date of Cano's departure.[60] This license suggests that the regulation of 1534 was enforced as it related to encomenderos. Other licenses indicate that the system did serve to control migration. During the period of the civil wars in Peru, perhaps in response to La Gasca's appeal in 1548, licenses were issued to people with acceptable reasons for going to Peru, or to those in the permitted categories of married men migrating with their families, or to merchants, but only upon the additional condition that they agreed to serve the king in any way they might be called upon. In some instances this promise was reinforced by posting a bond in New Spain to guarantee fulfillment. When permission to go to Peru might be given only for a visit, the limitation on stay in the southern colonies was backed by the requirement that a bond be posted to insure return within the stipulated period. In 1550 Juan Gaitán was forced to post such a bond, even though he traveled on official business.[61] The sanctity of marriage, so insisted upon by royal cédulas, was protected by requiring an onerous series of affidavits and a bond from married men who had proper reasons for travel.[62] Presumably the same requirements for travel to New Spain were enforced in the realms of Peru.

The effectiveness of the licensing system was perhaps especially apparent in enforcement of the regulations against taking Indians, whether slave or free, from one province to another. By interpretation the rule came to mean that an Indian servant might be taken on a journey to another province provided license were granted and bond posted for his return. A number of the licenses issued by Mendoza give this kind of permission, and such evidence as there is indicates that the same rule was observed in Peru.[63] That the control was enforced at least in part is evidence from the experience of Hernando de Villanueva in 1543. Villanueva had come to New Spain with an Indian man and woman, both natives of Peru, under a license issued by the lieutenant of the governor in Piura two or three years before 1543. The Indian, named Antonio, either fled or was kidnaped in New Spain. Not daring to return to Piura without him for fear of forfeiting the bond posted, Villanueva appealed to Mendoza, who ordered that the Indian be found and examined before a justice. If the Indian wished to return to Peru, he was to be delivered to Villanueva; if he declared himself unwilling to return, sworn testimony to that effect was to be given to Villanueva for presentation in Piura.[64] Enforcement of the regulations, as typified in this case, was apparently effective enough to prevent the development of any traffic in Indian slaves between the viceroyalties.

During the course of the sixteenth century the licenses issued in Mexico to travelers to Peru underwent a series of changes which illustrate the development of the controls over passenger movement.[95] The first licenses, issued by Antonio de Mendoza, were fairly elaborate documents setting forth the reasons for the voyage, the qualifications of the traveler in terms of royal regulations, and the permission of the viceroy, together with any conditions set. An invariable condition, in accordance with the royal cédula of 1537, was that the license to be valid must be endorsed by royal treasury officials attesting that the traveler owed nothing to the Crown. From the beginning licenses thus carried in their text a fairly detailed statement of the reasons for issuing them; this feature became characteristic of those issued in Mexico.

Luis de Velasco I instituted a number of modifications in the license form and the number of affidavits required. At some time within the first decade of his administration, probably within a year or two of taking over the viceregal post, he implemented the fiscal precautions ordered by the royal cédula of 1537 much more fully than had Mendoza. In addition to the endorsement of the royal treasury officials, the traveler had to obtain an affidavit from the fiscal of the audiencia that there was no suit pending against him for money owing the Crown and a further one from the official in charge of bienes de difuntos that he left no unsettled obligations in that field. The certification regarding the bienes de difuntos probably also covered the clause in the royal cédula of 1537 requiring an affidavit on the property of minors. Possible fraud in the use of licenses was made somewhat more difficult by a further innovation of Luis de Velasco I. Around 1560 licenses issued by him include a description of the traveler: age, stature, build, and coloring, distinguishing features such as scars and infirmities; this was intended to make impossible the substitution of another person. In licenses granted to people of quality or especially good character, such descriptions were omitted, perhaps as unnecessary or insulting when applied to persons of standing.

Later innovations in the Mexican licenses increased the number of necessary affidavits. Shortly after the establishment of the Holy Office in Mexico City, Viceroy Enríquez added the requirement that the traveler must secure a notation from the Inquisition that there was no case pending against him in that tribunal and that it had made a record of the license. The first surviving license with this type of notation was issued in 1576. At some time between 1576 and 1582 yet another affidavit was added to certify that the traveler owed nothing under the newly instituted tax of the *alcabala*.

Although evidence on licenses issued in Peru is much scantier, what we have indicates that Peruvian authorities required the same endorsements as in the Audiencia of Mexico.[66] This simultaneous enforcement in two widely separated colonies suggests that the originating factor was an instruction from the central government in Spain. In one, perhaps not too important, respect, licenses issued in Peru did differ markedly from those issued in Mexico: they were much terser, omitting all the detailed recital of petition, qualifications, and conditions. Some at least consisted merely of a single sentence.

In both viceroyalties, of course, the licenses issued to travelers going from one to the other domain followed the general form developed for all permits to travel. Licenses issued in Mexico City to travelers bound for the Philippines or the mother country show the same form and requirements as those issued to travelers bound for Peru. The licensing system in both viceroyalties, as indeed the entire system of control, was undoubtedly general for all travel and trade.

Royal control over trade and navigation was supplemented by one further inspection established by the Holy Office of the Inquisition in the 1570's. In the New World, as in Spain, the Inquisition was essentially a tribunal discharging Church functions but under such close royal supervision that it might well be regarded as more closely related to the Crown than to the Church. In New Spain, the establishment of the Holy Office led quickly to the appointment of commissioners at the two Pacific ports of Huatulco and Acapulco. The appointment was usually conferred on the curates. The commissioners were instructed to be the first to board entering vessels in order to make certain that there would be no evasion of their inspection of passengers, books, and articles of worship. The inspections were carried out conscientiously and have left us a remarkable record of ship arrivals.[67] Since Mexican practice was dictated from Spain, the Peruvian Inquisition must have followed the same organization and practices with little local variation.

In addition to the control and supervision discussed thus far, Mexico-Peru trade and navigation were subjected to regulation whenever they fell within the compass of the elaborate imperial, colonial, and municipal legislation dealing with purchase and transportation in both colonies. Only a few instances can be mentioned. In New Spain, merchants were subject to a requirement that they secure a viceregal license even before making their purchases. At most, they might make preliminary purchase agreements for completion when the license was issued. An additional license was needed to export the merchandise, but presumably this was issued as a matter of course once the license to purchase was granted.[68] The requirements implemented what amounted to a system of rationing of manufactures and other scarce commodities, for through it the viceroy was able to direct a crude allocation of goods in Mexico City, deciding how much might be shipped out of the city to each other city or colony. That any allocations for Peru were made at all testifies to the interest of Mexico City merchants and administrators in having the trade continue. At the other end of the voyage, in Peru and Ecuador, the merchants had to obey yet other regulations on proclamation and sale. In Peru, the audiencia in 1555 decreed that no merchandise imported into the realm, whether from Panama or Mexico, might be bought for resale. The ordinance, issued over the objections of the cabildo of Lima, sought to eliminate any middleman between the importing merchant and the retail purchaser.[69] It followed the pattern of the usual colonial and European rules against regrating, and probably had the usual lack of success. That there was more involved than the standard sixteenth-century prejudice against middlemen is apparent from an ordinance of the cabildo of Lima issued in 1564. Complaining that local artisans were buying articles brought from Panama and Mexico, probably to end competition between their own products and the imports, the cabildo forbade artisans to buy anything but raw materials.[70]

A further category of regulations that assumed some importance concerned Indians. In the first years of the navigation when roads were nonexistent or very bad and pack animals were scarce, travelers and merchants both in New Spain and in Peru used Indian bearers. The use of tamemes was strictly forbidden by a series of royal orders, the first of which was issued in December, 1528.[71] As so often happened in the Spanish Empire, the rigidity of the prohibition failed to take account of the fact that frequently there was no other way to move cargo and supplies. Another series of orders, therefore, permitted use of bearers wherever it was unavoidable. In such cases the authorities were to give licenses for each specific use and regulate the weight carried, distance traveled each day, and the pay. Furthermore, the Indians might be put to work only if willing—a restriction which few in either colony can have taken seriously. The standard weight carried by a bearer was two arrobas, his food, and its container, although this rule was subject to modification in accordance with local conditions.[72]

Under the dispensing amendments to the royal orders, tamemes were used widely in moving merchandise to west coast ports in the first years of navigation to Peru. Mendoza, toward the end of his administration, in a plea to the Crown for caution in forbidding the use of bearers, stated that the shortage of pack animals for carriage of supplies and goods to the coast made their use indispensable to Spanish traders.[73] As a favor to the Peruvian trade, Mendoza granted many licenses permitting the use of bearers to bring materials for shipbuilding, merchandise, and supplies to the Pacific ports.[74] He himself used large numbers of bearers, under license from his successor, to move luggage and supplies when he went to Huatulco en route to Peru.[75] During the first years of Velasco's administration, as the number of available pack animals greatly increased, there was less need to use bearers for the long hauls from Mexico City to Pacific ports. Bearers continued to be used at Huatulco, where local Indians were recruited by various means to bring supplies from the surrounding area. By then there could be little acceptable excuse for the practice, and in 1563 the alcalde mayor of the port and officials and encomenderos nearby were ordered not to permit such use in any circumstances.[76]

In Peru, the use of bearers was equally widespread in the first years after the Conquest,[77] but since most of the important Spanish centers were on or near the coast, the numbers of Indians used in the Mexico-Peru trade were less than in New Spain. Lima lay only two Spanish leagues, perhaps five miles, from its port at El Callao. Use of bearers in the coastal zones must have ended, once La Gasca's pacification of the colony permitted a rapid increase in beasts of burden. It is noteworthy that in both colonies the important factor in ending use of Indians as bearers was the development of roads and an increase in the number of mules and donkeys, which together made pack trains a far more efficient and inexpensive way of moving freight.

Mexico-Peru navigation and trade were thus subject to numerous controls. That they were enforced to a substantial extent has already been made clear. The mesh of this web of regulation by various governmental entities was kept wide, however, by a number of factors. The viceregal secretariats seem to have granted licenses with a considerable degree of generosity; since much of their revenue came from fees, they had an interest in issuing rather than refusing them. Furthermore, the dependence of most other officials upon fees meant that they, too, had a personal interest in furthering rather than hampering trade. There must have been few difficulties and irregularities, and these major in nature, which could not have been adjusted by suitable payments. Such additional payments, by and large, would have been fairly moderate, for extortionately high charges would have forced merchants and shipping to use alternate facilities. Finally, the long periods of waiting, enforced by the annual cycle of sailings between the viceroyalties, gave most people plenty of time to secure the basic licenses and clearances. If the sailing season was drawing to a close, officials would undoubtedly have been willing, except in unusually dubious instances, to speed up formalities for a suitable additional payment.

Taxation of the Mexico-Peru trade was perhaps even more flexible than regulation. During the first decades, the trade was not legally subject to customs duties as far as the home government was concerned, despite a royal cédula of 1532, issued for New Spain, ordering that *almojarifazgo* be collected on the "fruits of the land."[78] In New Spain, officials levied neither entry nor exit duties at Huatulco or any other Pacific port. In Peru, officials at El Callao collected duty on the cargo of the *Santa Cruz* on its two voyages of 1554 and 1555. Since almost all of the cargo consisted of products of New Spain, the levy was made on goods of New World origin, although it may also have been made on the few Spanish items carried. Unfortunately, the records of the marquesado shed no light on this point nor on the further one of the rate of levy. It must have been one of the two traditional rates: either 5 per cent as import tax or 7½ per cent on the ground that no tax had been paid in New Spain. Whatever the rate, there can be no doubt that in the 1550's almojarifazgo was being assessed at El Callao on intercolonial trade. The local treasury officials had justification in Spanish custom and in the cédula of 1532, if they knew of its existence. In all probability, the main justification was the simple fact that the royal treasury was desperately short of funds. For a number of years the home government seems to have been unaware that the levy was being made.[79]

The extension of almojarifazgo to intercolonial trade by direct order of the Crown came, after a long series of inquiries from 1559 to 1566. A series of cédulas issued between 1566 and 1568 ordered a general revision of customs schedules. Rates on goods already subject to tax were doubled; that on wine quadrupled. Spanish merchandise, wherever reshipped, was to be subject to an additional levy of 5 per cent on the increase in value at the port of entry. Colonial products and manufactures moving from one province to another by sea were to be taxed at 2½ per cent on exit and 5 per cent on entry; that is, at one-half the new rates for European goods.[80]

Implementation of the new schedule came rather slowly. Only in 1571 did Viceroy Enríquez issue the necessary instructions to the alcaldes mayores of Pacific ports. In his instructions, he set forth a series of rules for enforcement. The tax was to be assessed on the basis of sworn statements specifying items and amounts. Such statements must have appended to them a further statement of the tax collected, and must be filed. A certified list of the merchandise was to be given the exporter for presentation at the port of entry, but on this list only the prices of Spanish wares were to be given. This was a strange provision sure to invite fraud. Finally, since the principal exporters lived in Mexico City, they might pay the tax there.[81]

The inevitable questions on interpretations and omissions to which the instructions of 1571 gave rise were dealt with in a further series of instructions issued in October 1574. Negro slaves were declared subject to levies of 2½ per cent of value on exit and 5 per cent on entry. Spanish merchandise reworked in Mexico was to be assessed 2½ per cent on export on the increase in value. Since much merchandise of local origin was being exported as Spanish to avoid duty, a sworn statement listing all items in two categories by origin was to be required. Finally, since there had been much difficulty about the rule that prices were to be listed only for Spanish merchandise in the statement that must accompany exports, thenceforth all items were to have their values listed.[82] These amendments demonstrate that the instructions of 1571 were being applied.

In Peru, implementation of the cédulas of 1566–1568 must have come slightly earlier than in New Spain, for Francisco de Toledo, who made an inspection of customs collections along the coast north of El Callao, found much to complain of but did not mention failure to proclaim the new rates. He found that the 5 per cent levy on increase in value was being collected as 1 per cent of total value,[83] but after struggling to impose the formally ordained rate over the opposition of merchants and his own officials, he was finally forced to accede to the custom. The 1 per cent rate was still in force in 1615 when the Marqués de Montesclaros prepared his memoir for his successor.[84]

Further changes in the levy in Peru concerned Negro slaves and mercury. As late as 1571 no import tax was levied on Negroes brought to Peru from New Spain; indeed, until Enríquez's order of 1574 no export tax at all was levied in the Pacific ports of New Spain. Early in 1571 the audiencia and treasury officials in Lima, meeting in the absence of Toledo, decided, since no specific injunction could be found in any royal cédula, to impose standard import duties on Negro slaves on the ground that such was the practice at Seville.[85] This duty was in addition to a levy of 4 pesos a head already established by the city of Lima to pay expenses for the safekeeping of Negro slaves.[86]

On mercury shipped from Peru to New Spain, an export tax was collected in Peru during some years. Toledo, at least, ordered collection at the rate of 7½ per cent a quintal.[87] Upon arrival in New Spain, mercury was further liable to the import rate. Enforcement of this obligation came only after a long suit to determine whether it was subject to almojarifazgo, since the quinto had been paid on it in Peru. A royal decision in 1573 stated that duty must be collected regardless of any contrary decision by the Audiencia of Mexico.[88]

For the Mexico-Peru trade the schedules of 1566–1568 were scarcely onerous. But, as in the royal system of licensing, registry, and inspection, the extent to which the trade complied with the requirement depended upon the zeal of enforcing officers. Such evidence as we have, almost all relating to the Panama-Peru traffic for the period before trade in Chinese goods began to be restricted, indicates that the taxes were widely evaded. Much of the cargo shipped to Peru was landed on the coast north of Lima, a small amount being carried under sworn statement for landing at El Callao. Toledo named Paita as the principal center for smuggling in his day; later, much of the illegal landing was at points farther north on the coast of the Audiencia of Quito. Officials charged with collection, especially those at the small ports north of El Callao, were not trustworthy persons and were too poorly paid for effective enforcement or even for keeping proper records, as Toledo reported after his inspection of 1569–1570.[89] In such circumstances, bribery and official incompetence must have made the task of the smuggler easy. Direct frauds in the values listed on the statements accompanying cargo landing were also frequent enough to lead to repeated measures to enable the collectors to verify the truthfulness of the statements;[90] but even the treasury collectors were involved in a web of custom and accommodation which required them to assess goods for tax levy at far below the true value.[91] As for New Spain, we may guess that evasion was widespread there as well. Once the Crown began to place restrictions upon shipment of Chinese goods from New Spain to Peru, smuggling and fraud at both ends of the trade became far more lucrative and took place on a scale that can only be described as gigantic.

Customs duties were not the only taxes levied upon Mexico-Peru trade in the later decades of the sixteenth century. The trade was subject to various levies, including municipal ones, whenever a merchant and his wares fell within the orbit of a local tax schedule, as might happen when he entered a town. Among the general levies, perhaps the most important one, next to almojarifazgo, was the alcabala or sales tax. It was extended to New Spain on January 1, 1575, at a rate of 2 per cent upon Spanish products and local manufactures. The tax was payable every time merchandise changed hands. Peruvian opposition was sufficiently strong to suspend extension of the alcabala in the southern colonies until 1592.[92] The alcabala was actually a much heavier levy than the almojarifazgo, since it built up through successive transactions, and the merchants seem to have attempted evasion on a considerable scale. Such would be a reasonable interpretation of Enríquez' order requiring an affidavit on payment of alcabala before a license to leave New Spain would be valid. We are left with the impression that licensing, registry, and ship inspection were far more successfully enforced than taxation.

VII. THE END OF THE EARLY INTERCOLONIAL TRADE: THE PHILIPPINE TRADE

By 1585 a series of sweeping changes were already well under way in the Mexico-Peru traffic. Trade in Chinese goods was even then bringing great prosperity. This commerce became crucial in Mexico-Peru shipping for most of the remainder of the colonial period.

The story of the settlement of the Philippines and the opening of trade between the Spanish and Chinese has been told by William Lytle Schurz in his fine book, *The Manila Galleon.* In 1565 the pilot-monk Urdaneta finally found the long-sought return route from the Far East to New Spain by sailing far north to the zone of prevailing westerlies. His discovery made possible communication with the Philippines across the Pacific, and initiated two and a half centuries of sailings of the Manila galleons bearing silks, spices, and other goods from the East for consumption in America and Europe. Manila, founded in 1571, rapidly became a center of trade with the Chinese and other peoples of the Far East. As early as 1573 the first shipment of Chinese damasks, satins, silks of all colors, fine gilt Chinaware, and porcelain arrived at Acapulco. The traffic was then so new that Viceroy Enríquez was uncertain how much to tax the imports. Although he was inclined to sneer at the wares,[1] they found a ready sale, and ships returning from the Philippines carried increasingly large quantities.[2]

One of the first effects of the new trade was the rise of Acapulco as the principal Pacific port of New Spain. Legazpi's ships were built at La Navidad and left from there,[3] but Andrés de Urdaneta chose the excellent port of Acapulco for the Philippine ships even before the expedition sailed; he asked that a lighthouse be maintained after the first of July, 1565, until the fleet returned.[4] The port lies closer to Mexico City than Huatulco,[5] although the road passed through such mountainous, badly broken country that, in the later sixteenth century, the eighty leagues of road between the capital and Acapulco were held bad even by the tolerant standards of the day.[6] Nevertheless, roads were hardly good anywhere in sixteenth-century Mexico, and Acapulco had the supreme advantage of being the terminus of Philippine navigation with its coveted cargoes of Chinese wares. Inevitably trade began to shift from Huatulco, even the cacao ships being lured by the possibility of return cargoes of Chinese goods. By 1586 the total yield of royal customs at Huatulco was less than 1,000 pesos a year,[7]

[1] For notes to chapter vii, see pages 157–159.

a sum which suggests that imports and exports could not have been more than 30,000 pesos a year. Acapulco by then was handling the overwhelming proportion of cargo and passenger traffic. A few years later, in 1593, the royal customs collected in its port came to approximately 100,000 pesos for that year.[8] With the shift of trade, merchants, agents, and craftsmen also began to move away from Huatulco. Their migration was slowed by the fact that many of them had houses there and ranches and other properties nearby which they were reluctant to abandon. In 1587, the town, despite its small share of intercolonial trade, still had more than a hundred houses, although they were ramshackle structures of mud and wattle like virtually all others on the coast. The sack and burning of the town by Cavendish in that year[9] finally forced the townsfolk to leave, probably to follow the shipping to Acapulco. After 1587 Huatulco rapidly sank to the level of a small fishing settlement.

For Peruvian commerce, the effect of the opening of the Philippine trade was a rapid and eager adjustment to the new source of supply. Peru was short of manufactures and luxury goods in the very years that the silver output at Potosí was reaching previously unheard-of sums. Neither the galleons from Spain nor shipments of Mexican manufactures were able to meet the demands of the markets in Lima and Potosí. The Philippine trade offered a supply of luxury goods and even such necessities as iron and copper at prices far below those of imports from Spain or even the cheaper wares of Mexico. Part of the first shipment to arrive at Acapulco in 1573 probably was bought by Peru-bound merchants for reshipment, and much of subsequent cargoes must have been re-routed south.

For a few years there was even direct communication between the Philippines and Peru. The governor of the islands, operating under a royal cédula of April 14, 1579,[10] sent a ship laden with goods directly to El Callao in 1580 and another in 1581. Their pilots must have planned to follow the usual route to New Spain and then continue down the coast to South America. The first vessel never arrived in Peru. It may have been lost in the dangerous Pacific crossing or have ended its voyage in New Spain. The second vessel arrived in Peru in the summer of 1582 with a cargo of silks, porcelains, spices, iron, wax, and other wares. Of the cargo, the iron and spices—100 quintals of iron and 100 quintals of cinnamon, pepper, and cloves—came on royal account. All items arrived in good condition except for some of the cinnamon. The ship had to be dealt with by Enríquez, who as viceroy in New Spain, had welcomed the first shipment of silks in 1573.

He was inclined to look askance at the cargo as knicknacks of little value, but permitted it to be sold, using the proceeds on the royal share of the cargo to repair the vessel. Although he would not grant licenses to go to the Philippines, or meddle in any matters touching the islands, since they were under the jurisdiction of the viceroy of New Spain, he nevertheless permitted the vessel to use its license granted in Manila for the return.[11]

The voyage of 1582 must have raised bright hopes for a profitable direct trade. They were soon ended. As soon as Philip II heard of the plans for navigation between the Philippines and Peru, as he did first from reports by the governor of the Philippines, he issued instructions on June 11, 1582, forbidding all such navigation in the future and further charging the viceroy not to permit sale or purchase of goods from the Philippines in Peru.[12]

The prohibition on navigation between Peru and the Philippines put an end to direct trade. Neither the pleas of Peruvian merchants nor the arguments of the Marqués de Cañete, when he was viceroy of Peru, were able to bring King Philip to rescind the cédula. Cañete, in alliance with Lima merchants, proposed that three or four ships a year be allowed to make the voyage on condition that the wares imported pay duties at the rate of 25 per cent so that the revenue raised through these ships would bring the Crown more than it got from a fleet.[13] The king remained obdurate, although he did soften the prohibition to permit some trade in Chinese goods via New Spain.[14] In 1590 Cañete actually permitted a ship to sail for the Philippines, excusing his action on the ground that the galleons had not sailed that year and that Peru was short of merchandise, including iron and copper for the mines. A number of high officials in the viceregal government invested money in the venture. Cañete himself admitted sending 8,000 ducats on the vessel for investment on his own account, the amount being that of a permit he had to import merchandise each year from Spain without tax. In some embarrassment, he promised to pay all duties on his own goods unless the king were moved by his long services to instruct him not to.[15] The venture turned out to be a total loss, for the Portuguese authorities in the Far East seized the ship.[16] They may well have been acting under instructions issued by Philip II as King of Portugal. Cañete was rebuked by what amounted to return mail a year later, and the prohibition of 1582 was reissued in even stronger terms.[17]

The royal cédula of 1582 also forbade all import or sale in Peru of goods from the Philippines—a proviso which covered transshipments at Acapulco.

The promptness with which the order was issued suggests that the Crown officials in Spain had no intention from the first of permitting more than a limited trade across the Pacific, all Chinese goods to be consumed in Mexico. For a number of years, these officials must also have been unaware of the extent of transshipment in New Spain to Peru-bound vessels. Whatever their intentions and knowledge, the prohibitions on transshipment and sale in Peru remained a dead letter during the 1580's. Goods were embarked under registry and taxes collected on them as though no restrictions existed on the traffic.[18] The government of New Spain had at least the excuse that it was not formally notified of the royal will for some years; but in Peru, from the viceroy and audiencias down, all officials concerned were in open conspiracy to ignore Philip II's command. The situation makes for strange reading in the viceregal reports to the Crown.

In New Spain, Viceroy Villamanrrique, as though the trade were legal, imposed further customs levies on Chinese goods exported to Peru. The following year he issued a license to two residents of Mexico City, Captain Juan de Chapoya and Baltasar Rodríguez, to take to Peru a cargo of Chinese wares in a ship they were then building at Tehuantepec. He could hardly have refused the license since it was claimed on the basis of a royal cédula granted to the men at Barcelona on June 1, 1585. In his report to the king on the license, Villamanrrique commented that he understood that the prohibition related only to direct navigation between the Philippines and Peru, but that goods brought to New Spain might be reshipped in other vessels. He also reported in the same letter that reshipments to Peru of imports from the Philippines had become a very important part of Mexican trade.[19]

The royal answer must have surprised the viceroy. By a cédula issued November 11, 1587, he was roundly rebuked for permitting the ship of Chapoya and Rodríguez to take Chinese goods to Peru. It was not the royal will that there be such trade, ran the cédula, because of the many inconveniences which might result, and for that reason the trade had never been permitted until the governor of the Philippines sent two vessels to Peru and Villamanrrique gave the license to Chapoya and Rodríguez.[20] The imperial secretariat conveniently ignored its issuance of the first license to the two men. Whether deliberately or in genuine ignorance, it also showed little awareness of the extent of the entrepôt trade in Chinese wares to Peru.

As an officer of the Crown, Villamanrrique had to take some steps to enforce the cédula of 1587, even though any such measures were certain to encounter widespread resistance and evasion. While he was hesitating, a delegation from the cabildo of Mexico City called upon him to ask that Peruvian merchants be stopped from buying up imports from Spain for reshipment. Such re-export, they complained, had brought about scarcity and high prices in the capital.[21] It was an opportunity such as comes seldom; the viceroy obligingly promised a remedy. A few days later he issued a general ordinance regulating purchases for shipment to Peru. These had become so large, the order recited in a justificatory preamble, that they were draining New Spain of wares in spite of the fact that the last fleet from Spain was the largest known. Reshipments of goods from Spain were forbidden on the ground that Peru had a fleet for its special supply. Reshipments of goods from the Philippines, although not mentioned by the cabildo, were also forbidden on the ground that they fell under a direct royal injunction. The ban on reshipments was further justified to prevent loss of the second alcabala on retail sale to the royal treasury in New Spain. Trade between the colonies was not forbidden altogether; merchants were expressly informed that they could continue purchase of Mexican manufactures for shipment since they were the traditional export to Peru.[22]

Villamanrrique's ordinance left the Mexico City cabildo satisfied, and furnished evidence for the Crown that its cédula was being implemented. Aside from these useful effects, it had virtually no influence on the reshipment of either Chinese or Spanish merchandise to Peru, except perhaps to increase substantially the amount of bribery needed to get the merchandise registered and on board ship. A few years later the Mexico City cabildo complained of extensive reshipments of imports from Spain despite the ordinance.[23] At the other end of intercolonial navigation, the Marqués de Cañete, viceroy of Peru, reported in 1590 that cargoes of Chinese wares arrived openly and, far from being confiscated, were listed as legal imports. His report, which contained a plea for direct traffic between Peru and the Philippines, was sufficiently forceful to lead to some concession by the Crown.[24] Perhaps, too, wartime interruptions of fleet sailings to the New World made necessary some provision for the supply of Peru. In 1591, therefore, despite the rebuke of 1587 to Villamanrrique, Luis de Velasco II, then viceroy in Mexico City, was instructed to permit reshipment to Peru of such goods brought from the Philippines as were not needed for the supply of New Spain. He was, of course, to make sure that all taxes were paid.[25] This change of heart on the part of the imperial government lasted two years.

By the end of the 1580's, reshipment of Chinese goods had swollen the once modest interchange of Mexican wares for Peruvian silver to an enormous total. A series of reports by the Marqués de Cañete from 1590 to 1594[26] must have left the Council of the Indies and imperial secretariat with few illusions on what was happening. The failure to send out fleets in a number of years, he reported, left Peru badly short of Spanish imports. It also made trade difficult and unprofitable, since merchants, many of whom evidently sent specie to Spain for purchases, were forced to wait years for goods and a chance to recoup their investment. To the hazards of Peruvian trade by the long route to Panama and across the Atlantic to Spain were joined the burdens of an increasingly heavy taxation and the seizure of specie sent to Spain, for in 1590 Philip II met the needs of his treasury by impounding all specie which arrived at Seville from the New World. His agents, to be sure, gave promissory notes for everything taken, and he promised that the seizure would be the only one;[27] but, despite publication of his promise in Peru as elsewhere, merchants were scarcely reassured, since the needs of the royal treasury were not likely to be met by the one seizure. In contrast to the dangers and lack of profit in trade with Spain, the supply of Chinese goods which could be secured in New Spain promised handsome and easy returns. The distances to be traveled were much shorter and attended by far less danger from the king's enemies. Chinese wares were far more abundant, far cheaper than imports from Spain, and easier to sell. Merchants engaging in the Mexico trade could regain their capital with a substantial profit in a year or less, with much less chance of losing their fortunes and even their lives. Chinese silks and other textiles were so cheap, Cañete reported, that Indian caciques and even commoners were using them for clothing instead of cloth of local manufacture. The Chinese textiles sold for perhaps a ninth of the price of Spanish cloth in Peru. Textiles of Mexican manufacture were intermediate in price between the two. Even though no *flota* arrived in 1593, shops were still heavily stocked with unsold Spanish goods.

A paragraph in a letter from Cañete to Philip II written at Lima, April 12, 1594, provides a good summary of his observations:

The merchants of the entire realm (and particularly those of this city) complain continually of the multitude of taxes they pay in Spain and Panama, of the abuses and inconveniences they suffer, and of the lack of security for their property on the journey. As a result, they now make their purchases in New Spain, for the voyage between the port where purchases are made [Acapulco] and here avoids all the expense and risk of going to Spain. This year and last a dozen ships have sailed to Mexico, leaving this colony swept clean of silver. Although in my administration, your Majesty has been sent larger remittances on treasury account than in any other, remittances [to Spain] by private people are much smaller than before. The silver that used to be sent in the Tierra Firme fleets, goes now to New Spain.... Chinese merchandise is so cheap and Spanish goods so dear that I believe it impossible to choke off the trade to such an extent that no Chinese wares will be consumed in this realm, since a man can clothe his wife in Chinese silks for two hundred reales, whereas he could not provide her clothing of Spanish silks with two hundred pesos.

Although Cañete reported that Spanish goods could not be sold quickly because of the competition of Chinese wares, the complaints of Mexico City's cabildo that New Spain was stripped of European imports to stock Peru indicate that Peruvian merchants were still buying substantial quantities of Spanish wares in Mexico[24] and that the abundance of some of the Spanish goods in Peru in these years more probably resulted from supplementary imports via Acapulco. The southern colony, in effect, compensated for the failure of fleets to sail each year by outbidding the Spanish of the Audiencia of Mexico in their own territory. In Mexico City there were large stocks of goods, smuggled from Veracruz without declaration to municipal authorities, which could be bought for further smuggling or open export provided high enough prices were paid.[25] The statements by the viceroy of Peru and the cabildo of Mexico City may not be so directly contradictory as they seem, since part at least of the re-export of Spanish goods was in items like olive oil, iron, ironware, and paper, which the Philippine trade could not supply in sufficient quantity for colonial needs or at all. Cañete's report may have referred primarily to silks and other textiles which were directly competitive. There can be little doubt that imports from the Philippines did diminish the possible market for imports from Spain.

Cañete's letters indicate that many Peruvian merchants engaged in importing Spanish goods via Panama must have diverted their funds and ships to the safer and more profitable trade with New Spain. Although the small ventures which had characterized the trade earlier undoubtedly continued, the trade by the 1590's thus was characterized by the presence of wealthy large-scale operators, who were able to buy much or most of the cargo of the Manila galleons on the shore at Acapulco and reship the goods before they could be taken farther inland.[26] These merchants seem to have been Peruvians, even though the profits to be made on Chinese goods must have lured some wealthy Mexico City merchants into the trade.

By the 1590's the value of the Mexico-Peru trade, including reshipments of goods from the Manila galleons, was enormous. If Cañete was right in his comment that most of the specie exported from Peru by private people was going to New Spain to pay for goods there and that taxing Chinese imports at higher rates in El Callao would yield as much as the revenue on a flota, the silver involved in the Mexico-Peru trade must have been upwards of two million and perhaps even three million silver pesos. Most of this total represented payment for Chinese merchandise bought in Acapulco, the silver being sent on to the Philippines, where a large part of it was delivered to the Chinese. In the last four or five years of the century, the trade involved even larger amounts, for in 1602 the Mexico City cabildo instructed its agent at the Court of Madrid to inform the king that the silver lost to his realms through shipment to the Philippines and so eventually to the Chinese came to five million pesos a year and that in 1597 the specie sent from Acapulco reached the staggering total of twelve millions.[81] Since the bulk of these sums came from Peru, which took the greater part of the cargoes, the share of the southern viceroyalty in the trade would have been more than three millions and in the phenomenal year 1597 perhaps eight or ten.

These huge sums contrast with the modest 150,000 or 200,000 pesos of merchandise shipped from New Spain to Peru annually in the 1560's and early 1570's. The increase in overwhelming proportion came from the addition of goods from the Philippines, a trade in which New Spain played only a small part as the possessor of the port at which the Manila galleon landed its cargo. The manufactures of New Spain, which furnished the bulk of goods entering the trade in earlier years, continued to be bought and shipped. In terms of value, the amount shipped must have increased in a proportion between 50 and 100 per cent to a total of perhaps 300,000 silver pesos.[82] But, by the 1590's, colonial manufactures were a small proportion of the trade, perhaps no more than a tenth by value and in such years as 1597 less than that. The development of the Manila-Acapulco run thus changed the Mexico-Peru trade so greatly that it might be described as a new trade. The earlier forms of the trade which have been the concern of this study, continued, but were, in effect, buried in the fat of the new.

This very prosperity was to bring the ruin of the Mexico-Peru trade. The vast expansion of the trade in Chinese goods could hardly go unnoticed in Spain. The imperial government, with its mercantilist ideas and perennial need for funds, was certain to be concerned over the movement of vast sums to the Philippines, whence they disappeared into the specie-hungry Orient. It was also certain to react violently at any diminution in sales of Spanish goods since these supported the system of fleets so necessary in imperial communications and administration, and yielded it large revenues. The merchants of the Peninsula, especially those at Seville, who had managed to secure most of the silver of the New World by forcing an exchange of the goods shipped for the silver available, running up prices to whatever height necessary,[83] saw their lucrative monopoly ruined so long as the Philippine trade continued on such a scale, and found themselves still bound to meet the heavy charges on the sadly diminished fleets.[84] Furthermore, that any colony should become independent of the mother country for substantial supplies of merchandise, raised the perennial specter of renewed rebellion. From at least 1569 on, it was a continuing element of Crown policy that Peru be prevented from developing its own production of textiles and wine lest they diminish imports from the Peninsula and lest economic independence encourage ideas of detachment from political obedience.[85] When Cañete reported that Peru was peopled with Spaniards born in the colony, with no attachments to the home country, and that the colony was virtually self-sufficient in foodstuffs, including wine and sugar, and in coarser textiles, while the Philippine trade supplied it with silks and linens—all this to the ruin of Spanish trade—[86] he must have raised in the minds of Philip II and his counsellors vivid memories of the long years of rebellion and civil war in Peru. All peninsular interests and policy thus came to agreement: the Philippine trade must be curtailed, and colonies other than New Spain, especially Peru with its vast output of silver, must be kept as markets for Spanish goods.[87] This policy basically was agreed upon from the earliest years of the Philippine trade; the vast expansion of the trade in the 1590's merely proved that drastic measures would be needed to implement it.

The attempts of the Spanish Crown and merchants to protect the fleet system and Spanish markets in Peru can only be summarized here. In 1591 permission for a limited trade in Chinese goods between New Spain and Peru was coupled with a rigid order that navigation to the Philippines be restricted to New Spain. This permission for a limited reshipment of Chinese wares lasted only two years. In 1593 the shipment to all colonies other than New Spain, purchase, or even use of Chinese goods was forbidden. Trade between New Spain and the Philippines was restricted to two ships of 300 tons each, to be sailed for the benefit of the islanders, which might bring Chinese goods valued at 250,000 pesos to Acapulco each year and might return with 500,000 pesos in silver.[38] The order initiated a new phase of enforcement which aimed at containing the traffic by restricting the number of ships. Like most Spanish legislation on the Philippine trade, it was reissued at intervals of several years. It had little or no effect, if we may judge from the comments of the Mexico City cabildo, for in the years after it was issued, even larger quantities of silver were shipped to Manila.

In Peru, where the Marqués de Cañete warned the king tactfully but unmistakably that any prohibition on importation, sale, and use of Chinese goods almost certainly could not be enforced,[39] implementation of the new decrees was delayed by the reluctance of the viceroy to enforce them and by determined resistance on the part of the oidores, other officials concerned, and Peruvian merchants. Even Luis de Velasco II, during his term as viceroy of Peru, despite distinctly more active attempts to enforce the royal will,[40] was unable to halt the traffic. Once reshipment of Chinese merchandise from New Spain to Peru was declared illegal, merchants began a vast series of smuggling operations in connivance with royal officials. In 1597 Velasco reported to the Crown that one of the worst loopholes had turned out to be the claim of the Inquisition that cargo consigned to it and its familiars might not be inspected by treasury officials. Since the familiars were numerous and were friendly with merchants, substantial amounts of Chinese goods entered by this means alone. Much merchandise entered Peru as donations to religious foundations under the claim that such property was exempt from the royal ban. A great deal of Chinese merchandise was landed at small harbors and brought secretly to Lima, or was passed through the El Callao customs with the connivance of royal officials. Obviously the vast series of smuggling operations, which kept Peru amply supplied with Chinese merchandise through the 1590's and sent huge sums in silver to New Spain, could have been carried out only with the connivance of customs officials up and down the coast, the oidores of the audiencia, and probably the viceroy himself.[41] The normally conscientious Luis de Velasco II was rebuked in 1600 for laxness in the enforcement of the prohibitory decrees.[42] In New Spain, the purchase of Chinese goods and reloading on Peru-bound vessels also must have been carried out with the connivance of the port officials, the Audiencia of Mexico, and the viceroy.[43] Profits from the traffic were too large, the bribes too tempting, to be given up because of a Crown policy.

The imperial government and mercantile interests in Spain were, of course, fully aware that the forbidden trade not only continued but also continued in increasing volume. In 1604, after long consultations on measures to enforce the restrictive policy, a new series of decrees was issued to overhaul the entire system. Trade between the Philippines and New Spain was limited thenceforth to two vessels of 200 tons each. The new cédula contained numerous provisions designed to prevent fraud. Trade between New Spain and Peru was also to be placed under severe limitations as the only means for preventing reshipments of Chinese goods. The Crown would have been justified in ending all trade between the two colonies, ran the cédula, but had decided to allow three ships of 300 tons each to sail every year. They might carry products of the two viceroyalties for exchange but no specie whatever and they must go directly between El Callao and Acapulco without stopping at any other ports.[44] The terms of this restriction made it clear that at no time did the Crown or the Spanish merchants object to export to Peru of manufactures of the Audiencia of Mexico; their concern lay only with the flood of Chinese wares threatening Spanish markets and the system of fleets. Nevertheless, this cédula of 1604 was stringent enough to move the cabildo of Mexico City to protest, although earlier it had been unwilling to take an open stand against the prohibitory legislation.[45] Other cédulas issued in the same year tried to tighten enforcement by ordering that the ship's officers, royal inspector, treasury officials, and anyone else having part in the registry and inspection of vessels and their cargoes should be punished if any Chinese goods were discovered on a ship sailing from New Spain to Peru. The penalties for engaging in smuggling were made far more severe, even to perpetual banishment from the Indies and confiscation of the vessel carrying forbidden merchandise. As a measure to overcome lax infliction of penalties, a trustworthy oidor of the Audiencia of Lima was to be given special jurisdiction over all the cases arising in Peru under the prohibitory legislation.[46]

These measures may have had some success in diminishing the volume of the smuggling, but their success was limited and a great amount of prohibited goods continued to reach Peru. At intervals other cédulas attempted to strengthen the dam that royal policy required be maintained. In 1615 the clergy of the Indies were charged to cease assisting in the smuggling of goods and furnishing hiding places in their houses and convents.[47] Since the sale of confiscated Chinese goods at public auction proved still another and totally unexpected loophole, in 1617 the Crown ordered that Chinese goods seized as contraband must not be sold in Peru but must be shipped to Spain.[48] In 1633 another order declared that informers, who were entitled by law to a third of the contraband, were not to receive their share in the goods, since they could then sell these openly in Peru, but were to be paid in money.[49] Yet another cédula issued in 1621 ordered careful watch on the trade in asphalt from the Gulf of Guayaquil, since vessels from New Spain and Guatemala coming to get it were first loading Chinese merchandise at Acapulco.[50]

It was apparent to Spanish mercantile interests shortly after 1604 and to the imperial administration in Spain somewhat later that mere restrictive measures would not work so long as ships moved between the Audiencia of Mexico and Peru.[51] The cédula of 1604 permitted three vessels to make the annual voyage. In 1609 and 1620 these provisions underwent substantial modifications. The attempt to stop all specie from moving in the intercolonial trade having proved impossible, since Peru had little except silver that the Crown was willing to let enter the trade, permission accordingly was granted that specie to the extent of 200,000 ducats, approximately 300,000 pesos of eight reales, might be sent to Acapulco. To curb smuggling the number and size of vessels permitted to sail each year were reduced. In 1609 the number was cut to two of 200 tons and in 1620 to one of 200 tons. In the final version of the limited trade, as enacted in a cédula of March 28, 1620, at the demand of the Seville merchants, trade between the viceroyalties was limited to a single vessel of 200 tons, sailing from El Callao, which might bring 200,000 ducats in silver to Acapulco in a direct voyage without calling at any other ports, and might return to Peru with a cargo of manufactures and foodstuffs produced in New Spain.[52] Since even these measures did not succeed in shutting off the flow of Chinese goods into Peru, the Seville merchants, acting through their Consulado, pressed the Crown to forbid all trade between the viceroyalties. In 1631 this measure, inevitable under the policy of stopping Chinese imports into Peru, was finally accepted by the Crown. Trade and navigation between the two colonies were strictly prohibited and appropriate instructions to that effect were sent to the two viceroys. The first order of 1631, repeated on November 23, 1634, specified suspension during a trial period of five years.[53] The suspension was soon made indefinite; it lasted during the remainder of the seventeenth century and into the first decades of the Bourbon dynasty in the eighteenth.

NOTES

ABBREVIATIONS

Note.—The abbreviations for archives are followed by the names of the ramos; Roman numerals following the ramo refer to volumes.

AGI Archivo General de Indias, Seville.

AGN Archivo General de la Nación, Mexico.

BLT Transcript in The Bancroft Library, University of California, Berekeley.

DIE *Colección de documentos inéditos para la historia de España* (Madrid, 1842–1895).

DIHA *Colección de documentos inéditos para la historia de Hispano-América* (Madrid [1927–1932]).

DII *Colección de documentos inéditos, relativos al descubrimiento, conquista y organización de las antiguas posesiones españolas de América y Oceanía, sacados de los archivos del reino, y muy especialmente del de Indias* (Madrid, 1864–1884).

DIU *Colección de documentos inéditos relativos al descubrimiento, conquista y organización de las antiquas posesiones españolas de ultramar* (Madrid, 1885–1932).

GP Peru (Viceroyalty). *Gobernantes del Perú, cartas y papeles, siglo XVI; documentos del Archivo de Indias. Publicación dirigida per d. Roberto Levillier. ...* (Madrid, 1921–1926).

Jesús Archivo del Hospital de Jesús.

NOTES TO CHAPTER I: THE BEGINNINGS OF SHIPBUILDING AND NAVIGATION

[1] Whether or not there ever was sea communication between Mexico and Peru in pre-Conquest times is still a moot question. It seems reasonably certain that there was no such communication between the Inca empire and cultures of Anáhuac at the time of the Conquest. Chester S. Chard has summarized the evidence now available in an excellent article, "Pre-Columbian Trade Between North and South America," in the Kroeber Anthropological Society, *Papers*, No. 1 (Berkeley, 1950), 1–27. On the other hand, the presence of a number of common cultural phenomena in Ecuador and Peru and in Mexico, with no evidence that they have ever been present in the intervening lands, can only be explained at this time by postulating the existence of sea communication in the centuries before the establishment of the Aztec and Inca empires. The most important of such cultural phenomena is the smelting of copper and bronze, the development of which, stage by stage, can be traced in Peru but which appeared full-blown in Mexico at a period which Rivet and Arsandaux (*La Métallurgie en Amérique précolombienne*, pp. 178–187) tentatively place in the tenth and eleventh centuries A.D. The important point for present purposes is that, whatever may have existed earlier, the Spanish had to develop the Mexico-Peru navigation *ab ovo*.

[2] Gonzalo Fernández de Oviedo y Valdes, *Historia general y natural de las Indias, islas y tierrafirme del mar océano ...*, III, 58–64 (Lib. XXIX, cap. xii–xiii); Bartolomé de las Casas, *Historia de las Indias ...*, Lib. III, cap. lxxiv–lxxv; Angel de Altolaguirre y Duvale, *Vasco Núñez de Balboa*, pp. clvii–ix; "Relación de los sucesos de Pedrarias Dávila ... por ... Pascual de Andagoya, n.d. but *ca.* 1541, in Martín Fernández de Navarrete, ed., *Colección de los viages y descubrimientos que hicieron por mar los españoles desde fines del siglo XV ...*, III, 404; Dominic Salandra, "Pedrarias Dávila and the Spanish Beginnings on the Isthmus," unpublished thesis, University of California, Berkeley, pp. 189–194; Hubert Howe Bancroft, *History of Central America*, I, 441–450, 464–472.

[3] "Requerimiento hecho á Pedrarias en nombre de Gil González Dávila para que en cumplimiento de la Real cédula ... le entregasen los navíos construidos por Vasco Núñez de Balboa," Santa María del Antigua del Darién, February 4–9, 1520, in Altolaguirre, pp. 187–194; Oviedo, III, 65–66 (Lib. XXIX, cap. xiv); Bancroft, *History of Central America*, I, 480–482.

[4] Oviedo, III, 65–66, 97–114 (Lib. XXIX, cap. xiv and cap. xxi); Bancroft, I, 482–483.

[5] Cesáreo Fernández Duro, *Armada española desde la unión de los reinos de Castilla y de León*, I, 121, 194–195.

[6] "Requerimiento hecho á Pedrarias en nombre de Gil González Dávila ... ," Santa María del Antigua del Darién, February 4–9, 1520, in Altolaguirre, p. 188.

[7] Royal cédula to the lieutenant governor of Castilla del Oro, Burgos, September 6, 1521, *DII*, XXXVII, 297–298.

[8] "Relación de Pascual de Andagoya," in Navarrete, III, 420–422 ff.; Fernández Duro, I, 297–298.

[9] "Relación de Pascual de Andagoya," in Navarrete, III, 406.

[10] Oviedo, IV, 36 (Lib. XLII, cap. i); Antonio de Herrera y Tordesillas, *Historia general de los hecho de los castellanos en las islas i tierra firme del mar océano ...*, Dec. IV, 40 (Lib. III, cap. ii), Dec. V, 156–157 (Lib. VII, cap. ii); Lic. Francisco de Castañeda to the emperor, León, March 30, 1529 and October 5, 1529, in Manuel María de Peralta, ed., *Costa-Rica, Nicaragua y Panamá en el siglo XVI ...*, pp. 38–39, 64–66, 79–80; Castañeda to the emperor, Nicaragua [Leon?], May 30, 1531, in *DII*, XXIV, 181–182; "Relación de Pascual de Andagoya," in Navarrete, III, 413–416; "Instrucciones a los procuradores de la ciudad de Granada," Granada, July 10, 1527, and "Instrucciones a los procuradores de la ciudad de León," León, July 30, 1527, in León Fernández, comp., *Colección de documentos para la historia de Costa Rica ...*, IV, 8, 12–13; "Memorial dirigido a S.M. por el ayuntamiento de León de Nicaragua," 1531, in Fernández, p. 28; Cabildo of Granada, Nicaragua, to the emperor, November 24, 1544, in *DII*, VII, 556–558; Bancroft, *Central America*, I, 594, 607–609.

The agents sent by Granada and León to Spain in 1527 were instructed to defend the traffic in Indian slaves as the only means of support for the Spanish; the cities were concerned only by royal disapproval and the monopoly established by the royal governors and treasury officials. Only four years later, in 1531, the memorial of the city of León showed concern over the speed with which the Indian population of Nicaragua and surrounding areas was vanishing. In 1545 Lic. Diego de Herrera, who carried out the residencia of Rodrigo de Contreras, then governor of Nicaragua, reported that he had been informed that the province had had 600,000 Indians when discovered by the Spanish, of whom only 30,000 were left. Herrera to the emperor, Gracias á Dios, December 24, 1545, in *DII,* XXIV, 398–399. Most of the slaves exported from Central America were sent to Panama. The importance of Central America as source of supply for Panama may be estimated by the statistics showing origins of the slaves liberated at Panama in 1550 in Lesley Byrd Simpson, *Studies in the Administration of the Indians in New Spain. IV: The Emancipation of the Indian Slaves and the Resettlement of the Freedmen 1548–1553,* University of California Publications, Ibero-Americana: 16 (1940), p. 37. In addition, once the Spanish conquest of Peru began, large numbers of Central American Indians were sent to Peru as auxiliary soldiers or slaves, the distinction being rather much a matter of the conquerors' needs at the time of shipment or use. Lic. Cerrato to the emperor, Gracias á Dios, August 5, 1548, summarized in Squier MSS, The Bancroft Library, XXII, 81, and "Relación de Pascual de Andagoya," in Navarrete, III, 452.

[11] Letter in Peralta, p. 52.

[12] "Relación del descubrimiento y conquista de los reinos del Perú, y del gobierno y órden que los naturales tenian ... Hecha por Pedro Pizarro conquistador y poblador destos dichos reinos y vecino de la ciudad de Arequipa. Año 1571," *DIE,* V, 209–210.

[13] Lic. Francisco de Castañeda to the emperor, León, October 5, 1529, in Peralta, pp. 76–77; Herrera, Dec. IV, 131 (Lib. VII, cap. iv); Castañeda to the emperor, Nicaragua [Leon?], May 30, 1531, in *DII,* XXIV, 181–182; Cabildo of Granada to the emperor, Granada, November 24, 1544, in *DII,* VII, 557–562. On the fiber from cabuya, see Philip Laurence Wagner, "Nicoya: Historical Geography of a Central American Lowland Community," unpublished thesis, University of California, Berkeley, pp. 320–322.

[14] Herrera, Dec. V, 156–157 (Lib. VII, cap. ii). The statement that all of these were caravels is difficult to accept. Many may have been brigantines.

[15] Fernández Duro, I, 195.

[16] In *DII,* XLII, 83. Espinosa reported also that Alvarado's ships ranged downward from a *capitana* of 300 tons and that Almagro's *capitana* was 150 tons. The rest of the ships were 40–60 tons. Many brigantines were built and being built at Panamá. These figures probably do not include construction in the Audiencia of Mexico.

[17] Bancroft, *Central America,* II, 127–128.

[18] Ione Stuessy Wright, "Early American Voyages to the Far East, 1527–1565," unpublished thesis, University of California, Berkeley, pp. 147–148, 158–160; Ione Stuessy Wright, "The First American Voyage across the Pacific, 1527–1528. The Voyage of Alvaro de Saavedra Cerón," *The Geographical Review,* XXIX (July, 1939), 472–473; Cortés to the emperor, Coyoacán, May 15, 1522; Cortés to the emperor, Mexico City, October 15, 1524; Cortés to the emperor, Mexico City, September 11, 1526; Cortés to the emperor, Mexico City, September 3, 1526; in *Cartas y relaciones de Hernán Cortés al emperador Carlos V colegidas é ilustradas por Don Pascual de Gayangos,* pp. 268–269, 307–308, 372–373, 489–491.

[19] Cortés to Lic. Francisco Núñez, Puerto de Santiago en la Mar del Sur, June 20, 1533, in *Cartas y otros documentos de Hernán Cortés, novísimamente descubiertos ... e ilustradas por el P. Mariano Cuevas, S.J.,* pp. 110–112; Max L. Moorhead, "Hernán Cortés and the Tehuantepec Passage," *The Hispanic American Historical Review,* XXIX (August, 1949), 370–379.

[20] Wright, "Early American Voyages," p. 199; Cortés to the emperor, Texcoco, October 10, 1530, in Gayangos, pp. 504–505; Cortés to the emperor, Mexico City, April 20, 1532, in Hernando Cortés, *Escritos sueltos,* p. 194.

[21] Memorial of Cortés to the emperor, *ca.* 1540, in Cortés, *Escritos sueltos,* pp. 290–292.

[22] Cortés to the Council of the Indies, Mexico City, September 20, 1538, in *DII,* III, 535.

[23] Bancroft, *Central America,* II, 122–127; Henry Raup Wagner, *Spanish Voyages to the Northwest Coast of America in the Sixteenth Century . . . ,* p. 54.

[24] See letter of Diego Vázquez to Gonzalo Pizarro, La Puna, January 25, 1547, in Maggs Bros., *From Panamá to Peru,* p. 243; Ricardo Cappa, *Estudios críticos acerca de la dominación española en América,* X, 46–47.

[25] In 1538 when Cortés needed pilots, he sent to Panama to hire some. When he could get none there, he knew that none was available. Cortés to the Council of the Indies, Mexico City, September 20, 1538, in *DII,* III, 535.

[26] Relación de Pascual de Andagoya, in Navarrete, III, 416.

[27] Hernán Ponce de León, Hernando de Soto, and Sabastián de Benalcázar were lieutenants of Francisco Pizarro, who came from Nicaragua with ships, men, and Indians to aid in the conquest of Peru. "Relación del descubrimiento y conquista de los reinos del Perú ... por Pedro Pizarro ... ," 1571, *DIE,* V, 209–210; Jacinto Jijón y Caamaño, *Sebastián de Benalcázar,* I, 15–17. See also the letter of Benalcázar, San Miguel de Piura, November 11, 1533, in *DII,* XLII, 93–95.

[28] Juan de Segura to Lic. Juan de Altamirano, Acajutla, January 12, 1540, MS in AGN, Jesús, leg. 68, exp. 9; Juan de segura to Cortés, Panamá, September 15, 1539, *ibid.,* exp. 5.

NOTES TO CHAPTER II: THE ESTABLISHMENT OF COMMUNICATION AND TRADE

[1] "Parecer de Luis de Castilla, regidor de México," Mexico City, October 11, 1569, in Francisco del Paso y Troncosco, comp., *Papeles de Nueva España ...*, 2 ser., III, supplement, pp. 62–63. See also other opinions in the same series of inquiries, pp. 29–33; and Memorial of Mexico City to the viceroy, Marqués de Falces, February 10, 1567, and March 1, 1567, in Mexico (City), *Actas de cabildo*, VII, 330–331, 344–345; "Petición de la ciudad de México ...," presented to Juan de Ovando in Madrid, June 6, 1571, in Francisco del Paso y Troncoso, comp., *Epistolario de Nueva España*, XI, 118–119. François Chevalier, *La Formation des grands domaines au Mexique*, p. 41, gives an excellent account of the economic problem of the Spanish community at this time. It is notable that Cortés, who owned a number of slave gangs engaged in placer mining, and who ranked as one of the largest operators, continued work profitably until the 1540's. MS in AGN, Jesús, *passim.*

[2] Mexico (City), *Actas de cabildo*, II, 179 (Session of May 13, 1532).

[3] *Ibid.*, III, 89–90. See also George Kubler, *Mexican Architecture of the Sixteenth Century*, I, 72.

[4] Sessions of April 27 and 29, July 3, 4, 6, and 13, 1534, in Mexico (City), *Actas de cabildo*, II, 80–81, 92–94.

[5] Session of August 21, 1534, in *ibid.*, II, 96. The audiencia's prohibition paralleled and may have been based upon royal cédulas of May 4 and 21, 1534, Toledo, forbidding vecinos or settlers to leave the provinces or islands where they lived without license from the governor of the area. The penalty was to be loss of encomiendas and grants of lands. Pardon and restoration of grants might be given only by express royal permission; *DIU*, X, 208–210, 213–214. On February 27, 1575 Philip II reënacted these rules by reissuing the cédula of May 21, 1534; *DIU*, X, 215–217.

[6] See Audiencia of Mexico to the emperor, Mexico City, August 14, 1531, in *DII*, XLI, 129–130, urging that Nicaragua be made subject to Mexico because it was easily accessible from Mexico, especially by sea.

[7] Alvarado to the emperor, Guatemala City, May 17, 1536, in *DII*, XXIV, 234–235. The rush to Peru occurred in all of the older Spanish settlements on the Pacific coast of America. Nicaragua lost many inhabitants; even priests joined in the migration to the rich realms of Peru. Lic. Carrasco, bishop elect of León, to the Council of the Indies, n.p., n.d., in *DII*, V, 522–527.

[8] The story of Alvarado's expedition to Peru in 1534–1536, although intensely interesting, is marginal to this account. It is covered at some length in Bancroft, *History of Central Amercia*, II, 122–130; John Eoghan Kelly, *Pedro de Alvarado Conquistador*, pp. 186–201; Antonio de Herrera y Tordesillas, *Historia general*, Dec. IV, Lib. X, cap. xv (230:1–230:2), Dec. V, Lib. VI, cap. i (127:1–128:2), ff. See also Pedro Alvarado to the emperor, La Posesión, January 18, 1534, in *DII*, XXIV, 204–211; Alvarado to the emperor, Puerto Viejo, March 10, 1534, *ibid.*, XLI, 513–518; Diego de Almagro to the emperor, San Miguel de Piura, May 8, 1534, *ibid.*, XLII, 104–113; Francisco Pizarro and the royal treasury officials of Nueva Castilla to the Council of the City of Panama, Jauja, May 25, 1534, *ibid.*, X, 134–144; Alvarado to the emperor, Guatemala City, May 17, 1536, *ibid.*, XXIV, 211–236; Alvarado to the Council of the Indies, Guatemala City, November 20, 1536, *ibid.*, XXIV, 236–249.

[9] Herrera, Dec. IV, Lib. X, cap. xv (231:1–232:2).

[10] See above, note 5.

[11] As early as 1536 there may have been some back flow of Spaniards who had failed to find fortune in Peru. Alvarado to the Council of the Indies, Guatemala City, November 20, 1536, in *DII*, XXIV, 240–241. At this date the number of people returning must have been small relative to the number of those making their way to Peru.

[12] Cortés to the Council of the Indies, Calagua, February 8, 1535, in *Cartas y relaciones de Hernán Cortés al emperador Carlos V colegidas é ilustradas por Don Pascual de Gayangos*, pp. 531–534. The letter is also published in Hernando Cortés, *Escritos sueltos*, pp. 260–266.

[13] Herrera, Dec. V, Lib. VI, cap. xiii (150:1).

[14] *Ibid.*, Dec. IV, Lib. X, cap. xv (232:1–232:2).

[15] Francisco López de Gómara, *Historia de la conquista de México* ... ed. by Joaquín Ramírez Cabañas, cap cxcviii (II, 200); Francisco López de Gómara, *La historia general de las Indias* ... , cap. cxxvi: Herrera, Dec. V, Lib. VIII, cap. iv, v, vii, and x (188:2–190:2, 190:2–191:1,193:2–195:2, and 200:1–200:2). The two versions are not in complete agreement. López de Gómara lists as cargo for a second voyage what Herrera ascribes to the voyage of Grijalva. Whatever the exact quantities, it seems likely that, given the nature of the appeal, Cortés shipped men, food, and arms.

[16] Herrera, Dec. V, Lib. VIII, cap. v (190:1).

[17] MS, AGN, Jesús, leg. 270, exp. 8:85.

[18] López de Gómara and Herrera, as cited above. An excellent account of the Grijalva voyage may be found in Ione Stuessy Wright, "Early American Voyages to the Far East, 1527–1565," pp. 201–208. See also William Hickling Prescott, *History of the Conquest of Peru,* II, 63–65, 90–91. Agustín de Zárate, *Historia del descubrimiento y conquista de la provincia del Peru* ... , gives part of thte story of Francisco Pizarro's appeal for help, including a statement that an appeal was sent to Mendoza. In a brief sketch of the life of Carbajal, Zarate suggests that Mendoza assembled and sent aid. (Lib. III, cap. vi and vii and Lib. V, cap. xiv, in Barcia, *Historiadores primitivos* ... , III, 40:1–40:2, 41:2–42:1, and 94:1–94:2). Like most of Zarate's account, this story should be regarded as the gossip that reached his ears. One statement is trustworthy, since it would have been common knowledge, that despite his own preference for simple dress, Pizarro wore, on holidays, at the urging of his attendants, the fur robe that Cortés sent him by Grijalva, *ibid.,* Lib. IV, cap. ix (56:2–57:1). See also Diego Fernández of Palencia, *Primera parte de la historia del Perú,* I, 63, who gives the same story in condensed form.

[19] "Carta de recibo de Juan Chaves de ciertas escrituras del Señor marqués," Guatemala City, November 8, 1540, MS in AGN, Jesús, leg. 235, 2d ser., exp. 3.

[20] I follow the account of Diogo de Couto in João de Barros and Diogo de Couto, *Da Asia,* Dec. V, Lib. VI, cap. v (XII, 49–51). Diogo de Couto as archivist of the viceregal Portuguese archives at Goa must have based his account, which is considerably different from other versions, upon the testimony of survivors of the expedition in the Moluccas, taken down by Antonio Galvão, governor of Ternate, and forwarded to the Portuguese viceroy at Goa. There is no reason to doubt this story in view of Grijalva's great care to avoid sailing into the zone sold to the Portuguese by Charles V, a care which cost him his life since it led to the mutiny in which he was killed. Such care bears out the idea that Grijalva was still acting upon his instructions from Cortés; invasion of the Portuguese zone, with its consequence of imperial displeasure, would have been of concern to the marqués but would hardly have bothered an outlaw fleeing from justice. The story that Grijalva was fleeing because he had committed crimes may be dismissed as a cover. Cortés made mistakes about the loyalty of his men but would hardly be unaware of their acts. Galvão, the governor of the Moluccas at this time, in *The Discoveries of the World,* p. 200, written upon his return to Europe, years after these events, states that Cortés' plan was to carry out the voyage of discovery and find the way to the Moluccas before the new viceroy, Mendoza, could begin to outfit expeditions or demand a share. We may ascribe to Portuguese fear of intrusion in their zone the point about finding the way to the Moluccas, since a Cortés-financed expedition had already discovered it in 1526–1527.

[21] Galvão, pp. 200–205; Barros and Couto, Dec. V, Lib. VI, cap. v (XII, 49–51). Wright, "Early American Voyages," pp. 207–216, has a fine reconstruction of the events of the trans-Pacific voyage. Galvão suggests, although he does not state explicitly, that both ships made the transPacific voyage (pp. 201–205). His account is the basis for the versions in other Portuguese chroniclers. Fernão Lopes de Castanheda, *Historia do descobrimento e conquista da India pelos portuguezes,* liv. VIII, cap. clxxxi; Francisco d'Andrade, *Chronica do João III,* III, 264–265. Manuel de Faria e Sousa, *Asia portuguesa* ... , II, 306–307, is also based upon the published account of Galvão.

[22] López de Gómara, *Historia de la conquista de México,* Cap. clxxxviii. The various texts of López de Gómara differ on this point. I follow the Antwerp edition of 1554: " ... pero

huyó con ellas el Grijalva." Ramírez Cabañas in his critical edition arbitrarily altered the text by changing *el* to *de,* which gives a reading that Francisco Pizarro gave many rich gifts but fled with those brought by Grijalva. *Huyó,* however, is a term that would have been inaccurate if applied to Pizarro. Barcia, in his edition, preserves the sense of the edition of 1554 but corrects the Spanish to more ordinary usage by omitting *el.* The statement by López de Gómara probably reflects the bitterness of Cortés at the failure of Grijalva to send on the gifts in the companion vessel. It seems unlikely that news of the fate of Grijalva and his vessel reached Mexico or Spain before the middle 1540's. It came through the Villalobos expedition which passed near the waters where the Grijalva ship was lost and heard of the fate of the crew. See Herrera, Dec. VII, Lib. V., cap. ix (97:02).

[23] I follow the explicit statement in López de Gómara, cap. cxcviii (II, 200) and Barros and Couto, Dec. V, Lib. VI, cap. v (XII, 49). This agrees with the fact that in the winter of 1537–1538 there were in Mexico a pilot and seamen in the pay of Cortés who claimed to have sighted an island on a voyage which took them to Peruvian waters. See below, n. 25.

[24] Cédula of the queen to the royal treasury officials of New Spain, Valladolid, January 18, 1538, in Diego de Encinas, *Cedulario indiano ...* , III, 366–367.

[25] Antonio de Mendoza to Cortés, México, February 14, no year but 1538, MS in AGN, Jesús, leg. 68, exp. 331. The Galápagos Islands were discovered in 1535 by a vessel from Panamá. See chapter iii.

[26] "Carta de recibo de Juan de Chaves de ciertas escrituras del Señor marques," Guatemala City, November 8, 1540, MS in AGN, Jesús, leg. 235, 2d ser., exp. 3. At approximately the same time the fare for one man and luggage from Panama to Lima was 60 pesos de oro de minas. See the listing of the obligation of Juan de Mercado to Hernando Pizarro for transportation from Panama to Lima, June 13, 1537, in *The Harkness Collection in the Library of Congress. Documents from Early Peru,* item 13, pp. 32–36.

[27] Receipt of Juan Domingo for goods delivered by Capt. Palacios Rubios for the Marqués del Valle, Lima, April 10, 1538, in Rosenbach Co., *The Sea,* item 166. See also the summary of the same document made before it was removed from the Archivo del Hospital de Jesús in Francisco Fernández del Castillo, "Algunos documentos del Archivo del Marquesado del Valle (Hospital de Jesús)," in Sociedad mexicana de geografía y estadística, *Boletín,* XLIII (January–April, 1931), 36.

[28] MS in AGN, Jesús, leg. 68, exp. 331. At the time of this letter, Capt. Palacios Rubios must already have been at sea or in Peru. Since the letter mentions that the pilot and seamen of the ship sighting land were in Mexico at the time Mendoza wrote the letter, they must have made their voyage in the previous year. It seems likely, therefore, that they were the crew of the second ship of the Grijalva expedition. The only other possibility would be that Cortés sent an as yet unknown shipment in the middle of 1537, immediately after Grijalva, but the prevailing winds during the spring and summer, which were well-known to seamen by this time (see chap. iii), make it improbable that any ships sent out could have reached Peru during those seasons.

[29] Henry Raup Wagner, *The Spanish Southwest 1542–1794,* pp. 43–49; Herbert Eugene Bolton, *Coronado, Knight of Pueblos and Plains,* pp. 17–19.

[30] Cortés to the Council of the Indies, Mexico City, September 20, 1538, in Cortés' *Escritos Sueltos,* p. 281.

[31] See below, nn. 33, 34. The formal instrument may survive but has not been found in the Archivo del Hospital de Jesús.

[32] Power of attorney of Cortés to Alonso de Zamudio to collect debts in Peru, Cuernavaca, November 23, 1538, MS in AGN, Jesús, leg. 243, exp. 1:9. See below.

[33] Juan de Segura to Cortés, Panama, April 26, 1539, *ibid.,* leg. 68, exp. 6.

[34] Receipt for cargo of the *San Lázaro* issued by Juan Fernández de Ladrillero, master and pilot, Petacaltepec (New Spain), January 18, 1539, summarized in Rosenbach Co., *The Sea,* item 388; Inventory of the cargo of *San Lázaro,* Panama, April 18, 1539, summarized in Rosenbach Co., item 167; Fernández del Castillo, in Sociedad mexicana de geografía y estadística, *Boletín,* XLIII (January–April, 1931), 37; Cortés to Alonso de Zamudio, Cuernavaca, November 26, 1538, summarized in Rosenbach Co., item 166A.

[35] Juan de Segura to Cortés, Panama, April 26, 1539, MS in AGN, Jesús, leg. 68, exp. 6.

[36] *Ibid.;* Alsonso de Zamudio to Cortés, Panama, July 15, 1539, quoted at length in Lucas Alamán, *Disertaciones sobre la historia de la república megicana ...* , II, 69–73. The letter, no longer in the Archivo del Hospital de Jesús, is listed in Rosenbach Co., item 167A.

[37] Juan de Segura to Cortés, Panama, September 15, 1539, MS in AGN, Jesús, leg. 68, exp. 5. See also the letter of Zamudio, cited above, note 36. Segura wrote that the only item for which a favorable market could be found at Panama was sugar, which did not figure in the two shipments already made. He stated that he could sell up to 100 arrobas for at least 8 pesos de oro de minas the arroba if Cortés wished to send some before or during January, 1540, when the merchant fleet left Panama for Peru. The reason for the favorable market for sugar was that none had arrived in the ships from Spain.

[38] Juan de Segura to Cortés, Panama, September 26, 1539, summarized in Rosenbach Co., item 167B.

[39] "Carta de recibo de Juan de Chaves de ciertas escrituras del Señor marqués," Guatemala City, November 8, 1540, MS in AGN, Jesús, leg. 235, 2d ser., exp. 3.

[40] Juan de Segura to Lic. Juan de Altamirano, Acajutla, June 29, 1540, *ibid.,* leg. exp. 8.

[41] Juan de Segura to Lic. Juan de Altamirano, Acajutla, August 12, 1540, *ibid.,* leg. 68, exp. 9.

42 [42] See the two letters of Juan de Segura cited in notes 40 and 41. López de Gómara, *Historia de la conquista de México,* cap. cxcviii (II, 200).

[43] Prescott, II, 126–127.

[44] Licenses of Antonio de Mendoza to Blas de Simancas, mate of the *Todos Santos,* to use tamemes and to carry six Peruvian and Nicaragian Indians to Peru, Mexico City, November 14, 1542, MSS in AGN, Mercedes, I, fol. 194^{v}.

[45] Mexico City, November 21, 1542, *ibid.,* fol. 199^{r}–199^{v}.

[46] Mexico City, July 26, 1543, *ibid.,* II, fols. 128^{v}–129^{r}.

[47] Wagner, *Spanish Voyages,* pp. 74–75, 330; License of Mendoza to Bartolomé Ferrer [Ferrelo, the pilot of the Cabrillo expedition], Mexico City, October 23, 1543, MS in AGN, Mercedes, II, fol. 197^{v}

[48] License of Mendoza to Hernando de Villanueva, Mexico City, October 24, 1543, MS in AGN, Mercedes, II, fol. 199^{r}.

[49] I differ from Wagner (*Spanish Voyages,* pp. 74–75, 330), who declares that it was one of these ships that was seized in December, 1544.

[50] Nicolau de Albenino, *Verdadera relacion delo sussedido enlos Reynos e provincias del Peru ...* , fol. 4.

[51] Francisco Maldonado to Gonzalo Pizarro, Manta, January 3, 1545, La Gasca-Gonzalo Pizarro Correspondence, MSS in Huntington Library, II, fols. 498–499 (summarized in Maggs Bros., *From Panama to Peru,* p. 38); Hernando Bachicao to Gonzalo Pizarro, Manta, January 6, 1545, summarized in Maggs Bros., *op. cit.,* pp. 40–43; Diego Fernández, I, 152–153, 157. "Relación de lo acaecido en el reino del Perú con los abusos de Gonzalo Pizarro después de la prisión del virrey Blasco Núñez Vela," n.d., in *GP,* II, 289. See also Wagner, *Spanish Voyages,* pp. 74–75, 330. The galleon of Diego de Ocampo, which was not completed before 1544, could not have been one of the vessels of the Cabrillo expedition. See chapter iii.

[52] Fernando Montesinos, *Anales del Perú,* I, 172.

[53] Paso y Troncoso, *Epistolario,* IV, 233–235.

[54] Francisco Bernaldo de Quiros to the king, Mexico City, September 24, 1546, *ibid.,* IV, 242–244.

[55] From Tomebamba, in Maggs Bros., pp. 109–110.

[56] Lope de Ayala to Gonzalo Pizarro, Manta, October 7, 1546, La Gasca–Gonzalo Pizarro Correspondence, MSS in Huntington Library, II, fols. 631–632; Diego Vázquez to Gonzalo Pizarro, La Puna, October 13, 1546, MS, in *ibid.,* I, fols. 141–142; Bartolomé de Villalobos to Gonzalo Pizarro, Motape, December 30, 1546, summarized in Maggs Bros., p. 217. The preceding letters are summarized in the same catalogue on pp. 140 and 149, respectively. Moncibay

eventually was sent north by Gonzalo Pizarro with letters for Charles V, but these he promptly turned over to La Gasca. La Gasca to Gonzalo Pizarro, Jauja, December 16, 1547, in Maggs Bros., pp. 439–443.

[57] Bartolomé de Villalobos to Gonzalo Pizarro, Chira, November 21, 1546, summarized in Maggs Bros., p. 164.

[58] Montesinos, I, 176–177; Maggs Bros., pp. 361–365; Juan de Torquemada, *Primera [segunda, tercera] parte de los veinte i vn libros rituales i monarchia indiana ...*, Lib. V., cap. xi (I, 611:1–611:2). The army never sailed, since La Gasca informed Mendoza that he had assembled enough ships and men to succeed without further aid. In AGN, Mercedes, are a series of orders issued during 1550 and 1551 for settling the accounts and storing the arms of the expedition: III, fols. 32^{v}, 41^{v}, 44^{v}–46^{r}, 55^{v}, 168^{v}, 266^{v}–267^{r}, 358^{v}–359^{r}. The expedition was not only prepared in obedience to royal command but may also have been needed to preserve peace in Mexico, for as long as a rebel regime successfully maintained itself in Peru, the hold of the royal government on New Spain was not completely secure. Despite Mendoza's conciliatory suspension of the New Laws in Mexico, a number of disaffected Spaniards, some enraged at the failure of the Crown to grant encomiendas in perpetuity, others hoping for personal profit from the disturbance, sent messages of encouragement to Gonzalo Pizarro or made their way to Peru to throw in their lot with his. A *relator* of the royal audiencia in Mexico City, Hernando de Herrera, wrote to offer his services to Gonzalo. Among the people of lesser degree in New Spain there was actually a plot in 1549 for a revolt. The plot was quickly discovered and the leaders, Juan Román, a stockingmaker, Juan Venegas, and an unnamed Italian were brought to confession and execution in Mexico City. Others implicated in the revolt attempted to flee to Peru but many were seized on the roads, especially at the City of Oaxaca and the ports. "With this purge," commented the historian Torquemada, "the land [New Spain] was quieted and cleansed and those who were found not to be implicated in this disloyalty were held in great esteem." It is doubtful that an abortive revolt as late as 1549 was an affair of magnitude; more likely Mendoza gladly took advantage of an incident involving people without important connections or embarrassing claims to social standing for a public display of severity. That he had crushed a revolt, whereas Peru had been engulfed by one would increase his standing with the royal councillors in Spain. Torquemada, Lib. V, cap. xi (I, 610:2–611:1); Hernando de Herrera, *relator* of the Audiencia of Mexico, to Gonzalo Pizarro, Mexico City, June 12, 1546; Juan Ortiz de Guzmán to Gonzalo Pizarro, Manta, November 26, 1545; Bartolomé de Villalobos to Gonzalo Pizarro, Chira, November 21, 1546; Lope Sánchez de Valdivieso to Gonzalo Pizarro, Paita, March 28, 1547; summarized in Maggs Bros., pp. 106, 170, 164, 301.

[59] See La Gasca to the Council of the Indies, Lima, May 2, 1549, in *GP*, I, 181.

NOTES TO CHAPTER III: THE PORTS, ROADS, AND ROUTES OF THE MID-CENTURY

[1] This description is based upon United States Hydrographic Office, *Sailing Directions for the West Coasts of Mexico and Central America*... (H. O. No. 84) ed. of 1937, pp. 257–258; United States Hydrographic Office, *Chart No. 877 (Harbors of Guatulco, Santa Cruz, and Tangola Tangola from a Survey by the U.S.S. Tuscarora in 1877)*; Gaspar de Vargas, "Relación de Guatulco y su partido," n.d. but not later than 1580, in Paso y Troncoso, *Papeles de Nueva España* ..., 2 sér., IV, 233–234, 237; Fray Bernardo Albuquerque, "Relación de la gente que ay en todo este obispado de la ciudad de antequera del Valle de guazaca desta nueva españa asi de españoles como mestizos e yndios pa ynbiar al Real consejo de yndias de su magt ...," *ca.* 1571, MS in AGI, Audiencia de Méjico, leg. 357 (60-4-22).

[2] Cortés to the emperor, Mexico City, April 20, 1532, in Gayangos, 513–514; Cortés to the emperor or the Council of the Indies, March 12, 1532; Royal cédula of the queen to the Audiencia of Mexico, Seville, October 17, 1532; Cortés to the emperor or the Council of the Indies, November 12, 1532; Royal cédula of the queen to the Audiencia of Mexico, Madrid, February 16, 1533; in Rosenbach Co., *The Sea,* items 162, 163, 164, 165.

[3] Hubert Howe Bancroft, *The Native Races of the Pacific States of North America,* II, 388. See also chap. i.

[4] Many of the accounts of the operations of this shipyard are in AGN, Jesús, *passim*. See also Cortés, "Memorial que dió al Rey ...," Madrid, June 25, 1540, *DIE,* IV, 213. A careful account of the water passage from Coatzacoalcos to the divide and the haul to the Pacific coast, as well as the possible sites of the shipyard has been written by Max L. Moorhead, "Hernán Cortés and the Tehuantepec Passage," *The Hispanic American Historical Review,* XXIX (August, 1949), 370–379.

[5] Luis de Velasco to the emperor, Mexico City, February 21, 1552, in Paso y Troncoso, comp., *Epistolario de Nueva España,* VI, 141.

[6] "Recompensa de la villa de Tehuantepec que se incorporó en la real corona," June 8, 1563, 51 ff., MS in AGN, Jesús, leg. 235. The royal cédula ordering the retrocession and compensation was issued at Toledo, December 16, 1560.

[7] See Juan López de Velasco, *Geografía y descripción universal de las Indias* ..., p. 239. This was based on information received in Spain during the 1560's and the first years of the 1570's. The work lists Acapulco as a port but one which was still so unimportant that it did not merit a lengthy description. La Navidad was described as the probable center for the Philippine trade, since the first fleet sent there had left from it. *Ibid.*, pp. 246–247.

[8] *Ibid.*, p. 239; U. S. Hydrographic Office, *Sailing Directions for the West Coasts of Mexico and Central America,* pp. 28–33, 254–267.

[9] Inventory of cargo of *San Lázaro,* Panama, April 18, 1539, and Juan de Segura to Córtes, Panama, September 26, 1539, in Rosenbach Co., items 167 and 167B.

[10] Cortés, "Memorial pidiendo residencia contra Don Antonio de Mendoza," 1543, in Cortés, *Escritos sueltos,* pp. 334–335; Wagner, *Spanish Voyages to the Northwest Coast of America in the Sixteenth Century,* pp. 54–56.

[11] MSS in AGN, Mercedes, I–VIII, *passim;* Indios, II, *passim;* and General de Parte, I–II, *passim*.

[12] Receipt for 14 pesos of fine gold to Juanés de Mancitorres and Roldán, Tehuantepec, November 8, 1539, MS in AGN, Jesús, leg. 201, *hoja suelta.*

[13] See the account of the building of a galleon by Diego de Ocampo in this same chapter. Order of Mendoza to Christóbal de Chávez, corregidor of the port of Huatulco, Mexico City, November 8, 1542, MS in AGN, Mercedes, I, fol. 189^{v}.

[14] "The Admirable and Prosperous Voyage of the Worshipfull Master Candish ...," in Hakluyt, *The Principal Navigations,* XI, 320–321.

[15] My comments and map are based on these sources: Order of Antonio de Mendoza to the corregidor of Izúcar and those of Acatlán and Huajuápam, Mexico City, December 2, 1542, MSS in AGN, Mercedes, I, fols. 204^{v}–205^{r}; Order of Mendoza to the Cabildo of Coatzacoalcos, Mexico City, September 22, 1543, *ibid.*, II, fols. 163^{r}; Order of Mendoza for repair of the

road from Antequera to Tehuacán, Mexico City, April 22, 1544, *ibid.*, fol. 334^v; Order of Luis de Velasco to the alcalde mayor of Oaxaca to have repaired the roads leading out of the city of Antequera to Guatemala, Huatulco, and the Mixteca, Mexico City, August 16, 1560, *ibid.*, V, fols. 83^r–83^v; Order of Velasco I to the alcalde mayor of Oaxaca to have the road from Antequera to the port of Huatulco placed in repair. Mexico City, May 19, 1561, MS, *ibid.*, V, fol. 324^v; Orders for the repair of roads issued to the corregidores of Nochixtlán, Justlahuaca, and Teposcolula, September 15, 1550, *ibid.*, III, fols. 188^r–189^r; "Relación del pueblo de Miaguatlán," 1580, "Relación de Cuicatlán," September 15, 1580, and "Relacion de Guaxilotitlán," March 10, 1581, in Paso y Troncoso, *Papeles*, IV, 123–124, 184, 197; Expediente on the *congregación* and *deslinde* of Tanatepec, Nanacaltepec, and near-by towns, 1603, MS in AGN, Tributos, II, exp. 2; "Descripcion de Tetiquipa Rio-Honda, hecha por el Señor Christoval de Salas," n.d. but *ca.* 1580, in *Revista mexicana de estudios históricos*, II (1928), app., 117. *Relación breve y verdadera de algunas cosas de las muchas que sucedieron al padre fray Alonso Ponce ...*, I, 258–272, 273–289, 491–498, 503–507; Certified copy of orders of Mendoza on building and repairing roads in New Spain for use in his defense in the *visita* of Tello de Sandoval, Mexico City, October 31, 1546, 12 ff., MS in AGI, Justicia, leg. 259. Most freight was carried by pack train, but carts were used to some extent. The order of Luis de Velasco of August 16, 1560 cited above states that *carretas* were used on the roads, but this can only have been done in the valleys.

My reconstruction of the roads from Mexico City to Huatulco involves a great deal of guesswork. The orders listed above make it clear that one of the royal highways from Mexico City to Oaxaca passed through Izúcar, Acatlán, and Huajuápam. The rest of the reconstruction of that route involves a consideration of terrain, the importance of Teposcolula and Yanhuitlán in the sixteenth century, and the existing *caminos de herradura* which antedate the motor road. The highways from Puebla to Tehuacán and Oaxaca and from Oaxaca to Tehuantepec are traced in detail in the *Relación de Ponce;* that from Oaxaca to Huatulco ran down the central valleys of Oaxaca to Miahuatlán. From there it must have used the pass of San José del Pacifico to reach Río Hondo.

[16] Moorhead, *loc. cit.;* Juan de Toledo to Lic. Altamirano, Tehuantepec, August 31, 1540, MS in 4 fols., AGN, Jesús, leg. 202; Pedro de Ahumada to Nicolás de Cazana, Tehuantepec, March 16, 1554, *ibid.*, leg. 68, exp. 172; Pedro de Ahumada to Nicolás de Cazana, Mexico City, July 27, 1554, *ibid.*, leg. 68, exp. 183; Vasco de Gutiérrez to Nicolás de Cazana, Coatzacoalcos, October 3, [1554?], *ibid.*, leg. 68, exp. 307. The viceregal license to Antonio Núñez, merchant to transport via the Río de Alvarado to Villa Alta and Antequera, Mexico City, July 13, 1563, *ibid.*, Mercedes, VI, 339^v, indicates use of yet another river route from the Veracruz coast to supply Villa Alta and Oaxaca City.

[17] License of Mendoza to Gonzalo de las Casas to use tamemes, Mexico City, November 13, 1550; Order of Luis de Velasco to Gonzalo de las Casas, Mexico City, December 3, 1550; Order of Velasco that tamemes needed by Mendoza for his trip to Huatulco be provided under the usual safeguards, Mexico City, December 3, 1550; License of Luis de Velasco to Francisco de Torres to use tamemes to move the personal clothing and other effects of Mendoza via the Isthmus of Tehuantepec to Huatulco, Mexico City, December 15, 1550; License of Luis de Velasco to Martín de Arratia and Juan de Vargas to employ tamemes, Mexico City, December 16, 1550; MSS in AGN, Mercedes, III, fols. 234^r, 237^r, 237^r–237^v, 243^r–243^v, and 243^v.

[18] The description of winds and sailing seasons is based on: Alexander von Humboldt, *Essai politique sur le royaume de la Nouvelle-Espagne*, I, 312–314 (liv. I, chap. iii); IV, 386, 394–403 (liv. I, chap. xii); López de Velasco, 82–84, 402–403; "Relación de ... Pascual de Andagoya," in Navarrete, *op. cit.*, III, 449–450; U. S. Hydrographic Office, *Sailing Directions for the West Coasts of Mexico and Central America*, pp. 27–34; *idem, Sailing Directions for South America*, III, 38–42 (H. O. No. 174, ed. of 1938); *Viage Qve don Juan de Herrera y Montemayor hizo el año de MDCXVII des. Mexico al reyno del Piru y ciudad de Lima*, MS in Biblioteca Nacional de México, 10–7–503, fols. 1–14. United States Department of Agriculture, Weather Bureau, *Atlas of Climatic Charts of the Oceans.*

[19] *Historia natural y moral de las Indias*, Lib. III, cap. viii (p. 158).

[20] Humboldt, IV, 402 (liv. V, chap. xii).

[21] *Primera [segunda, tercera] parte de los veinte i vn libros rituales i monarchia indiana ...*, Lib. V, cap. xi (I, 610:2).

[22] Humboldt, IV, 402 (liv. V, chap. xii); Pascual de Gayangos in *Cartas y relaciones de Hernán Cortés*, p. 277 n.; Wright, "Early American Voyages to the Far East, 1527–1565," p. 206.

[23] MS in AGN, Mercedes, I, fol. 189^{v}.

[24] *Ibid.*, II, fols. 205^{r}–205^{v}.

[25] Francisco Maldonado to Gonzalo Pizarro, Manta, January 3, 1545, La Gasca–Gonzalo Pizarro correspondence, MSS in the Huntington Library, II, fols. 498–499 (summarized in Maggs Bros., *From Panama to Peru*, p. 38). See chap. i.

[26] See chap. ii.

[27] Fray Tomás de Berlanga to the emperor, Puerto Viejo, April 26, 1535, in *DII*, XLI, 538–543. See also La Gasca to the Council of the Indies, Lima, May 2, 1549, in *GP*, I, 168–190.

[28] Letter to the king, Guatemala, April 14, 1579, in Peralta, pp. 576–577.

[29] The account of landfalls and places along the South American coast is based upon the account of the voyage of Herrera y Montemayor, 1617, cited above, note 18, the accounts of Diego de Ocampo's vessel, the voyages of the Cortés family shipping in the 1550's (discussed in chap. iv), and the following reports on the movement of one vessel from Mexico along the South American coast in the winter of 1546–1547: Lope de Ayala to Gonzalo Pizarro, Manta, October 7, 1546; Diego Vazquez to Gonzalo Pizarro, La Puna, October 13, 1546; Bartolomé de Villalobos to Gonzalo Pizarro, Chira, November 21, 1546; Bartolomé de Villalobos to Gonzalo Pizarro, Motape, December 30, 1546; Martín de Olmos to Gonzalo Pizarro, Guanape, February 5, 1547; all summarized in Maggs Bros., pp. 140, 149, 164, 217, 252.

[30] López de Velasco, pp. 444–446; U. S. Hydrographic Office, *Sailing Directions for South America*, III, 366–369.

[31] López de Velasco, p. 447; U. S. Hydrographic Office, *Sailing Directions for South America*, III, 362–365.

[32] López de Velasco, p. 448; U. S. Hydrographic Office, *Sailing Directions for South America*, III, 355.

[33] López de Velasco, p. 443.

[34] *Ibid.*; U. S. Hydrographic Office, *Sailing Directions for South America*, III, 343–344.

[35] López de Velasco, p. 471; U. S. Hydrographic Office, *Sailing Directions for South America*, III, 329–332.

[36] López de Velasco, p. 468.

NOTES TO CHAPTER IV: THE TRADING VENTURES OF THE CORTES ESTATE

[1] "Obligado que hizo el señor Juan de Toledo a Pascualín, sobre el navío Santa Cruz," Tehuantepec, November 30, 1540, in AGN, *Boletín,* XXI (1950), 13–14. The manuscript is in AGN, Jesús, leg. 270, exp. 5.

[2] Letters of Juan de Toledo to Lic. Juan de Altamirano, Tehuantepec, May 12, 1540, June 26, [1540], and August 31, [1540], MSS in AGN, Jesús, leg. 202, *hojas sueltas* without expediente number.

[3] Citation of power of attorney issued to Pedro de Ahumada Sámano, Yanguas, October 14, 1551, in power of attorney issued by Pedro de Ahumada Sámano to Nicolás Ortiz de Ybargüen, Port of Huatulco, February 22, 1554, MS certified copy, in AGN, Jesús, leg. 243, exp. 2:125.

[4] "Testamento de Hernán Cortés, Marqués del Valle de Oaxaca, Capitán General y Conquistador de la Nueva España," October 11–12, 1547, in *DIE,* IV, 239–277.

[5] MS in AGN, Jesús, *passim,* especially leg. 243, exp. 1.

[6] "Testamento de Hernán Cortés," October 11–12, 1547, in *DIE, IV,* 239–277; "Resumen de los autos del pleito seguido por los indios de Coyoacán ... " and the accompanying *probanza, ca.* 1561, in *Documentos inéditos relativos a Hernán Cortés y su familia* (AGN, *Publicaciones,* XXVII, 343–390); Codices of the suit of the Indians of Cuernavaca against the Marqués del Valle, in AGN, Jesús, leg. 276. Accounts of Simón Pasca, majordomo of the Marquesado in Mexico City, 1550–1554, MS in AGN, Jesús, leg. 98, exp. 6, which show substantial payments to Indian towns by order of the audiencia.

[7] Ahumada to Juan Bautista de Marín, Mexico City, July 31, 1556, MS in 4 fols., and "Relación de las haciendas y granjerías que el Marqués, mi señor, tiene en esta Nueva España y en tierras de su estado," December 12, 1556, MS in 4 fols., in AGN, Jesús, leg. 202, *hojas sueltas,* and leg. 267, exp. 26 respectively.

[8] "Información acerca de la rebelión de los indios Zacatecas y Guachichiles a pedimento de Pedro de Ahumada Sámano," February 15, 1562–October 5, 1562, in *DIHA,* I, 237–358. Ahumada spent more than 26,000 pesos on the war—an enormous sum.

[9] This power of attorney is cited in that issued by Pedro de Ahumada Sámano to Nicolás Ortiz de Ybargüen, port of Huatulco, February 22, 1554, MS certified copy, in AGN, Jesús, leg. 243, exp. 2:125.

[10] Cited in the judgment of the Audiencia of Mexico in the suit of Marcos Borjes de Acosta against the Marqués del Valle, Mexico City, June 3–30, 1569, MS in AGN, Jesús, leg. 218, exp. 36.

[11] "Marín—gastos de los navíos para el Perú," December, 1554, (MS in part of AGN, Jesús, leg. 228, exp. 2) published in AGN, *Boletín, XXI* (1950), 14–16.

[12] Receipt of Antonio Díaz, second mate of the *San Lázaro,* Tehuantepec, April 10–May 27, 1554, and certificate of Diego Núñez, notary, on registry of the shipment in the *San Lázaro* to the port of Huatulco, Tehuantepec, June 23, 1554, MSS in AGN, Jesús, leg. 201, *hojas sueltas.* Accounts of Simón Pasca, majordomo in Mexico City, 1550–1554, *ibid.,* leg. 98, exp. 6.

[13] Unless otherwise specified the following account of the voyage of the *San Pedro* and the first two voyages of the *Santa Cruz* is based upon the accounting for the first two voyages of the *Santa Cruz* preserved in MS in AGN, Jesús, leg. 235, series 2, exps. 7 and 8.

[14] License of Luis de Velasco I to the galleon *Santa Cruz* to go to Peru, Mexico City, March 5–6, 1555, MS in AGN, Mercedes, IV, fol. 123^{v}.

[15] "Obligación de Alvaro Muñoz, piloto del *San Pedro,*" port of Huatulco, January 31, 1554, MS in 1 fol. in AGN, Jesús, leg. 270, exp. 8:2.

[16] "Marín—gastos de los navíos para el Perú," December, 1554, (MS in part of AGN, Jesús, leg. 228, exp. 2) published in AGN, *Boletín,* XXI (1950), 14–16.

[17] See Consulate of the Sea, cap. 130–131. Such merchandise was normally exempt from jettison.

[18] "Sobrecarta de venta de la tercera parte del galeón *Santa Cruz,*" Antequera, December 28, 1554, MS in 2 fols., in AGN, Jesús, leg. 235, exp. 2.

[19] "Obligación de Alvaro Muñoz, piloto del *San Pedro,*" port of Huatulco, January 31, 1554, MS in 1 fol. in AGN, Jesús, leg. 270, exp. 8:2.

[20] "Memoria de lo que debe el galeon San p° y la cargoçon que llebo ques a cargo de Ju[n] albarez de luna capitan del dho galeon ...," 1556, MS in 2 fols., in "Cuentas de Pedro de Ahumada, 1550–1567," MS in 33 fols. in AGN, Jesús, leg. 229, exp. 1.

[21] "Marín—gastos de los navíos para el Perú," December, 1554 (MS in part of AGN, Jesús, leg. 228, exp. 2) published in AGN, *Boletín,* XXI (1950), 14–16.

[22] *Ibid.*

[23] Pedro de Ahumada to Juan Bautista de Marín, n.d. but probably November, 1553, MS in 1 fol., and Ahumada to Nicolás de Cazana, Tehuantepec, March 16, 1554, MS in 1 fol., in AGN, Jesús, leg. 228, exp. 3:43, and leg. 68, exp. 172.

[24] Power of attorney issued by Pedro de Ahumada Sámano to Nicolás Ortiz de Ybargüen, port of Huatulco, February 22, 1554, MS certified copy, in AGN, Jesús, leg. 243, exp. 2:125.

[25] "Memoria de lo que debe el galeon San p° y la cargoçon que llego ques a cargo de Ju[n] albarez de luna capitan del dho galeon ...," 1556, MS in 2 fols., in "Cuentas de Pedro de Ahumada, 1550–1567," MS in 33 fols., in AGN, Jesús, leg. 229, exp. 1.

[26] *Ibid.;* Ahumada to Juan Bautista de Marín, MS in 1 fol., *ibid.,* leg. 228, exp. 3:43.

[27] *Probanza* on the lack of responsibility of Lorenzo Ladrón de Guevara for the loss of thirteen mules, Lima, February 22, 1555, MS, *ibid.,* leg. 247, *atado* 2, *hojas sueltas.*

[28] San Miguel de Piura, May 24–25, 1554, MS, *ibid.,* leg. 243, exp. 2:125.

[29] See the last pages of chapter iv.

[30] See chapter vi.

[31] MS in AGN, Mercedes, IV, fol. 123[v].

[32] Peru (Viceroyalty), *Audiencia de Lima, Correspondencia de presidentes y oidores,* foreword by J. de la Riva-Agüero, pp. xxiv–liii.

[33] The transfer and acceptance are incorporated in a certified copy of the power of attorney issued to Nicolás Ortiz de Ybargüen, MS in AGN, Jesús, leg. 243, exp. 2:125.

[34] *Ibid.,* leg. 247, *atado* 2, *hojas sueltas.*

[35] In addition to the entry in the accounts of the *Santa Cruz,* the receipt of Captain Alonzo de Montalbán for payment, Guayaquil, November 3, 1555, is extant in the Cortés family records, MS in 1 fol., *ibid.,* leg. 68, exp. 184.

[36] Consulate of the Sea, cap. 249.

[37] Ahumada to Juan Bautista de Marín, Apozol, March 11, 1556, MS in AGN, Jesús, leg. 202, *hojas sueltas.*

[38] The note dated Mexico City, September 18, 1556, is preserved in MS, *ibid.,* leg. 235, exp. 2. The same expediente also contains an acknowledgment of receipt of the slaves for sale and of the promissory notes due in Peru for collection.

[39] "Memoria de lo que debe el galeon San p° y la cargoçon que llebo ques a cargo de Ju[n] albarez de luna capitan del dho galeon ...," 1556, MS in 2 fols., in "Cuentas de Pedro de Ahumada," 1550–1567, MS in 33 fols., in AGN, Jesús, leg. 229, exp. 1. Accounts of Simón Pasca, Majordomo in Mexico City, 1550–1554, *ibid.,* leg. 98, exp. 6.

[40] Ahumada to Juan Bautista de Marín, Apozol, March 11, 1556, *ibid.,* leg. 202, *hojas sueltas.*

[41] MS in 4 fols., *ibid.,* leg. 267, exp. 26.

[42] The viceregal license to sail was issued as early as September 7, 1556, MS in AGN, Mercedes, IV, fol. 378[r].

[43] "Relacion de la carga q ba en el galeon sta cruz q salio de p xx de hebro 1557," MS in AGN, Jesús, leg. 235, series 2, exp. 4.

[44] *Ibid.,* leg. 235, exp. 10:9. A partial list of the merchandise shipped has been published by Francisco Fernández del Castillo, "Algunos documentos del archivo del Marquesado del Valle (Hospital de Jesús)," Sociedad mexicana de geografía y estadística, *Boletín, XLIII* (1931), 38–39.

[45] Order of Ahumada to Juan Bautista de Marín to enter discharge, and charge against the Marqués del Valle, 8,154 pesos for silver sent to Veracruz, Mexico City, October 22, 1558, MS in AGN, Jesús, leg. 228, exp. 3:203.

[46] The two notes are dated Mexico City, February 25, 1559, for 1,000 silver pesos and Mexico City, March 10, 1559, for 200 silver pesos, MSS, *ibid.*, leg. 235, exp. 2.

[47] See below, nn. 51, 52, and accompanying text.

[48] The judgment of the audiencia together with its recapitulation of the contents of the allegations and receipts for payment are preserved in *ibid.*, leg. 218, exp. 36.

[49] Bancroft, *History of Mexico,* II, 580.

[50] Power of attorney issued by Martín Cortés, Mexico City, February 1, 1566, MS in AGN, Jesús, leg. 243, exp. 2:9.

[51] Port of Huatulco, April 6, 1566, *ibid.*, leg. 235, exp. 2.

[52] Promissory note of Lorenzo Ladrón de Guevara in favor of Juan Gómez de Zorita, Antequera, February 3, 1557, and notation of appeal to the Audiencia of Lima for assistance in collection, Lima, August 22, 1566, *ibid.*, leg. 270, exp. 8:46.

[53] "Relación de lo que valieron las rentas del Marqués del Valle en los años de 1568 y 1569, hecha por Juan de Cigorondo, contador de dicho Estado," Mexico City, January 10, 1570, in Paso y Troncoso, *Epistolario de Nueva España,* XI, 57–60.

[54] Inventories and rental agreements on the marquisate properties of the Peñol de Xico, 1570–1574, MSS in AGN, Jesús, leg. 273, exp. 4:8.

NOTES TO CHAPTER V: THE TRADE AT MATURITY

[1] Mexico (City), *Actas de cabildo,* VI, 167.

[2] Lima, *Libros del cabildo,* V, 198.

[3] Peru (Viceroyalty), *Audiencia de Lima. Correspondencia,* I, 142.

[4] MS in AGN, Mercedes, IV, fol. 90^{r-v}.

[5] *Ibid.,* fol. 90^{v}.

[6] MS notation, *ibid.,* fol. 98^{v}.

[7] MS notation, *ibid.,* fol. 123^{v}.

[8] October 14, 1555, MS, *ibid.,* fol. 242^{v}.

[9] MS notation, January 30, 1556, *ibid.,* fol. 304^{r}.

[10] MS notation, March 11, 1556, *ibid.,* fol. 317^{r}.

[11] July 16, 1556, MS, *ibid.,* fol. 366^{v}.

[12] September 7, 1556, *ibid.,* fol. 378^{r}.

[13] October 26, 1560, *ibid.,* V, fols. 137^{v}–138^{r}.

[14] December 31, 1560, *ibid.,* fol. 197^{r}.

[15] March 1, 1561, *ibid.,* fol. 254^{r}.

[16] See above, n. 4. December 14, 1565, *ibid.,* VIII, fols. 219^{v}–210^{r}.

[17] October 26, 1560, and January 25, 1564, *ibid.,* V, fols. 137^{v}–138^{r} and VII, fol. 299^{v}.

[18] See chapter iv. The license to sail was issued at Mexico City on April 22, 1563, *ibid.,* VI, fols. 201^{r}–201^{v}.

[19] Ricardo Cappa, *Estudios críticos,* X, 46–47, 76–77; Juan Pablo Carrión to the king, Mexico City, November 11, 1564, in Paso y Troncoso, *Epistolario,* X, 50–53; "The Admirable and Prosperous Voyage of Worshipfull Master Thomas Candish . . . Written by Master Francis Pretty . . . ," Hakluyt, XI, 313–318; Villamanrique to the king, Mexico City, October 28, 1587, MS in AGI, 58-3-10 (BLT); Wagner, "Nicoya," unpublished thesis, University of California, Berkeley, pp. 334–335. See also chapter i.

[20] Moya y Contreras to the king, Mexico City, May 8, 1585, in Paso y Troncoso, *Epistolario,* XII, 142.

[21] Viceroy Enríquez to the king, Mexico City, December 5, 1572, and Conde de Coruña to the king, Mexico City, April 1, 1581, both in Spain. Ministerio de Fomento, *Cartas de Indias,* pp. 294–295 and 337–338, respectively; Memoria of Luis de Velasco II to Monterrey, *ca.* October, 1595, MS in AGI, 58-3-13 (BLT).

[22] Cappa, X, 92–93; "Relacion de lo que se le ha de hazer al Señor Presidente de los puertos de la bahia de Esparça y puerto de Sanct Jhoan ... " Esparza, July 14, 1591, in Peralta, *Costa-Rica, Nicaragua y Panamá en el siglo XVI,* pp. 642–643.

[23] Order of Velasco I to royal treasury officials to advance 300 silver pesos to Andrés de Cauches and Martín de Goiti, Mexico City, April 4, 1560, and order of Velasco I to royal treasury officials to pay 2,000 silver pesos to Lope de Molina, Mexico City, October 3, 1560, MSS in AGN, Mercedes, V, fols. 18^{v} and 116^{v}–117^{r}, respectively. For want of workmen only part of the gear needed could be manufactured in Nicaragua, so that pita was sent to New Spain for the manufacture of the remainder.

[24] Coyoacán, April 2, 1550, MS in AGN, Mercedes, III, fol. 32^{v}.

[25] *Recopilación de leyes de Indias,* Lib. IX, Tít. XLIV, ley 1; Enríquez to the king, Lima, February 12, 1583, in *GP,* IX, 238.

[26] *GP,* XI, 290–301. The measurement was of cubic content. Fifty-five arrobas or one ton equaled the space occupied by two water casks of standard size. In terms of English cubic feet, the ton came to 53.44 cubic feet. (M. Oppenheim, *A History of the Administration of the Royal Navy . . . ,* I, 53 n.) This ton was the so-called *tonelada de Sevilla,* which was one-fifth smaller than the *tonel de Vizcaya.*

[27] "Extract from the Declarations of John Drake," March 24, 1584, in Zelia Nuttall, *New Light on Drake,* pp. 26–31; "The Admirable and Prosperous Voyage of Worshipfull Master Thomas Candish . . . Written by Master Francis Pretty," Hakluyt, XI, 301–324. The Englishmen, of course, calculated in their own ship's tons, which were each of 60 cubic feet (Oppenheim, I, 30 and 53 n.) or about 15 per cent larger than the Spanish one of the period.

The ships of the Manila trade were larger. The *Santa Ana* was 700 tons. Another ship, diverted from the Philippine navigation to carry Enríquez from New Spain to Peru, was 450 tons. Enríquez to the king, Lima, October 28, 1581, in *GP,* IX, 56.

[28] License to Luis de Velasco I for a voyage to Peru, Mexico City, November 23, 1554, MS in AGN, Mercedes, IV, fols. 90ʳ–90ᵛ. Ships in the Pacific carried much smaller crews than was required by royal ordinance for vessels in the Atlantic. Paul Taylor, "Spanish Seamen in the New World During the Colonial Period," *The Hispanic American Historical Review,* V (November, 1922), 642–643.

[29] See chapter iv.

[30] License issued April 22, 1563, Mexico City, MS in AGN, Mercedes, VI, fol. 201ʳ–201ᵛ.

[31] Mexico City, February 23, 1566, *ibid.,* VIII, fols. 254ᵛ–255ʳ.

[32] License to sail, issued at Mexico City, December 14, 1565, *ibid.,* fols. 219ᵛ–220ʳ.

[33] License issued at Coyoacán, April 2, 1550, *ibid.,* III, fol. 32ᵛ.

[34] License issued at Mexico City, October 26, 1560, *ibid.,* V, fols. 137ᵛ–138ʳ.

[35] License issued at Mexico City, January 25, 1564, *ibid.,* VII, fol. 299ᵛ.

[36] License to the *San Jerónimo,* Mexico City, November 23, 1554, *ibid.,* IV, fol. 90ʳ–90ᵛ.

[37] License to *La Concepción,* Mexico City, December 31, 1560, *ibid.,* V, fol. 197ʳ.

[38] License to the *San Lorenzo,* Mexico City, October 26, 1560, *ibid.,* V, fols. 137ᵛ–138ʳ.

[39] License to *La Concepción,* Mexico City, February 23, 1566, *ibid.,* VIII, fols. 254ᵛ–255ʳ.

[40] License to the *Santa Cruz,* Mexico City, March 5–6, 1555, *ibid.,* IV, fol. 123ᵛ.

[41] License to the *San Juan de los Frailes,* Mexico City, March 1, 1561, *ibid.,* V, fol. 254ʳ.

[42] License to *La Magdalena,* Mexico City, October 14, 1555, *ibid.,* IV, fol. 242ᵛ.

[43] License to *La Concepción,* Mexico City, December 31, 1560, *ibid.,* V, fol. 197ʳ.

[44] "Visitas de navíos en Acapulco," 1581–1587, MS in AGN, Inquisición, CLXIX, exp. 3, no. 4.

[45] *Ibid.,* No. 5. Master Pretty reported that the Cavendish expedition encountered a Greek pilot, a Fleming, and a "coaster" [pilot and master] born in Marseilles. Hakluyt, XI, 309–327; "Sumaria relacion que hizo el Doctor Castilla ...," 1588, in *GP,* XI, 132.

[46] *Recopilación,* Lib. IX, Tít. XLIV, ley xi; Diego de Encinas, *Cedulario indiano ...*, I, 451.

[47] Some of the licenses issued in the 1540's give permission to take Indians on voyages to Peru. In 1542 Blas de Simancas was given permission to take three Indians from Peru and Nicaragua for the ship's service. In 1543 Bartolomé Ferrelo was licensed to take fourteen Indian and Negro slaves on his voyage to Peru for ship's service, but the Indians, if natives of New Spain, had to be brought back. MSS in AGN, Mercedes, I, fol. 194ᵛ and II, fol. 197ᵛ, respectively.

[48] An interesting instance of the escape of a Peruvian Indian brought by his master to Mexico occurred in 1543. See p. 107.

[49] MS in AGN, Mercedes, IV, fol. 90ʳ–90ᵛ.

[50] License issued at Mexico City, November 23, 1554, *ibid.,* fol. 90ᵛ.

[51] A sailor's contract with Cortés, which follows what seems to have been a standard form, may be found in AGN, Jesús, leg. 203, *hojas sueltas.* It is dated Mexico City, March 18, 1539. See also "Cuenta de lo que ha gastado el Marqués del Valle con los oficiales é marineros é gente de guerra del armada que salió á descubrir en el Mar del Sur, desde el puerto de Santiago, en 29 de octubre de 1533, de que fué por capitán Diego Becerro," 1535, *DII,* XII, 298–313.

[52] Haring, *Trade and Navigation Between Spain and the Indies in the Time of the Hapsburgs . . . ,* pp. 317–318. See also the description of payment of the crew members of the *Santa Cruz* in chapter iv and the references to the Consulate of the Sea made there.

[53] López de Velasco, pp. 301 and 327.

[54] Letter of Bachiller Alonso Muñoz, commissioner of the Inquisition in Acapulco, to the Inquisition in Mexico City, Acapulco, March 10, 1587, MS in AGN, Inquisición, CLXIX, exp. 3.

[55] License to the *San Jerónimo* to return to Peru, Mexico City, November 23, 1554, MS in AGN, Mercedes, IV, fol. 90ʳ–90ᵛ.

[56] License to *La Concepción,* chartered by León and his associates, to go to Peru, Mexico City, February 23, 1566, *ibid.*, VIII, fols. 254^{v}–255^{r}.

[57] "Visitas de navíos en Acapulco," 1581–1587, MS in AGN, Inquisición, CLXIX, exp. 3, No. 4.

[58] See, for example, the license issued to *Nuestra Señora de la Concepción,* Bautista Natarén master, Mexico City, July 16, 1556, MS in AGN, Mercedes, IV, fol. 366^{v}.

[59] License issued at Mexico City, January 17, 1580, MS in AGN, General de parte, II, fol. 126^{v}.

[60] Nuttall, pp. 199–200. Zárate came to Mexico City from Spain in 1578. Cappa, X, 185–193.

[61] License to go to Peru issued at Mexico City, December 5, 1587, MS in AGN, General de parte, III, fol. 229^{v} (exp. 491); "Visitas de navíos en Acapulco," 1581–1587, MS in AGN, Inquisición, CLXIX, exp. 3.

[62] The surviving license relating to Mendoza's transfer was issued to Gil Ramírez Dávalos and Francisco Duartes, a Spanish servant, three Negroes, one Negress, and an "indio de la India de Portugal," the last a slave of Francisco de Mendoza, the viceroy's son. Order of Luis de Velasco I to the alcalde mayor of Huatulco, January 12, 1551, MS in AGN, Mercedes, III, fols. 254^{v}–255^{r}.

[63] Coruña to the king, Mexico City, April 1, 1581, Spain. Ministerio de Fomento, *Cartas de Indias,* pp. 337–338.

[64] License issued September 25, 1582, Mexico City, MS in AGN, Indios, II, fol. 6^{r} (exp. 23).

[65] License issued January 17, 1580, Mexico City, MS in AGN, General de parte, II, fol. 126^{v}.

[66] License issued March 7, 1580, Mexico City, MS in AGN, General de parte, II (no fol.).

[67] The Inquisition of Mexico to its commissioner in Acapulco, Mexico City, January 29, 1583, MS in AGN, Inquisición, CXXXIII, exp. 5.

[68] Memorial of Don Hernando Cortés, presented in Valladolid *ca.* 1605, in Hernando Cortés, *Cartas,* ed. by Mariano Cuevas, pp. 289–294.

[69] Notations of licenses issued to Fray Andrés de Navarrete and Fray Juan de León of the Order of Nuestra Señora del Carmen, Mexico City, January 10, 1581, MS in AGN, General de parte, II, fol. 264^{v}. Fray Juan de León came to New Spain from Peru, since he brought with him a Peruvian mestizo servant. License issued to Pedro Rodríguez, Mexico City, January 26, 1581, *ibid.,* fol. 272^{v}.

[70] For example, license of Luis de Velasco I to García Escudero and his son, Mexico City, November 8, 1554; and notations of licenses issued December 14, 1554, to Cristóbal de Molina, and December 20, 1554, to Juan de Yarto, MSS in AGN, mercedes, IV, fols. 82^{v}–83^{r} and 95^{v}, respectively.

[71] For example, license issued to Pero Martínez de Bequedo, his wife, their nephew, and a Negro slave, Mexico City, October 12, 1560, *ibid.,* V, fol. 122^{r}.

[72] MS in AGN, General de parte, II, fols. 289^{v}–290^{r}.

[73] *Ibid.,* I, fol. I, 105^{v}.

[74] *Ibid.,* II, fol. 97^{r}.

[75] *Ibid.,* Mercedes, VIII, fol. 245^{r}–245^{v}.

[76] *Ibid.,* General de parte, II, fol. 85^{r}–85^{v}.

[77] *Ibid.,* Mercedes, VI, fol. 40^{r}.

[78] Jose Toribio Medina, *La imprenta en Lima ...*, I, XXIV–XXVI.

[79] License issued at Mexico City, June 18, 1576, MS in AGN, General de parte, I, fol. 203^{v}.

[80] License issued at Mexico City, April 6, 1554, *ibid.,* Mercedes, IV, fol. 1^{v}.

[81] MS in *ibid.,* Mercedes, V, fol. 173^{r}.

[82] *Ibid.,* General de parte, I, fol. 179^{r}–179^{v}.

[83] *Ibid.,* Mercedes, VII, fol. 390^{v}.

[84] *Ibid.,* VIII, fol. 225^{r}.

[85] *Ibid.,* fols. 195^{v}–196^{r}.

[86] Viceregal order to the alcalde mayor of Acapulco and other justices Mexico City, December 3, 1579, MS in AGN, General de parte, II, fol. 94^{r}; License issued at Mexico City, September 13, 1579, *ibid.,* fol. 70^{r}.

[87] License issued at Mexico City, November 5, 1575, *ibid.*, I, fol. 51^r.

[88] License issued at Mexico City, November 10, 1575, *ibid.*, fol. 57^v.

[89] License issued at Mexico City, August 3, 1576, *ibid.*, fol. 224v.

[90] License issued at Mexico City, September 11, 1576, *ibid.*, fol. 242^r–242^v.

[91] License issued at Mexico City, October 31, 1579, *ibid.*, II, fol. 81^r–81^v.

[92] License issued at Mexico City, February 26, 1583, *ibid.*, Indios, II, fol. 127^v (exp. 547).

[93] License issued at Mexico City, October 5, 1582, *ibid.*, fol. 14^r (exp. 57).

[94] License issued at Mexico City, September 22, 1580, *ibid.*, General de parte, II, fol. 248^r–248^v.

[95] Notation of license, Mexico City, July 31, 1556, *ibid.*, Mercedes, IV, fol. 366^v.

[96] License issued at Mexico City, November 7, 1575, *ibid.*, General de parte, I, fol. 53^r–53^v.

[97] License issued at Mexico City, April 13, 1576, *ibid.*, fols. 167^v–168^r.

[98] License issued at Mexico City, January 7, 1564, *ibid.*, Mercedes, VII, fol. 274^v.

[99] May 2, 1549, Lima, in *GP*, I, 181–183. See also Montesinos, *Anales*, I, 109–113, 195; Cobo, *Historia del Nuevo Mundo*, II, 352–355, 362, 378, 393–395, 408–410 *et passim;* El Inca Garcilaso de la Vega, *Primera parte de los comentarios reales*, I, 323–339 (Lib. IV, cap. xvi-xxx).

[100] Lima, January 28, 1560, *GP*, I, 347–351.

[101] Letter to the king, Lima, February, 1567, *ibid.*, III, 234.

[102] Letter to the king, Lima, October 28, 1581, *ibid.*, IX, 59.

[103] The question of amount of specie produced during the sixteenth century in the various Spanish colonies in America has long attracted the attention of scholars. It is still far from solution. Some of the more recent studies on the subject are: Earl J. Hamilton, "Imports of American Gold and Silver into Spain, 1503–1660," *The Quarterly Journal of Economics*, XLIII (May, 1929), 436–472; *idem*, *American Treasure and the Price Revolution in Spain, 1501–1650*, pp. 11–45; Clarence H. Haring, *Trade and Navigation*, pp. 329–337; *idem*, "American Gold and Silver Production in the First Half of the Sixteenth Century," *The Quarterly Journal of Economics*, XXIX (May, 1915), 433–479; Bailey W. Diffie, *Latin American Civilization: Colonial Period*, pp. 102–108, 366–367. In this connection, see also "Razón certificada ... de las sumas que por razón de los Reales derechos de Quintos y Diezmos han contribuido los caudales sacados del famoso cerro de *Potosí*, desde el año de 1556, en que se dió principio de sus labores mineralogicos, hasta 31 de diciembre de 1783 ... ," *DIE*, V, 170–184; and the table of shipments of royal treasure from New Spain to Seville published in Gómez de Cervantes, *La vida económica y social de Nueva Epaña al finalizar el siglo XVI*, 188, and in Haring, *Trade and Navigation*, p. 332.

[104] Letter to the king, Lima, February, 1567, *GP*, III, 234. See also Francisco de Barrionuevo, governor of Panama, to the emperor, Panama, December 23, 1533, in *DII*, XLI, 505–510.

[105] As is evident from the large amount of Spanish wares reëxported from Mexico to Peru.

[106] Simpson, *Exploitation of Land in Central Mexico in the Sixteenth Century*, University of California Publications, Ibero-Americana : 36 (1952), pp. 13–15, 24–25, *et passim;* Borah, *Silk Raising in Colonial Mexico*, University of California Publications, Ibero-Americana : 20 (1943), pp. 15–38; Henry Hawks, "A Relation of the Commodities of Nova Hispania, and the Maners of the Inhabitants," 1572, Hakluyt, IX, 384–391. See the discussion of manufactures exported from New Spain below.

[107] *Relación breve y verdadera de algunas cosas ... que sucedieron al padre fray Alonso Ponce*, I, 403–404; López de Velasco, p. 296; "Relacion de las Rentas que su Magd. tiene en las provincias de Guatemala, honduras y nicaragua," 1574, *Colección de documentos referentes a la historia colonial de Nicaragua*, p. 78. "Relacion hecha por el licenciado Palacio al rey D. Felipe II ... ," Guatemala City, March 8, 1576, *DII*, VI, 14–15.

[108] Chevalier, *La Formation des grands domaines au Mexique*, p. 194; Haring, *Trade and Navigation*, p. 211. See also chapter iv on the Marquesado del Valle.

[109] Cédula of the princess, Valladolid, October 29, 1556, in Vasco de Puga, fol. 198^r.

[110] The testimony is published in Paso y Troncoso, *Papeles de Nueva España*, 2 ser., III, supplement, pp. 62–65, 156–158, 173, 206–208, *passim*.

[111] Manuel Moreyra Paz Soldán, "La tesorería y la estadística de acuñación colonial en la Casa de moneda de Lima," in Universidad Católica del Perú, Instituto de Investigaciones Históricas, *Cuadernos de estudios,* II, No. 4, pp. 5–6. The anarchy was so general that books of rules for handling the various circulating media were published. Juan Diez Freile, *Sumario cõpẽdioso de las quẽtas de plata y oro q̃ en los reynos del Piru son necessarias a los mercaderes: y todo genero de tratantes. Cõ algunas reglas tocantes al Arithmetica ...* (Mexico City, 1556), listed in José Toribio Medina, *La imprenta en México,* I, 88–90; and Juan de Belveder, *Libro general de las reduciones de plata, y oro de diferentes leyes y pesos, de menor á mayor cantidad, y de sus interesses á tanto por ciento, con otras reglas, y auisos muy necessarios para estos Reynos del Piru ...* (Lima, 1597).

[112] López de Gómara, *Historia de la conquista de México,* II, 293–294 (cap. ccxlix). Garcilaso de la Vega, *Primera parte de los commentarios reales,* I, 323–339 (Lib. IX, cap. xvi-xxx); "Relacion del Virrey de Nueva-España, sobre los servycios personales que facian los yndios en aquellas provincias," date given as 1537 but more probably 1547 or 1548, in *DII,* XLI, 152–153. See also chapter ii on shipments in the 1530's and 1540's.

[113] Emilio Romero, *Historia económica del Perú,* pp. 120–121; Cappa, V, 282–284.

[114] Lima, *Libros del cabildo,* IV, 174. Session of June 16, 1554.

[115] Letter to the Council of the Indies, Lima, May 2, 1549, in *GP,* I, 181.

[116] *Primera parte de los comentarios reales,* I, 336 (Lib. IX, cap. xxviii).

[117] Cappa, V, 282–284; Chevalier, pp. 95, 170.

[118] At the time of Henry Hawks' travels through New Spain in the 1560's, sweetmeats and preserves were still being shipped to Peru. "A Relation of the Commodities of Nova Hispania, and the Maners of the Inhabitants," 1572, Hakluyt, IX, 386. Such exports do not appear in the export licenses for the 1570's and 1580's.

[119] The following description is based primarily upon the lists of exports contained in the following: Partnership agreement between Pedro del Río and the Marquesado del Valle, Mexico City, February 4, 1556, MS in AGN, Jesús, leg. 235, exp. 10:9; License to Juan Báez and his family to go to Peru with merchandise valued at 6,000 pesos, Mexico City, November 24, 1575; Partial list of merchandise being exported by Martín Ruíz de Ayaldeburu, *ca.,* October 1, 1579; List of merchandise in permit issued to Juan de Valdinvalle, October 30, 1579; License issued to Diego Delicana and his wife, Mexico City, December 10, 1579; List of merchandise being carried by Isidro de Segovia, *ca.* January 3, 1580; List of merchandise bought by Domingo Ortiz for export to Peru, December 24, 1580; List of merchandise to be taken to Peru by Miguel Pérez de Acarreta, Mexico City, January 18, 1581; MSS in AGN, General de parte, I, fols. 74^{r}–75^{v} (?); II, fols. 42^{v}, 77^{v}–79^{v}, 97^{r}, 309^{r}–309^{v}, 308^{v}, 268^{v}–269^{r}. MS in AGN, Civil, MDCCIII, exp. 1, has a list of books shipped to Peru in January, 1577. Further comments on the trade are in the reports of the oidores of the Audiencia of Mexico, Villalobos, Doctor Orozco, and Villanueva, to the king, Mexico City, June 5, 8, and 15, 1564, MSS in AGI, Audiencia de Méjico, leg. 207 (59-6-13). This description omits goods received via the Philippine trade, which are discussed in chapter vii.

[120] Lima, *Libros del cabildo,* VII, 243, 469–470. (Sessions of March 3, 1572 and June 12, 1573.)

[121] *Recopilacion de leyes ... de Indias,* Lib. IX, tít. xxvi, ley xviii.

[122] Order of Antonio de Mendoza to the royal treasury officials in Mexico that in future properly marked silver be accepted for minting, Mexico City, July 26, 1543, MS in AGN, Mercedes, II, fols. 128^{v}–129^{r}; Doctor Orozco to the king, Mexico City, June 8, 1564, MS in AGI, Audiencia de Méjico, leg. 207 (59-6-13).

[123] Rental agreement between Diego de Molina and Alonso Baca de Andrada on the haciendas of the Peñol de Xico, property of the Marquesado del Valle, Mexico City, May 1, 1574, and annexed inventories of livestock and buildings, 1569–1574, MSS in AGN, Jesús, leg. 273, exp. 4:8. See chapter iv.

[124] The evidence for this point is the failure of Spanish colonial writers to mention the potato. In this connection, see also Salaman, *The History and Social Influence of the Potato,* pp. 1–2.

[125] Mexico (City). *Actas de cabildo,* VI, 299–300, 340, 491; VII, 10, 37, 330–331, 344–351 (Sessions of August 8, 1557, September 19, 1558, October 3, 1561, January 9, 1562, April 29, 1562, February 10, 1567, and March 1, 1567); cédulas of the princess to the royal treasury officials in Seville and those in New Spain, Valladolid, March 4, 1559, in Encinas, *Cedulario,* III, 416–417.

[126] Guillermo Lohmann Villena, "Enrique Garcés, descubridor del mercurio en el Perú, poeta y arbitrista," *Anuario de estudios americanos,* V, 444–454; Gwendolin Cobb, "Potosí and Huancavelica," unpublished thesis, University of California, Berkeley, pp. 24–25; "Memorial y relacion de las minas de azogue del Pirú," Huancavelica, April 20, 1607, *DII,* VIII, 422–423; Royal cédulas to the viceroys of Peru and New Spain, Madrid, November 14, 1562, Encinas, III, 417–418.

[127] Mexico (City). *Actas de cabildo,* VII, 381–382 (Session of December 19, 1567); Fernando Montesinos, *Anales del Perú,* p. 21.

[128] Mexico (City). *Actas de cabildo,* VII, 410 (Session of August 27, 1568. Moya de Contreras to the President of the Council of the Indies, Mexico City, August 31, 1574, in Paso y Troncoso, *Epistolario,* XI, 172–173.

[129] "Instrucción para Corte," Mexico City, October 3, 1561, in Mexico (City). *Actas de cabildo,* VII, 491; Agreement of Alonso Baco de Andrada as governor of the Marquesado del Valle to pay 1,200 pesos for twelve quintals of Peruvian mercury, Mexico City, April 20, 1574, MS in AGN, Jesús, leg. 270, exp. 7:42. The Marquesado bought the mercury for use in its mines at Tasco. See also Montesinos, II, 21. An inquiry made in 1591 to establish costs for comparison with mercury imports from China, gave the following breakdown for Peruvian mercury per quintal:

Cost at Huancavelica	40/0/0		oro de minas
Transportation to the sea at Chincha (pack train)	4/		
Packaging (*badanas y hilo*)	2/	–	2/4
Sea freight to El Callao	/4		
" " " Acapulco	2/	–	2/4
Transportation to Mexico City (pack train)	4/		
	52/4	–	53/4

("La ynformacion que se hiço Para del azogue de China," Mexico City, October 21, 1591, MS in AGI, 58-3-11 (BLT).) A selling price of 100 silver pesos a quintal would come to 60/4 gold pesos or a profit of but 7 to 8 gold pesos per quintal. If the testimony was true, competition among merchants cut profits on mercury to about 15 per cent of cost unloaded in Mexico City, a very low rate indeed.

[130] Cédula of the princess to the treasury officials of New Spain, Valladolid, March 4, 1559, Encinas, III, 416–417.

[131] Letter of the king to the viceroy of New Spain, May 18, 1572, and letter of the king to the royal treasury officials in Mexico, May 26, 1572, both quoted in Encinas, III, 420–421 and 467.

[132] Royal cédula declaring monopoly of mercury shipments from Peru to New Spain, Madrid, May 26, 1573; and extracts of letter of the king to viceroy of Peru, December 1, 1573, both in Encinas, III, 420–421 and 419–420; *Recopilación,* Lib. VIII, tít. XXIII, ley 1; Montesinos, II, 52, 58–59.

[133] Montesinos, II, 52.

[134] *Ibid.,* pp. 50–51, 58–59; Cobb, "Potosí and Huancavelica," pp. 39–41 and 123–143; Lohmann Villena, "Enrique Garcés," *Anuario de estudios americanos,* V, 448–454; Letters of Francisco de Toledo to the king, Cuzco, March 25, 1571 and March 1, 1572, La Plata, November 30, 1573, and letter of Toledo to Cardinal de Sigüenza, Potosí, March 20, 1573, in *GP,* III, 476–484, 580–592, V, 151–157, 4–5. On mercury production, see below.

[135] Mexico City, August 8, 1576, MS in AGN, General de parte, I, fol. 226v.

[136] Mexico City, September 19, 1576, *ibid.,* fols. 248r–248v.

[137] García de Mendoza to the king, Lima, April 27, 1590, in *GP*, XII, 114–116; Cobb, "Potosí and Huancavelica," p. 56.

[138] Marqués de Cañete to the king, Lima, January 16, 1593, in *GP*, XII, 326–327.

[139] Royal cédula, Madrid, May 26, 1573, in Encinas, III, 424–425.

[140] Marqués de Cañete to the king, Lima, January 16, 1593, in *GP*, XII, 326–327.

[141] Enríquez to the king, Mexico City, January 9, 1574, in *Cartas de Indias*, p. 303.

[142] Lic. Ramírez de Cartagena to the king, Lima, April 16, 1573; Enríquez to the king, Lima, February 17, 1583; García de Mendoza to the king, Lima, April 27, 1590; and as Marqués de Cañete to the king, Lima, January 16, 1593, May 18, 1593, El Callao, April 12, 1594, Lima, January 20, 1595; Velasco II to the king, El Callao, April 16, 1598; in *GP*, VII, 169–171; IX, 256; XII, 114–116, 326–327; XIII, 42–43, 138, 252–253; XIV, 108.

[143] The Marqués de Cañete reported on November 20, 1593, that between 1590 and 1593, mercury in the amount of 5,500 quintals had been shipped. *GP*, XIII, 112.

[144] "Relación que el príncipe de Esquilache hace al Señor Marqués de Guadalcázar ... ," 1621, Peru. *Memorias de los virreyes* ... , I, 133–134.

[145] Letter of June 15, 1564, MS in AGI, Audiencia de Méjico, leg. 207 (59-6-13).

[146] The Marqués de Cañete reported to the royal secretary, Juan de Ibarra, in 1592 that taxes on imports from New Spain had yielded as much revenue as would have been received from imports brought from Spain in the fleet. Lima, April 28, 1592, in *GP*, XII, 242–243.

[147] Expediente on the need for Bernardino Martínez, bookdealer, to go to Peru to collect for books sent to an agent for sale, 1580, MS in AGN, Civil, MDCCIII, exp. 1.

[148] License to Alonso Ortega, Mexico City, December 13, 1565, *ibid.*, Mercedes, VIII, fol. 218v.

[149] As in the instance of the *San Jerónimo;* see the first section of this chapter.

[150] Marqués de Cañete to the king, Lima, December 30, 1590 and April 28, 1592, in *GP*, XII, 203–204, and 242–243.

[151] See the discussion of ownership of vessels in this chapter. See also chapter vii.

[152] Notation of license to return to Peru issued by the Audiencia Gobernadora to Diego López de Toledo, merchant, and one servant, Mexico City, December 11, 1565, MS in AGN, Mercedes, VIII, fol. 216v.

[153] "Visitas de navios en Acapulco," 1581–1587, *ibid.*, Inquisición, CLXIX, exp. 3.

[154] Marqués de Cañete to the king, El Callao, April 12, 1594, in *GP*, XIII, 136.

NOTES TO CHAPTER VI: REGULATION AND TAXATION

[1] *Recopilación,* Lib. IX, Tít. XLIV, ley i; Encinas, *Cedulario indiano,* IV, 122–123.

[2] *Recopilación,* Lib. IX, Tit. XLIV, ley vi.

[3] *Ibid.,* ley iii.

[4] Haring, *Trade and Navigation,* pp. 30–31; Order of Mendoza appointing Pedro Pantoya inspector of ships at Huatulco, Mexico City, May 22, 1543, MS in AGN, Mercedes, II, fols. 79^r–79^v.

[5] Haring, *op. cit.,* pp. 59–60.

[6] See, for example, the "Registro del *San Lázaro,* surto en Acapulco, para salir rumbo a Panamá," October 30, 1538, MS in 13 fols., AGN, Jesús, leg. 203.

[7] *Recopilación,* Lib. IX, Tít. XXXIII, ley xxxii. Encinas, IV, 215–216, gives the text of the order but under the date of 1572.

[8] *Recopilación,* Lib. IX, Tít. XXXIII, ley xxiii. On December 10, 1566, Philip II extended the rules of registry by applying specifically to the Pacific navigations the order that no one might register any property of whatever kind in the name of another person. *Ibid.,* Tít. XLIX, ley x; Encinas, IV, 217.

[9] *Recopilación,* Lib. IX, Tít. XLIV, ley ix.

[10] *Ibid.,* Tít. XXXV, ley lv.

[11] On pilots, ibid., Tít. XXIII, leyes xiv-xvi; on seamen, ibid., Tít. XXV, ley xii. The prohibition was specifically reiterated for the Pacific in an instruction of July 17, 1572, to the viceroy of Peru. Encinas, *op. cit.,* I, 451; *Recopilación,* Lib. IX, Tít, XLIV, ley xi. That part of the intention of the order of 1572 was to keep information about the Pacific navigations secret is evident from a clause that no pilot or ship's master of the Pacific navigations might go to Spain without express royal license. See also the forebodings of Francisco de Zárate in his report to Enríquez on Drake, Realejo, April 16, 1579, Peralta, pp. 583–584. (Nuttall's translation [*New Light,* p. 209] is a bit odd at this point.)

[12] See chapter v.

[13] Medina del Campo, October 28, 1480, cited in full in a cédula of Prince Philip to the Audiencia of New Granada, Valladolid, September 17, 1548, Encinas, I, 433–434.

[14] Royal cédula to the House of Trade, Burgos, September 9, 1511, Encinas, I, 396–397. In 1552, the rule was changed by an order that no one might migrate to the Indies without express royal license. *Ibid.,* I, 440.

[15] Toledo, May 21, 1534, *ibid.,* I, 411.

[16] *Ibid.,* IV, 285–286, I, 433–434.

[17] La Gasca to the Council of the Indies, Lima, September 25, 1548, *GP,* I, 119–120.

[18] Draft of a letter by La Gasca to Prince Philip or to the Council of the Indies, Villamuriel, October 17, 1554, Maggs Bros. pp. 540–543.

[19] Extract by Muñoz of a letter of the Marqués de Cañete to the king, December 27, 1555, *DII,* III, 561–562. Cañete to the king, Paita, April 15, 1556, *GP,* I, 266–267.

[20] *Ibid.;* Cañete to the Council of the Indies, Lima, October 28, 1560, in *GP,* I, 371.

[21] Conde de Nieva to the king, Lima, June 16, 1561; Francisco de Toledo to the king, Lima, February 8, 1570; Toledo to the king, Lima, December 12, 1577; in *GP,* I, 386–387, III, 364–365, VI, 14–15; Memorials of Cristobal Maldonado to the king, *ca.* August 1574, *DIE,* XCIV, 372 and 390 (the marginal comments on the memorials summarize the Crown's policy); Montesinos, *Anales del Perú,* II, 104; Chevalier, *La Formation des grands domaines au Mexique,* p. 29.

[22] MS in AGI Audiencia de Méjico, leg. 1089, Registro 1548, fols. 71–72.

[23] Puga, *Provisiones,* fol. 170^v–171^r.

[24] Encinas, *op. cit.,* I, 406. The order was repeated in 1551; *ibid.,* pp. 266–267, 422.

[25] *Ibid.,* pp. 406–407.

[26] *Ibid.* In 1568 the Crown ordered the exile of all undesirables in spite of the issuance of a general amnesty. *Ibid.,* pp. 266–267, 422–423.

[27] *Ibid.,* pp. 407–408.

[28] Badajoz, June 3, 1580, in *GP*, IX, 20–21.

[29] Issued at San Lorenzo, March 31, 1584, *ibid.*, X, 23.

[30] For a comment on the effect of such orders, see the letter of the Audiencia of Lima to the king, Lima, January 27, 1573, *ibid.*, VII, 146. The audiencia complained that the power vested in the viceroy and audiencias to exile without trial led to extortion and great injustice. The threat that it would be used forced treasury officials to honor all requisitions, however improper. The Conde del Villar suspended the application of such cédulas during his administration. Letter to the king, Lima, April 25, 1588, *ibid.*, XI, 69 and 91.

[31] The monarchs of Bohemia to the president and oidores of the Audiencia of New Spain, Valladolid, July 7, 1550, Puga, fols. 125^v–126^r. Puga gives the date as 1551, but it appears as 1550 in the MS copy in AGI, Audiencia de Méjico, leg. 1089, *Registro* 1548, fols. 259^r–260^v. The *Recopilación* also gives the date as 1550, Lib. VII, Tít. III, ley I.

[32] *Recopilación*, Lib. VII, Tít. III, ley I; Puga, fols. 179^v–180^v.

[33] *Recopilación*, Lib. I, Tít. VII, ley xiv.

[34] *Ibid.*, Lib. VII, Tít. III, leyes I and viii; Lib. II, Tít. I, ley xiv; Lib. III, Tít. III, ley lix.

[35] Puga, fol. 36^r.

[36] Encinas, IV, 323; *Recopilación*, Lib. VI, Tít. I, ley xlviii.

[37] Puga, fols. 164^v–165^r.

[38] *Recopilación*, Lib. I, Tít. XVI, ley xv.

[39] *Ibid.*, Lib. IX, Tít. XXVI, ley lxx.

[40] *Ibid.*, ley lxix.

[41] Encinas, I, 381; *Recopilación*, Lib. II, Tít. XXXIII, leys I and xxxvii.

[42] Cédula of the queen to the royal treasury official of New Spain, Valladolid, January 18, 1538, Encinas, III, 366–367.

[43] Paso y Troncoso, *Epistolario*, III, 260–261.

[44] "Memorial pidiendo residencia contra Don Antonio de Mendoza," *ca.* 1543, Cortés, *Escritos sueltos*, pp. 334–335.

[45] Issued at Mexico City, October 11, 1542, MS in AGN, Mercedes, I, fols. 167^v–168^r.

[46] Issued at Mexico City, July 23, 1550, *ibid.*, III, fol. 128^v.

[47] License to Francisco Heres and ship *San Juan*, Mexico City, June 6, 1542, and license to Pedro de Malta, Mexico City, October 11, 1542, *ibid.*, I, fols. 59^v–60^r, and 168^r.

[48] Order of Mendoza to Alonso de Canseco, corregidor of Huatulco, Mexico City, December 24, 1543, *ibid.*, II, fols. 236^v.

[49] The license of Mendoza to the carabelón of Francisco Pilo to go to Peru (Coyoacán, April 2, 1550, *ibid.*, III, fol. 32^v) specifically instructed the corregidor of Amula to carry out the registry and inspection. See also in this regard, the order of Luis de Velasco empowering Juan Gallego, vecino of Oaxaca and corregidor of Huamelula, to exercise the powers of the alcalde mayor of the town and port of Huatulco so that vessels and passengers going to Peru could be registered, etc., notwithstanding the illness of the incumbent alcalde mayor, Pedro Pachecho, Mexico City, November 20, 1554, *ibid.*, IV, fols. 88^v–89^r.

[50] It was customary for each alcalde mayor of the port of Huatulco to have the right to appoint one alguacil with a yearly salary of 130 pesos de oro común, paid from the revenues of vacant corregimientos and alguacilazgos. Order of Luis de Velasco to the royal treasury officials to pay the past alguaciles their salaries, Mexico City, June 6, 1561, *ibid.*, V, fol. 344^v.

[51] Order of Luis de Velasco to the alcalde mayor of the port of Huatulco, Mexico City, June 4, 1556, *ibid.*, IV, fols. 361^r–361^v.

[52] Order of Mendoza issued at Mexico City, May 22, 1543, *ibid.*, II, fol. 79^r–79^v.

[53] Villamanrrique to the king, Mexico City, February 23, 1586, MS in AGI, 58-3-9 (BLT).

[54] See license of Antonio de Mendoza to Hernando de Villanueva, Mexico, October 24, 1543, MS in AGN, Mercedes, II, fol. 199^r. Villanueva had come to New Spain with a license issued by Sebastián de la Gama, lieutenant of the governor of Piura.

[55] See, for example, the notation of the license granted to Pedro Meleado to return to Peru since he brought a license issued by La Gasca, Mexico City, November 8, 1554, MS in AGN, Mercedes, IV, fol. 86^v; Lic. Ramírez de Cartagena to the king, Lima, April 16, 1573, in *GP*, VII, 171.

[56] See the instance of the *Santa Cruz* in chapter iv.

[57] Lima. *Libros de cabildo,* IV, 517–519.

[58] The price was 8,000 pesos of *plata ensayada* (equal to gold pesos), but it was reduced to 6,000 pesos when the post turned out to be less remunerative than it had been represented to be. When Enríquez took over the administration of Peru, he was ordered to establish for sale to the highest bidder, an escribanía del Mar del Sur with jurisdiction over ship's registry. He found that the proposal conflicted with rights of Andrada, but suggested that the king consider the possibility of establishing three such posts, one each at El Callao, Panama, and New Spain, to divide notarial jurisdiction over registry for the entire Pacific coast. The discussion over what might be established dragged on for a decade. In 1592 the Crown ordered that a single post be created and sold for El Callao, but the second Marqués de Cañete, then viceroy of Peru, warned that as long as a separate escribano de registro existed at Panama, any other post was worth little. As a result of his advice, a joint El Callao–Panama jurisdiction was created and sold in 1595 to Diego de la Presa for 40,000 ducats, payable in two annual installments. The Panama office was to be handled by a lieutenant. Enríquez to the king, Lima, February 17, 1583; Cañete to the king, Lima, May 18, 1593 and May 13, 1595; in *GP,* IX, 261–262; XIII, 145–146 and 337.

[59] On the first and second voyages of the *Santa Cruz,* both inspection and registry were carried out by Diego de Porras, alguacil mayor of the port. See the accounts of the *Santa Cruz,* MS in AGN, Jesús, leg. 235, exp. 8.

[60] Issued at Mexico City, November 21, 1542, MS in AGN, Mercedes, I, fol. 199ʳ–199ᵛ.

[61] License issued to Juan Gaitán, Mexico City, March 19, 1550, MS in AGN, Civil, MCCLXXI, exp. 187–189; license issued to García Escudero and his son, Mexico City, November 8, 1554; license issued to Antonio de Hinojosa and his household, Mexico City, November 9, 1554; license issued to Pedro de Segura, merchant, Mexico City, March 14, 1555; MSS in AGN, Mercedes, IV, fols. 82ᵛ–83ʳ, 85ᵛ, and 125ᵛ.

[62] The full documentation of such a permission is available in the case of Bernardo Martínez, bookdealer, October–November, 1580, MSS in AGN, Civil, MDCCIII, exp. 1, and General de parte, II, fols. 289ᵛ–290ʳ. That this was customary procedure is apparent from the earlier license issued to Juan Alvarez, married merchant of Mexico City, Mexico City, October 24, 1560, MS in AGN, Mercedes, V, fol. 132ʳ.

[63] License of Mendoza to Bartolomé Ferrer, Mexico City, October 23, 1543; and license to Blas de Simancas, Mexico City, November 8, 1542, MSS in AGN, Mercedes, II, fols. 197ᵛ and I, 194ʳ, respectively. For Peru, see the discussion in chapter v on passengers.

[64] Order of Mendoza to the justices of New Spain, Mexico City, October 24, 1543, *ibid.,* fol. 199ʳ.

[65] The following discussion is based upon licenses in AGN, Mercedes, I–VIII; General de parte, I–II; and Indios, II.

[66] A license issued by the Audiencia of Lima, October 8, 1571, is in AGN, Civil, MDCCIII, exp. 1.

[67] This discussion is based upon the following manuscripts, all in AGN, Inquisición: letter of the inquisitors of Mexico City to Juan Zorrilla de la Concha, curate of Acapulco, advising him of his appointment as commissioner and congratulating him on the inspection of the *San Juan Bautista,* newly arrived from the Philippines, Mexico City, January 8, 1582 (CXXXII, exp. 12 or fol. 96); instruction to the commissioner at the port of Acapulco, Mexico City, January 8, 1582 (CXXXII, exp. 23 or fols. 109–114); fragment of a general instruction for the inspection of ships in the Pacific, 1586 (CXL, exp. 8); letters of the inquisitors of Mexico City to the commissioner at the port of Huatulco, Mexico City, April 27, 1587 and August 14, 1587 (CXLII, exp. 15); letter of Pedro de Balmaseda, commissioner at Acapulco, to the Holy Office in Mexico City, Acapulco, March 14, 1589 (CXLII, exp. 62); inspections of ships in Acapulco harbor, 1581–1587 (CLXIX, exp. 3–5); questionnaire to be used in the inspection of the fleet arriving at Veracruz, 1583 (CLXIX, exp. 4). The general questionnaire for use in Pacific ports is unfortunately truncated, but it can be pieced out by reference to the questionnaire issued for use at Veracruz and the reports of ship inspections at Acapulco. The categories of questions

were as follows: 1. The name of the vessel, what port it belonged to, and under what license and registry it sailed? 2. When the ship had left its home port, what other harbors it had called at, what other ships it had met en route, and what people it had dealt with in the voyage? 3. What foreigners were on board, how and when they came there, and if they traveled with license and were duly entered on the ship's register? 4. What preaching, catechism, and prayers had been used during the voyage and the names of saints prayed to for protection? (This item may have involved a not unshrewd assumption that people in danger from tempest would revert to the beliefs they cherished most?) 5. What books had been used for prayer and leisure reading, what languages they were written in, and whether any were known to be forbidden? 6. Were there any books, declared or undeclared, in the cargo and what additional books had been taken on board during the voyage? 7. What images were on board and what were the inscriptions on them? 8. Had any person on board done or said anything contrary to the teachings of the Church?

[68] A number of such licenses for the years 1554–1556 may be found in AGN, Mercedes, IV. See, as examples, the license issued on December 20, 1554, to Juan de Yarto, which combines both permissions in a single license (fol. 195^{v}); and the license to purchase issued to Francisco Muñoz, April 13, 1556 (fol. 329^{v}). Muñoz had already selected the merchandise he wanted and by virtue of the license could now purchase his selections. This permission was good for thirty days, probably the customary time limit.

[69] Lima, *Libros de cabildo,* IV, 315 (meeting of August 2, 1555).

[70] *Ibid.,* VI, 250 251 (meeting of July 14, 1564).

[71] *Recopilación,* Lib. VI, Tít. XII, ley vi; Puga, fols. 34^{r}–34^{v} and 200^{v}–201^{v}.

[72] *Recopilación,* Lib. VI, Tít. XII, leyes x and xv; Encinas, IV, 308–310; Puga, fols. 89^{r}, 105^{r}–106^{r}.

[73] "Relacion del Virrey de Nueva-España, Don Antonio de Mendoza, sobre los servycios personales que facian los yndios en acquellas provyncias," date given as 1537 but more probably 1547, *DII,* XLI, 152–153.

[74] AGN, Mercedes, I–III, *passim.*

[75] Orders of November 13, 1550; December 3, 1550; December 15, 1550; December 16, 1550; and January 15, 1551, *ibid.,* III, fols. 234^{r}, 237^{r}, 243^{r}–243^{v}, 243^{v}, and 259^{r}–259^{v} for the provision of such bearers.

[76] Order of June 30, 1563, *ibid.,* VI, fols. 293^{v}–294^{r}.

[77] Montesinos, I, 113.

[78] Cédula of the queen to the Audiencia of Mexico, etc., Segovia, October 15, 1532, Puga, fol. 80^{v}.

[79] It may have been collection at El Callao, among others, which brought forth orders that no customs duty might be levied without express royal enactment. *Recopilación,* Lib. VIII, Tít. XV, ley xli (1563 and 1571).

[80] Instructions to the Conde de Nieva and commissioners, Ghent, July 23, 1559, *Nueva colección de documentos inéditos para la historia de España y de sus Indias,* VI, 9–19; Philip II to the treasury officials in New Spain and Tierrafirme, Madrid, August 4, 1561, quoted in a similar order to the treasury officials in Peru and Chile, Madrid, 458–459, Encinas, III, 458–459; Francisco de Morales to the king, May 12, 1563; May 17, 1563; May 20, 1563; May 23, 1563; *DIHA,* I, 399–405, 368, 369, 389–391; Villalobos to the king, Mexico City, June 5, 1564; Orozco to the king, Mexico City, June 8, 1564; Villanueva to the king, Mexico City, June 15, 1564, MSS in AGI, Audiencia de Méjico, leg. 207 (59-6-13); *Recopilación,* Lib. VIII, Tít. XV, leyes I, ix, x, xi, xiii; Encinas, III, 448–453.

[81] Orders to the alcaldes mayores of Acapulco and Tehuantepec, May 2, 1571 and July 9, 1571, in Fonseca and Urrutia, V, 29–35.

[82] Fonseca and Urrutia, V, 35–44.

√[83] Toledo to the king, Lima, February 8, 1570, in *GP,* III, 323–327.

[84] Peru (Viceroyalty), *Memorias de los virreyes,* I, 51.

[85] Dr. Cuenca to the king, Lima, February 6, 1571, in *GP,* VII, 10–11; *Recopilación,* Lib. VIII, Tít. XV, ley xviii.

[86] Lima. *Libros de cabildo,* VI, 243 and 469–470.

[87] Lic. Ramírez de Cartagena to the king, Lima, April 16, 1573, in *GP,* VII, 169–171. Toledo did not let much mercury leave Peru.

[88] See chapter v.

[89] Toledo to the king, Lima, February 8, 1570, in *GP,* III, 323–327; Toledo to the king, Cuzco, March 25, 1571, *ibid.,* III, 469–471; Toledo to the king, Cuzco, March 1, 1572, *ibid.,* III, 569–572; Lima, *Libros de cabildo,* VII, 243.

[90] Cédulas of Philip II to the treasury officials of Panama, Madrid, May 26, 1573 and San Lorenzo, January 12, 1576, and cédula to the Audiencia of Panama, Madrid, May 26, 1573, Encinas, III, 475–477.

[91] Francisco de Guerra y Céspedes to the king and Council of the Indies, Lima, April 30, 1603, *DIE,* LII, 491–492.

[92] *Recopilación,* Lib. VIII, Tít. XIII, ley 1; Encinas, III, 436; Fonseca and Urrutia, II, 5–9. The alcabala was imposed in the Audiencias of Quito, Lima, and Charcas only with great difficulty. See the reports of Cañete to the king, August 1, 1592; January 13, 1593; January 20, 1593; May 18, 1593; November 15, 1593; November 20, 1594; and April 12, 1594, in *GP,* XII, 319, 321 ff.; XIII, 12–13, 43–44, 58–60, 107–108, 134, 143.

NOTES TO CHAPTER VII: THE END OF THE EARLY INTERCOLONIAL TRADE

[1] Enríquez to the king, Mexico City, December 5, 1573, Spain, Ministerio de Fomento, *Cartas de Indias,* pp. 290–291.

[2] Schurz, *The Manila Galleon,* p. 27.

[3] Order of Luis de Velasco to the royal treasury officials in Mexico City to advance funds for the purchase of asphalt, cables, and rigging in Nicaragua for ships being built at La Navidad, Mexico City, April 4, 1560, MS in AGN, Mercedes, V, fol. 18ᵛ; Schurz, p. 371.

[4] Order of the Audiencia Gobernadora to Andrés Orejón, alcalde mayor of Acapulco, to maintain a lighthouse for the Far Eastern expedition, Mexico City, July 12, 1565, MS in AGN, Mercedes, VIII, fol. 71ʳ.

[5] Schurz, pp. 371–373.

[6] Luis de Velasco II to the king, Mexico City, August 14, 1595, MS in AGI, 58-3-12 (BLT).

[7] Villamanrrique to the king, Mexico City, February 23, 1586, *ibid.,* 58-3-9 (BLT).

[8] Luis de Velasco II to the king, Mexico City, April 6, 1594, *ibid.,* 58-3-11 (BLT).

[9] See the account of the voyage of Cavendish in Hakluyt, XI, 320–321.

[10] Spain, Consejo de Indias, *Extracto historial,* fol. 247ᵛ.

[11] Enríquez to the king, Lima, August 6, 1582 and February 12, 1583, *GP,* IX, 107–108 and 236–237. I accept Enríquez' direct statement that only one ship reached Peru. The discrepancy in dates of the sailings of the two vessels in the royal cédula and Schurz, p. 366, is probably due to the length of time the ships took to make the crossing.

[12] Enríquez to the king, Lima, February 12, 1583, *GP,* IX, 236–237.

[13] Letter to the king, Lima, February 26, 1590, *ibid.,* XII, 101–102. Cañete raised the almojarifazgo on Chinese imports via New Spain from the former 5 per cent to 15 per cent.

[14] Paragraph of a letter from the king to Cañete, February 6, 1591, and royal cédula to Luis de Velasco II, Madrid, February 27, 1591, Encinas, I, 283–285; *Recopilación,* Lib. IX, Tít. XLV, ley v.

[15] Cañete to Juan de Ibarra, Lima, April 28, 1592, *GP,* XII, 242–243.

[16] Cañete to Juan de Ibarra, El Callao, April 12, 1594, *ibid.,* XIII, 151–152.

[17] Royal cédulas, Madrid, December 18, 1591, Encinas, I, 284–285; *Recopilación,* Lib. IX, Tít. XLV, ley v.

[18] Cañete to the king, Lima, February 26, 1590, *GP,* XII, 101–102; also see below.

[19] Villamanrrique to the king, Mexico City, February 23, 1586, MS in AGI, 58-3-9 (BLT); Schurz, pp. 366–368. The additional tax brought the import duty to 10 per cent.

[20] Royal cédula to Villamanrrique, November 11, 1587, cited in the cédula to Luis de Velasco II, Madrid, February 27, 1591, in Encinas, I, 283–284.

[21] Mexico (City), *Actas de cabildo,* IX, 317 (Session of January 13, 1589).

[22] Copy of ordinance issued January 23, 1589, sent to Spain, MS in AGI, 58-3-11 (BLT).

[23] Mexico City, *Actas de cabildo,* XIII, 112–114 (Sessions of January 23 and 26, 1598).

[24] Cañete to the king, Lima, February 26, 1590, *GP,* XII, 101–102.

[25] Royal cédula to Luis de Velasco II, Madrid, February 27, 1591, Encinas, I, 283–284.

[26] Letters to the king, Lima, February 26, 1590; December 30, 1590; January 17, 1593; November 20, 1593; El Callao, April 12, 1594; all in *GP,* XII, 101–102; 203–204; 336; XIII, 115; 136; and Cañete to Juan de Ibarra, Lima, April 28, 1592, *GP,* XII, 242–243. The description which follows is based upon these letters. See also the petition of the cabildo of Lima to the viceroy, May 25, 1599, on the need for the trade in Chinese goods to supply Peru because of failure of shipments from Spain. Lima, *Libros de cabildo,* XIII, 267–271. The Lima cabildo also claimed that a substantial share of imports from the Audiencia of Mexico consisted of manufactures of that realm.

The merchants of New Spain also complained of economic difficulties because of losses through war and storm and infrequency of fleets. Mexico (City), *Actas de cabildo,* XI, 157 (Session of August 30, 1593).

[27] For a description of the seizure of specie at Seville, see Haring, *Trade and Navigation,* pp. 173–174. This was merely one in a series of such seizures under Hapsburg rule.

[28] Mexico City. *Actas de cabildo,* IX, 317; XIII, 112–114; XV, 47 (Sessions of January 13, 1589; January 23 and 26, 1598; and May 6, 1602).

[29] For evidence on frauds in declarations, see *ibid.,* XIII, 234–235 (Session of October 5, 1598).

[30] *Ibid.,* XIII, 112 (Session of January 23, 1598).

[31] *Ibid.,* XV, 47 (Session of May 6, 1602).

[32] It seems likely that the later restriction of Mexico-Peru trade to a purchase value of 200,000 ducats in colonial products in Acapulco was based upon an estimate of the amount by value of manufactures and other products of the Audiencia of Mexico shipped in the trade. See below. One of the interesting developments of the trade was an increase in exports of Mexican silk textiles—woven of Chinese yarn primarily. Borah, *Silk Raising,* pp. 89–90.

[33] Haring, pp. 136–137.

[34] On the position of the Seville merchants, see the letter of the cabildo of Lima to that of Mexico City, October 18, 1599, in Mexico City. *Actas de cabildo,* XIV, 32 (Session of December 17, 1599); Marqués de Montesclaros to the king, Lima, April 12, 1612, *DII,* VI, 298–314; "Extracto del asiento de avería de 1618," Seville, March 3, 1618, article 33, in Cespedes, *La avería,* p. 168; and Haring, pp. 123–154.

[35] On the Spanish policy of maintaining political dependence through economic dependence, see Cappa, *Estudios,* VI, 18; Enríquez to the king, acknowledging instructions to prevent the development of competing Peruvian industries, Lima, February 15, 1583; Conde del Villar to the king, acknowledging instructions to hinder the development of local wine and textile industries, Lima, April 25, 1588; Cañete to the king, explaining his reasons for not carrying out the Crown order to uproot all grapevines in Peru, El Callao, May 27, 1592; all in *GP,* IX, 249; XI, 67–69; XII, 299–300.

[36] Letter to the king, Lima, December 30, 1590, *GP,* XII, 203–204.

[37] See the review of Spanish policy in the letter of the Cardinal Archbishop of Seville to the king, Seville, October 28, 1603, *DIE,* LII, 565–572. The letter also contains a discussion of means for destroying the wine industry in Peru.

[38] *Recopilación,* Lib. IX, Tít. XLV, leyes vi, lxviii, and lxxi. Letter of the king to the Cardinal Archbishop of Seville, Valladolid, September 21, 1603, cited in the answer of the archbishop, Seville, October 28, 1603, *DIE,* LII, 565–566.

[39] See above, pp. 120–122.

[40] Luis de Velasco II to the king, El Callao, April 11, 1597 and Lima, December 7, 1600, *GP,* XIV, 44 and 299.

[41] Schurz, "Mexico, Peru, and the Manila Galleon," *The Hispanic American Historical Review,* I (1918), 399–402; Marqués de Montesclaros to the king, Lima, December 14, 1612, *DII,* VI, 340–344; Letter of the king to the Cardinal Archbishop of Seville, Valladolid, September 21, 1603, cited in the answer of the archbishop, Seville, October 28, 1603, *DIE,* LII, 565–566; Luis de Velasco II to the king, El Callao, April 11, 1597, *GP,* XIV, 44; Haring, pp. 149–151.

[42] Royal cédula to the Viceroy of Peru, Bosque de Balsain, October 4, 1600, *DII,* XIX, 124–125.

[43] This fact was pointed out to the king by the Marqués of Montesclaros in a letter of December 14, 1612, Lima, *DII,* VI, 340–344.

[44] Royal cédulas, Valladolid, December 31, 1604, quoted in full in Mexico City. *Actas de cabildo,* XVI, 206–213. The *Recopilación* and the Consejo de Indias, *Extracto historial* obscure the story of the evolution of restrictive measures.

The terms of the cédulas of 1604 would seem to have prohibited reëxport of Spanish goods from Mexico to Peru. Nevertheless, in March, 1607, another cédula expressly forbade such reshipment to protect the trade via Panama. Solórzano Pereira, *Política Indiana,* V, 27 (who gives the date as March 15) and Schäfer, *El consejo real y supremo de las Indias,* II, 343 (who quotes an account of Dr. Salcedo in MS, AGI, Indiferente general, leg. 856, giving the date as March 5).

[45] Mexico (City). *Actas de cabildo*, XVI, 213 (Session of December 2, 1605). See also *ibid.*, XIV, 32 (Session of December 17, 1599) *et passim*. For evidence of the hostility of the Mexico City cabildo to the purchase of Chinese goods by the Peruleros, see *ibid.*, XIII, 112 (Sessions of January 23 and 26, 1598).

[46] *Recopilación*, Lib. IX, Tít. XLV, leyes lxix, lxx, and lxxvi.

[47] *Ibid.*, ley lxxii.

[48] *Extracto historial*, fols. 248^{v}–249^{r}. The order was repeated in a royal cédula of July 30, 1627.

[49] *Recopilación*, Lib. IX, Tít. XLV, ley lxxiii.

[50] *Ibid.*, ley lxxvii.

[51] See above, note 45. Montesclaros in his report to the king, Lima, December 14, 1612, stated explicitly that only by ending all commerce between the colonies could the smuggling be stopped. As a compromise between the conflicting interests of Peninsular and Peruvian merchants, he suggested cutting the trade to one ship a year. *DII*, VI, 340–344.

[52] "Memorial dado al rey en su real Consejo de las Indias por D. Juan Grau y Monfalcón, procurador general de las Islas Filipinas ... ," *ca.* 1637, *DII*, 447–448; *Recopilación*, Lib. IX, Tít. XLV, ley lxxviii. The language of the article, quoted in the *Recopilación*, suggests that the restriction to 200,000 ducats was contained in the cédula of June 10, 1609, which limited the navigation to two vessels of 200 tons each.

[53] *Recopilación*, Lib. IX, Tít, XLV, ley lxxviii. The prohibition was repeated in the instructions to the Conde de Chinchón, March 29, 1636 and may have been made indefinite at that time. See also the Memorial of Grau y Monfalcón, *ca.* 1637, *DII*, 447–448; Solórzano Pereira, V, 27.

BIBLIOGRAPHY

BIBLIOGRAPHY

This bibliography is arranged according to the following classification:

Manuscript and archival materials
  Archival materials
  Other manuscripts, including theses
Printed materials
  Documents, laws, and legislative records
  Books and articles

For archives, only ramos and collections are listed because of the number and variety of archival materials used; full document citations are given in the footnotes.

MANUSCRIPT AND ARCHIVAL MATERIALS

ARCHIVAL MATERIALS

Archivo General de Indias, Seville (AGI)
Audiencia de Méjico.
Justicia.
Patronato.
(These ramos were consulted through film and transcripts in The Bancroft Library, University of California, Berkeley, and film in the Department of Geography, University of California, Berkeley.)
Archivo General de la Nación, Mexico (AGN)
Archivo del Hospital de Jesús.
Civil.
General de parte.
Indios.
Inquisición.
Mercedes.
Tributos.

OTHER MANUSCRIPTS, INCLUDING THESES

Baird, William Harrell. "The Beginnings of shipbuilding in America." Unpublished M.A. thesis, University of California, Berkeley, 1938.
Cobb, Gwendolin Ballantine. "Potosí and Huancavelica. Economic Bases of Peru, 1545 to 1640." Unpublished Ph.D. thesis, University of California, Berkeley, 1947.
Salandra, Dominic. "Pedrarias Dávila and the Spanish Beginnings on the Isthmus." Unpublished Ph.D. thesis, University of California, Berkeley, 1933.
"Viage Qve don Iuan de Herrera y Montemayor hizo el año de M.DCXVII des. Mexico al reyno del Piru y ciudad de Lima y aduersos sucesos del. Vtil y prouechoso para todos los que se derrotaren en la costa de tierrafirme." MS, Biblioteca Nacional de México, 10-7-503.
Wagner, Philip Laurence. "Nicoya: Historical Geography of a Central American Lowland Community." Unpublished Ph.D. thesis, University of California, Berkeley, 1953.
Wright, Ione Stuessy. "Early American Voyages to the Far East, 1527–1565." Unpublished Ph.D. thesis, University of California, Berkeley, 1940.

PRINTED MATERIALS

DOCUMENTS, LAWS, AND LEGISLATIVE RECORDS

Archivo General de la Nación, Mexico. *Documentos inéditos relativos a Hernan Cortes y su familia* (*Publicaciones*, XXVII). Mexico City, 1935.
Barriga, Victor M., ed. *Documentos para la historia de Arequipa*. Arequipa, 1939–1940. 2 vols.
Charcas (Audiencia). *La Audiencia de Charcas. Correspondencia de presidentes y oidores, documentos del Archivo de Indias. Publicación dirigida por d. Roberto Levillier. ... Prólogo de d. Adolfo Bonilla y San Martín.* ... Madrid, 1918–1922. 3 vols.

Colección de documentos inéditos, relativos al descubrimiento, conquista y organización de las antiguas posesiones españolas de América y Oceanía, sacados de los archivos del reino, y muy especialmente del de Indias. Madrid, 1864–1884. 42 vols.

Colección de documentos inéditos relativos al descubrimiento, conquista y organización de las antiguas posesiones españolas de ultramar. ... Madrid, 1885–1932. 25 vols.

Colección de documentos inéditos para la historia de Hispano-América. Madrid, [1927–1932]. 14 vols.

Colección de documentos inéditos para la historia de España. ... Madrid, 1842–1895. 112 vols.

Colección de documentos referentes a la historia colonial de Nicaragua. Recuerdo del centenario de la independencia nacional. 1821–1921. Managua, [1921].

[Consulate of the Sea]. *Codigo de las costumbres maritimas de Barcelona, hasta aqui vulgarmente llamado Libro del Consulado. Nuevamente traducido al castellano con el texto limosin restituido á su original integridad y pureza; e ilustrado con varios apéndices, glosarios, y observaciones históricas. por d. Antonio de Capmany, y de Monpalau, secretario perpetuo de la Real academia de la historia.* ... Madrid, 1791.

Cortés, Hernando. *Cartas, y otros documentos de Hernán Cortés, novísamente descubiertos en el Archivo general de Indias de la ciudad de Sevilla, e ilustrados por el P. Mariano Cuevas, S.J.* Seville, 1915.

———. *Cartas y relaciones de Hernan Cortés al emperador Carlos V colegidas é ilustradas por don Pascual de Gayangos.* Paris, 1866.

———. *Escritos sueltos. Colección formada para servir de complemento a las "Cartas de relacion."* Mexico City, 1871.

Encinas, Diego de, comp. *Cedulario indiano recopilado por ... Reproduccion facsimil de la edicion unica de 1596 con estudio e indices de Alfonso Garcia Gallo.* Madrid, 1945. 4 vols.

Fernández, León, comp. *Coleccion de documentos para la historia de Costa Rica.* ... San José, Costa Rica, 1881–1907. 10 vols.

Gayangos, Pascual de. See Cortés, Hernando. *Cartas y relaciones* ...

Hakluyt, Richard, comp. *The Principal Navigations, Voyages, Traffiques & Discoveries of the English Nation, Made by Sea or Over-land to the Remote and Farthest Distant Quarters of the Earth at any Time Within the Compass of these 1600 Yeeres,* ... (Works issued by the Hakluyt Society. Extra series). Glasgow, 1903–1905. 12 vols.

The Harkness Collection in the Library of Congress. Documents from Early Peru. The Pizarros and the Almagros. 1531–1578. Washington, D.C., 1936.

Icaza, Francisco A. de, comp. *Conquistadores y pobladores de Nueva España, diccionario autobiográfico sacado de los textos originales.* ... Madrid, 1923. 2 vols.

Lima. *Cabildo. Libros de cabildos de Lima.* ... *Descifrados y anotados per Bertram T. Lee; prólogo del dr. José de la Riva-Agüero.* Lima, 1935–1948. 16 vols.

Maggs Bros., comps. *From Panama to Peru. The Conquest of Peru by the Pizarros, the Rebellion of Gonzalo Pizarro and the Pacification by La Gasca. An Epitome of the Original Signed Documents to and from the Conquistadors, Francisco, Gonzalo, Pedro, and Hernando Pizarro, Diego de Almagro, and Pacificator La Gasca Together with the Original Signed MS. Royal Decrees.* London, 1925.

Mexico (City). *Actas de cabildo del ayuntamiento de México.* Mexico City, 1884–1905. 77 vols.

Navarrete, Martín Fernández de, ed. *Colección de los viages y descubrimientos que hicieron por mar los españoles desde fines del siglo XV, con varios documentos inéditos concernientes á la historia de la marina castellana y de los establecimientos españoles en Indias.* ... Madrid, 1825–1837. 5 vols.

Nueva colección de documentos inéditos para la historia de España y de sus Indias. Publícanla don Francisco de Zabálburu y don José Sancho Rayón. Madrid, 1892–1896. 6 vols.

Nuttall, Zelia, ed. *New Light on Drake. A Collection of Documents Relating to His Voyage of Circumnavigation 1577–1580. Translated and Edited by* ... (The Hakluyt Society Publications, series 2, vol. 34). London, 1914.

Pardo, J. Joaquin, comp. *Prontuario de reales cédulas, 1529–1599.* Guatemala City, 1941.

Paso y Troncoso, Francisco del, ed. *Epistolario de Nueva España, 1505–1818.* ... Mexico City, 1939–1942. 16 vols.

———, ed. *Papeles de Nueva España ... 2a sér., Geografía y estadística.* Mexico City, 1905–1906. 6 vols.

———, ed. *Papeles de Nueva España ... Segunda série tomo III suplemento.* (Biblioteca Aportación Histórica). Mexico City, 1946–1947.

Peralta, Manuel María de, ed. *Costa-Rica, Nicaragua y Panamá en el siglo XVI su historia y sus limites segun los documentos del Archivo de Indias de Seville, del de Simancas, etc.* ... Madrid and Paris, 1883.

Peru (Viceroyalty). *Audiencia de Lima. Correspondencia de presidentes y oidores. Documentos del Archivo de Indias. Publicación dirigida por d. Roberto Levillier.* ... Vol. I: 1549–1564. Madrid, 1922.

———. *Gobernantes del Perú, cartas y papeles, siglo XVI; documentos del Archivo de Indias. Publicación dirigida por d. Roberto Levillier.* ... Madrid, 1921–1926. 14 vols.

———. *Memorias de los vireyes que han gobernado el Peru durante el tiempo del coloniaje español.* Lima, 1859. 6 vols.

———. *Relaciones de los vireyes y audiencias que han gobernado el Perú.* ... Lima, 1867–1872. 3 vols.

Puga, Vasco de. See Spain. *Provisiones* ...

Real Academia de la Historia, Madrid. *Cortes de los antiguos reinos de Leon y de Castilla.* ... Madrid, 1861–1903. 5 vols.

Rosenbach Co., The. *The Sea. Books and Manuscripts on the Art of Navigation, Geography, Naval History, Shipbuilding, Voyages, Shipwrecks, and Mathematics, Including Atlases, Maps and Charts.* Philadelphia and New York, 1938.

Sandoval, Fernando B., comp. "El astillero del Carbón en Tehuantepec 1535–1566," Archivo General de la Nación, Mexico, *Boletín*, XXI (1st quarter of 1950), 1–20.

Serrano y Sanz, Manuel, ed. *Relaciones históricas y geográficas de América Central* (*Colección de libros y documentos referentes á la historia de América*, VIII). Madrid, 1908.

Spain. *Provisiones cedulas instrucciones para el gobierno de la Nueva España.* ... Edited and compiled by Vasco de Puga (*Colección de incunables americanos*, III). Madrid, 1945.

———. *Recopilación de leyes de los reynos de las Indias, mandadas imprimir y publicar por la magestad católica, del rey don Carlos II. nuestro señor,* ... 2d ed.; Madrid, 1756. 4 vols.

Spain. Consejo de Indias. *Extracto historial del expediente que pende en el Consejo real, supremo de las Indias, a instancia de la ciudad de Manila, y demás de las Islas Philipinas, sobre la forma en que se ha de hacer, y continuar, el comercio, y contratacion de los texidos de China en Nueva-España: Y para la mejor comprehension, distinguiendo, y separando tiempos, se notan los lances de esta dependencia desde el descubrimiento de las Islas Philippinas, y concesion de su comercio, con todo quanto ha ocurrido hasta el presente de officio, y á instancia del Consulado, y comercio de España. Formado, y adjustado de orden del rey, y acuerdo del mismo consejo, y á costa de su magestad por un ministro de la tabla.* ... Madrid, 1736.

Spain. Ministerio de Fomento. *Cartas de Indias.* ... Madrid, 1877.

BOOKS AND ARTICLES

Acosta, José de. *Historia natural y moral de las Indias en que se tratan las cosas notables del cielo, y elementos, metales, plantas y animales dellas: y los ritos, y ceremonias, leyes y gobierno y guerras de los indios.* ... New ed. with prologue by Edmundo O'Gorman. Mexico City, 1940.

Aiton, Arthur Scott. *Antonio de Mendoza, First Viceroy of New Spain* ... Durham, North Carolina, 1927.

Alamán, Lucas. *Disertaciones sobre la historia de la república megicana, desde la época de la conquista que los españoles hicieron á fines del siglo XV y principios del XVI de las islas y continente americanos hasta la independencia.* ... Mexico City, 1844–1849. 3 vols.

Albenino, Nicolau de. *Verdadera relacion delo sussedido enlos reynos e prouincias del Peru desde la yda a ellos del virey Blasco Nuñes Vela hasta el desbarato y muerte de Gonçalo Piçarro (Sevilla, 1549). Reproduction fac-simile avec une introduction de José Toribio Medina.* (Université de Paris. *Travaux et mémoires de l'Institut d'Ethnologie,* XI). Paris, 1930.

Alessio Robles, Vito. *Acapulco en la historia y en la leyenda.* Mexico City, 1932.

Altolaguirre y Duvale, Angel de. *Vasco Nuñez de Balboa.* Madrid, 1914.

Anderson, Romola and R. C. *The Sailing Ship.* New York, 1926.

Andrade, Francisco d'. *Chronica do João III.* New ed. Coimbra, 1796. 4 vols.

Antúñez y Acevedo, Rafael. *Memorias históricas sobre la legislación y gobierno del comercio de los españoles con sus colonias en las Indias Occidentales.* ... Madrid, 1797.

Artiñano y de Galdácano, Gervasio de. *La arquitectura naval española (en madera). Bosquejo de sus condiciones y rasgos de su evolución.* Madrid and Barcelona, 1920.

Bancroft, Hubert Howe. *History of Central America. San Francisco,* 1883–1887. 3 vols.

———. *History of Mexico.* San Francisco, 1883–1888. 6 vols.

———. *The Native Races of the Pacific States of North America....* New York, 1875–1876. 5 vols.

Barcia Carballido y Zúñiga, Andrés González de, comp. *Historiadores primitivos de las Indias Occidentales, que juntó, traduxó en parte, y sacó á luz, ilustrados con eruditas notas y copiosos indices,* ... Madrid, 1749. 3 vols.

Barlow, Robert Hayward. *The Extent of the Empire of the Culhua Mexica* (University of California Publications, Ibero-Americana: 28). Berkeley, California, 1949.

Barón Castro, Rodolfo. *La poblacion de El Salvador. Estudio acerca de su desenvolvimiento desde la época prehispánica hasta nuestros dias.* ... Madrid, 1942.

Barros, João de, and Couto, Diogo de. *Da Asia.* New ed. Lisbon, 1777–1788. 13 pts. in 24 vols.

Belveder, Juan de. *Libro general de las redvciones de plata, y oro de diferentes leyes y pesos, de menor á mayor cantidad, y de sus interesses á tanto por ciento, con otras reglas, y auisos muy necessarios para estos reynos del Piru.* ... Lima, 1597.

Bolton, Herbert Eugene. *Coronado, Knight of Pueblos and Plains.* Albuquerque, New Mexico, 1949.

Borah, Woodrow. *Silk Raising in Colonial Mexico.* (University of California Publications, Ibero-Americana: 20). Berkeley, California, 1943.

Cappa, Ricardo. *Estudios críticos acerca de la dominación española en América.* Madrid, 1889–1897. 20 vols.

Casas, Bartolomé de las. *Historia de las Indias ... ahora por primera vez dada á luz por el marqués de la Fuensanta del Valle y d. José Sancho Rayón.* Madrid, 1875–1876. 5 vols.

Céspedes del Castillo, Guillermo. *La averia en el comercio de Indias (Publicaciones de la Escuela de Estudios Hispano-Americanos de la Universidad de Sevilla,* XV). Seville, 1945.

Chard, Chester S. "Pre-Columbian Trade between North and South America," *Kroeber Anthropological Society Papers,* No. 1 (Berkeley, California, 1950), pp. 1–27.

Chevalier, François. *La Formation des grands domaines au Mexique. Terre et société aux XVIe–XVIIe siécles* (Université de Paris. *Travaux et mémoires de l'Institut d'Ethnologie,* LVI). Paris, 1952.

Cieza de León, Pedro. *La crónica del Perú* [actually *Primera parte de* ...] in *Biblioteca de autores españoles desde la formación del lenguaje hasta nuestros dias,* ed. by Ribadeneyra, XXVI (Madrid, 1862), pp. 349–458.

Cobb, Gwendolin Ballantine. "Supply and Transportation for the Potosí Mines, 1545–1560," *The Hispanic American Historical Review,* XXIX (January, 1949), 25–45.

Cobo, Bernabé. *Historia de la fundación de Lima* in Lima, Peru. Concejo Provincial. *IV centenario de la fundacion de la ciudad. Monografías históricas sobre la ciudad de Lima.* Lima, 1935. 2 vols.

———. *Historia del Nuevo Mundo ... publicada por primera vez con notas ... de d. Marcos Jiménez de la Espada.* Seville, 1890–1893. 4 vols.

Colmeiro, Manuel. *Historia de la economía política en España.* Madrid, [1863]. 2 vols.

Díaz del Castillo, Bernal. *Historia verdadera de la conquista de la Nueva España ... Unica edición hecha según el códice autógrafo. La publica Genaro García.* Mexico City, 1904. 2 vols.

Diffie, Bailey W. "Estimates of Potosí Mineral Production, 1545–1555," *The Hispanic American Historical Review,* XX (May, 1940), 275–282.

———, with the assistance of Justine Whitfield Diffie. *Latin American Civilization: Colonial Period.* Harrisburg, Pa., 1945.

Dorantes de Carranza, Baltasar. *Sumaria relación de las cosas de la Nueva España, con noticia individual de los descendientes legítimos de los conquistadores y primeros pobladores españoles ... La publica por primera vez el Museo nacional de México, paleográfiada del original por el Sr. d. José María de Agreda y Sánchez.* Mexico City, 1902.

[Drake, *Sir* Francis, *1st Bart.*] *The World Encompassed by Sir Francis Drake, Being His Next Voyage to That to Nombre de Dios. Collated With An Unpublished Manuscript of Francis Fletcher, Chaplain to the Expedition. With Appendices Illustrative of the Same Voyage, and Introduction by W. S. W. Vaux, Esq., M. A.* (The Hakluyt Society Publications, series 2, vol. 16). London, 1854.

Faria e Sousa, Manuel de. *Asia portuguesa* ... (translated from Spanish by Isabel Ferreira do Amaral Pereira de Matos and María Vitória Garcia Santos Ferreira, with an introduction by M. Lopes d'Almeida) New ed. Pôrto, 1945–1947. 6 vols. in 5 pts.

Fernández, Diego. *Primera parte de la historia del Perú por ... vecino de Palencia,* ed. by Lucas de Torre. 2d ed.; Madrid, 1913. 2 vols.

Fernández del Castillo, Francisco. "Algunos documentos del Archivo del Marquesado del Valle (Hospital de Jesús)," *Boletín de la Sociedad mexicana de geografía y estadística,* XLIII (January–April, 1931), 17–40.

Fernández Duro, Cesáreo. *Armada española desde la unión de los reinos de Castilla y de León.* ... Madrid, 1895–1903. 9 vols.

Fonseca, Fabián de, and Urrutia, Carlos de. *Historia general de real hacienda, escrita ... por orden del virey, conde de Revillagigedo. Obra hasta ahora inedita y que se imprime con permiso del supremo gobierno.* ... Mexico City, 1845–1853. 6 vols.

Galvão, Antonio. *The Discoveries of the World, from Their First Original unto the Year of Our Lord 1555 by Antonio Galvano, Governor of Ternate. Corrected, Quoted, and Published in England, by Richard Hakluyt, (1601). Now Reprinted, with the Original Portuguese Text: and Edited by Vice-Admiral Bethune, C. B.* (The Hakluyt Society Publications, series 1, vol. 30). London, 1862.

Garcilaso de la Vega, el Inca. *Primera parte de los Commentarios reales, que tratan, de el origen de los Incas, reies qve fveron del Perú, de sv idolatria, leies, y govierno, en paz, y en guerra: de svs vidas, y conquistas: y de todo lo que fue acquel imperio, y su republica, antes que los españoles pasaron á él.* ... 2d ed. rev.; Madrid, 1723.

Gómara, Francisco López de. *Historia de Mexico, con el descvbrimiento de la nueva España, conquistada por el muy illustre y valeroso principe don Fernando Cortes, marques del Valle.* ... 3d ed.; Antwerp, 1554.

———. *Historia de la conquista de México.* ... With Introduction and Notes of Joaquín Ramírez Cabañas. Mexico City, 1943. 2 vols.

———. *La historia general de las Indias, con todos los descubrimientos y cosas notables que han acaecido en ellas, dende que se ganaron hasta agora,* ... 3d ed.; Antwerp, 1554.

———. *Historia general de las Indias,* ... In Barcia, *Historiadores primitivos* ... , II.

Gómez de Cervantes, Gonzalo. *La vida económica y social de Nueva España al finalizar el siglo XVI. Prólogo y notas de Alberto María Carreño.* Mexico City, 1944.

Gómez de Orozco, Federico. "Las primeras comunicaciones entre Mexico y Peru," in Universidad Nacional Autónoma de México, Instituto de Investigaciones Estéticas, *Anales* ... , No. 7 (1941), 65–70.

Häbler, Konrad. *Die wirtschaftliche Blüte Spaniens im 16. Jahrhundert und ihr Verfall.* ... Berlin, 1888.

Hamilton, Earl J. *American Treasure and the Price Revolution in Spain, 1501–1650....* Cambridge, Mass., 1934.

———. "Imports of American Gold and Silver into Spain, 1503–1660," *Quarterly Journal of Economics,* XLIII (May, 1929), 436–472.

Haring, Clarence Henry. "American Gold and Silver Production in the First Half of the Sixteenth Century," *Quarterly Journal of Economics,* XXIX (May, 1915), 433–479.

———. *Trade and Navigation Between Spain and the Indies in the Time of the Hapsburgs...* Cambridge, Mass., 1918.

Harrisse, Henry. *The Discovery of North America, A Critical, Documentary, and Historic Investigation, with an Essay on the Early Cartography of the New World....* Paris and London, 1892.

Herrera y Tordesillas, Antonio de. *Historia general de los hechos de los castellanos en las islas i tierra firme del mar oceano. Escrita por ... coronista mayor de sv. md. de las Indias y sv coronista de Castilla. ...* 2d ed.; Madrid, 1726–[1727]. 9 vols. in 4.

Humboldt, Alexander von. *Essai politique sur le royaume de la Nouvelle Espagne.* 2d ed.; Paris, 1825–1827. 5 vols.

Jijón y Caamaño, Jacinto. *Sebastián de Benalcázar.* Quito, 1936. Vol. I.

Jiménez de la Espada, Marcos. "Las islas de los Galápagos y otras más á poniente," *Boletín de la Sociedad geográfica de Madrid,* XXXI (1891), 351–402.

Kelly, John Eoghan. *Pedro de Alvarado, Conquistador.* Princeton, 1932.

Kidder, Alfred II. "South American Penetrations in Middle America," in *The Maya and Their Neighbors.* New York, 1940. Pp. 441–459.

Kubler, George. *Mexican Architecture of the Sixteenth Century.* New Haven, 1948. 2 vols.

Leonard, Irving Albert. *Books of the Brave, being an Account of Books and of Men in the Spanish Conquest and Settlement of the Sixteenth-Century New World.* Cambridge, Mass., 1949.

Lohmann Villena, Guillermo. "Enrique Garcés, descubridor del mercurio en el Peru, poeta y arbitrista," *Anuario de estudios americanos* (Escuela de estudios hispano-americanos de Sevilla), V (1948), 439–482.

———. "Hernán Cortés y el Peru," *Revista de Indias,* IX (Madrid, 1948), 339–340.

———. "Hernán Cortés y el Peru," in Spain. Consejo Superior de Investigaciones Científicas. Instituto Gonzalo Fernández de Oviedo. *Estudios cortesianos. IV centenario de Hernán Cortés.* Madrid, 1948. Pp. 339–340. [Same article as above.]

Lopes de Castanheda, Fernão. *Historia do descobrimento e conquista da India pelos portuguezes.* 3d ed.; Coimbra, 1924–1933. 9 vols. in 4.

López de Velasco, Juan. *Geografía y descripción universal de las Indias, recopilada por el cosmógrafo-cronista ... desde el año de 1571 al de 1574. ...* Madrid, 1894.

Lothrop, Samuel K. "South America As Seen from Middle America," in *The Maya and Their Neighbors,* New York, 1940. Pp. 417–429.

The Maya and their Neighbors. New York, [1940].

Means, Philip Ainsworth. *Fall of the Inca Empire and the Spanish Rule in Peru: 1530–1780....* New York and London, 1932.

Medina, José Toribio. *La imprenta en Lima (1584–1824).* Santiago, Chile, 1904–1907. 4 vols.

———. *La imprenta en México (1539–1821).* Santiago, Chile, 1907–1912. 8 vols.

Mendiburu, Manuel de. *Diccionario historico-biografico del Peru, formado y redactado por ... Parte primera que corresponde a la epoca de la dominacion española. ...* Lima, 1874–1890. 8 vols.

Mendieta, Gerónimo de. *Historia eclesiástica indiana. ...* ed. by Joaquín García Icazbalceta. Mexico City, 1870.

Milla y Vidaurre, José *Historia de la América Central desde el descubrimiento del país por los españoles (1502) hasta su independencia de la España (1821). ...* Guatemala City, 1879–1882. 2 vols.

Montesinos, Fernando. *Anales del Perú.* Madrid, 1906. 2 vols.

Moorhead, Max I. "Hernán Cortés and the Tehuantepec Passage," *The Hispanic American Historical Review,* XXIX (August, 1949), 370–379.

Moreyra y Paz-Soldan, Manuel. *Estudios sobre el trafico maritimo en la epoca colonial.* Lima, 1944.

———. "La tesorería y la estadística de acuñación colonial en la casa de moneda de Lima," in Universidad Católica del Perú. Instituto de Investigaciones Históricas, *Cuadernos de estudios,* II, No. 4 (September, 1942), 3–56.

Oppenheim, M. *A History of the Administration of the Royal Navy and of Merchant Shipping in Relation to the Navy.* Vol. I. MDIX–MDCLX. London and New York, 1896.

Oviedo y Valdés, Gonzalo Fernández de. *Historia general y natural de las Indias, islas y tierrafirme del mar océano.* ... ed. by José Amador de los Ríos. Madrid, 1851–1855. 3 pts. in 4 vols.

Pardo, J. Joaquín. *Efemerides para escribir la historia de la muy noble y muy leal ciudad de Santiago de los caballeros del reino de Guatemala.* Guatemala City, 1944.

Penrose, Boies. *Travel and Discovery in the Renaissance,* Cambridge, Mass., 1952.

Ponce, Alonso [wrongly ascribed to]. *Relacion breve y verdadera de algunas cosas de las muchas que sucedieron al padre fray Alonso Ponce en las provincias de la Nueva España. ...* Madrid, 1873. 2 vols.

Porras Barrenechea, Raúl. "El contador Agustín de Zárate," *Mercurio peruano,* XXIII (Lima, September, 1941), 499–505.

Portillo y Díez de Sollano, Alvaro de. *Descubrimientos y exploraciones en la costa de California.* Madrid, 1947.

Prescott, William Hickling. *History of the Conquest of Peru with a Preliminary View of the Civilization of the Incas.* 2d ed.; London, 1847. 2 vols.

Quirino da Fonseca, ——. *A caravela portuguesa e a prioridade tecnica das navegaçoes henriquinas.* Coimbra, 1934.

Revista mexicana de estudios históricos. Mexico City, 1927–1928. 2 vols.

Rada, José Jacinto. *"México y Perú en la historia americana," Boletín de la Sociedad mexicana de geografía y estadística,* XLVI (1938), 265–294.

Rivet, Paul, and Arsandaux, H. *La Métallurgie en Amérique précolombienne* (Université de Paris. *Travaux et mémoires de l'Institut de l'Ethnologie,* XXXIX). Paris, 1946.

Romero, Emilio. *Historia economica del Perú.* Buenos Aires, 1949.

———. *Historia economica y financiera del Peru. Antiguo Peru y virreynato.* Lima, 1937.

Salaman, Redcliffe N. *The History and Social Influence of the Potato . . .* Cambridge, 1949.

Sandoval, Fernando B. *La industria del azúcar en Nueva España* (Universidad Nacional Autónoma de México, Instituto de Historia, *Publicaciones. ...* XXI). Mexico City, 1951.

Schäfer, Ernst. "Comunicaciones maritimas y terrestres de las Indias españolas," *Anuario de estudios americanos* (Escuela de estudios hispano-americanos de Sevilla), III (1946), 969–983.

———. *El consejo real y supremo de las Indias. Su historia, organización y labor administrativa hasta la terminación de la casa de Austria. Seville, 1935–1947.* 2 vols.

Schurz, William Lytle. *The Manila Galleon.* New York, 1939.

———. "Mexico, Peru, and the Manila Galleon," *The Hispanic American Historical Review,* I (1918), 389–402.

Simpson, Lesley Byrd. *Exploitation of Land in Central Mexico in the Sixteenth Century* (University of California Publications, Ibero-Americana:36). Berkeley, California, 1952.

———. *Studies in the Administration of the Indians in New Spain. IV: The Emancipation of the Indian Slaves and the Resettlement of the Freedmen 1548–1553* (University of California Publications, Ibero-Americana: 16). Berkeley, California, 1940.

Solórzano Pereira, Juan de. *Política indiana. ...* 2d ed.; Madrid and Buenos Aires, [1930]. 5 vols.

[Suárez de Peralta, Juan]. *Noticias históricas de la Nueva España ... ,* ed. by Justo Zaragoza. Madrid, 1878.

Taylor, Paul S. "Spanish Seamen in the New World during the Colonial Period," *The Hispanic American Historical Review,* V (1922), 631–661.

Torquemada, Juan de. *Primera [segunda, tercera] parte de los veinte i vn libros rituales i monarchia indiana, con el origen y guerras, de los indios occidentales, de sus poblaçones, descubrimiento, conquista, conuersion, y otras cosas marauillosas de la mesma tierra* ... Madrid, 1723, 3 vols.

United States Department of Agriculture. Weather Bureau. *Atlas of Climatic Charts of the Oceans.* Washington, D.C., 1938.

United States Hydrographic Office. *Sailing Directions for South America. Volume III (West Coast): Golfo Corcovado to the Gulf of Panama Including Off-lying Islands (H. O. No. 174).* 4th ed.; Washington, D.C., 1938.

———. *Sailing Directions for the West Coasts of Mexico and Central America from the United States to Colombia Including the Gulfs of California and Panama (H. O. No. 84).* 8th ed.; Washington, D.C., 1938.

Veita Linaje, José de. *Norte de la contratacion de las Indias Occidentales.* ... Seville, 1672. 2 vols. in 1.

Wagner, Henry Raup. *The Spanish Southwest 1542–1794, An Annotated Bibliography.* Berkeley, California, 1924.

———. *Spanish Voyages to the Northwest Coast of America in the Sixteenth Century....* (California Historical Society, Special Publications, No. 4). San Francisco, 1929.

Whitaker, Arthur Preston. *The Huancavelica Mercury Mine. A Contribution to the History of the Bourbon Renaissance in the Spanish Empire.* Cambridge, Mass., 1941.

Wright, Ione Stuessy. "The First American Voyage across the Pacific, 1527–1528. The Voyage of Alvaro de Saavedra Ceron." *The Geographic Review,* XXIX (1939), 472–482.

Zárate, Agustín de. *Historia del descvbrimiento y conqvista de la provincia del Perv, y de las guerras, y cosas señaladas en ella, acaecidas hasta el vencimiento de Gonçalo Piçarro, y de sus sequaces, que en ella se rebelaron, contra su magestad.* in Barcia, *Historiadores primitivos* ..., III.

www.ingramcontent.com/pod-product-compliance
Lightning Source LLC
LaVergne TN
LVHW090947080826
845145LV00003B/920